National Think Tank 2020 (12)

Editor-in-Chief Cai Fang
Associate Editor-in-Chief Li Xinfeng, Zhao Jianying, Guo Jianshu

Research Reports on the Elimination of Poverty in China
—Qinba Mountain Area, Shaanxi Province

He Degui, Yao Guimei, Xu Rong, Wu Xueyan

Translated by Yang Xiaofeng, Zeng Ashan

中国社会科学出版社
CHINA SOCIAL SCIENCES PRESS

图书在版编目(CIP)数据

中国脱贫攻坚调研报告. 秦巴山区篇 = Research Reports on the Elimination of Poverty in China—Qinba Mountain Area, Shaanxi Province：英文／何得桂等著；杨晓峰，曾阿姗译. —北京：中国社会科学出版社，2020.5

(国家智库报告)

ISBN 978 - 7 - 5203 - 6864 - 3

Ⅰ.①中…　Ⅱ.①何…②杨…③曾…　Ⅲ.①扶贫—调查报告—中国—英文　Ⅳ.①F126

中国版本图书馆 CIP 数据核字(2020)第 145648 号

出 版 人	赵剑英
项目统筹	王　茵
责任编辑	张冰洁　王玉静
责任校对	乔镜蕫
责任印制	李寡寡

出　　版	中国社会科学出版社
社　　址	北京鼓楼西大街甲 158 号
邮　　编	100720
网　　址	http://www.csspw.cn
发 行 部	010 - 84083685
门 市 部	010 - 84029450
经　　销	新华书店及其他书店

印　　刷	北京君升印刷有限公司
装　　订	廊坊市广阳区广增装订厂
版　　次	2020 年 5 月第 1 版
印　　次	2020 年 5 月第 1 次印刷

开　　本	710×1000　1/16
印　　张	17.75
字　　数	221 千字
定　　价	88.00 元

Give Full Play to the Role of Think Tanks to Promote Friendly Cooperation between China and Africa

—*The General Preface to the Library of the China-Africa Institute*

We are witnessing major changes unfolding in the world, changes unprecedented in a century. With the in-depth development of world multipolarization, economic globalization, social informatization and cultural diversity, peace, development, cooperation and mutual benefit have become the common aspirations of human society; and it is the common wish of people from all countries to build a community with a shared future for mankind. At the same time, humankind is faced with many common challenges, typified by fierce power politics among major countries, continuous regional conflicts, terrorism, development imbalance, climate change, rising unilateralism and protectionism. China, as the largest developing country in the world, is a builder, contributor and upholder of the cause of peace and development of mankind. The 19th National Congress of the Communist Party of China held in October 2017 has led China to a new great journey of development. Guided by Chinese President Xi Jinping Thought on Socialism with Chinese Characteristics for a New Era, the Chinese people are making continued efforts to achieve the Two Centenary Goals of China and the Chinese dream of the great rejuvenation of the Chinese nation, and to make new and greater contributions to mankind. Africa, the continent with the largest number of developing countries, is one of the important forces in safeguarding world peace and promoting global development. In recent years, Africa has made the admirable advances on the road of pursuing sustainable self-development and strength through unity, changing from a "hopeless continent" for the West to a "continent with a future full of hope," and a "running lion." African countries are actively exploring development paths that suit their own national conditions, and the African people are forging ahead to realize *The Agenda 2063* and the African dream of peace and prosperity.

China and Africa boast a deep-running friendship and have long formed a community with a shared future. China attaches great importance to the development of China-Africa relations. In March 2013, Xi Jinping visited Africa, also his first trip abroad as national leader. He also chose Africa for his first overseas visit in July 2018 after he was elected to a second term. Over the past six years, Xi has visited the African continent four times and arrived in eight African countries, including Tanzania, South Africa and Senegal, showing the world that China cherishes the traditional friendship with Africa and values highly the continent and China-Africa relations. In 2018, the Beijing Summit of the Forum on China-Africa Cooperation was successfully held. At this summit, Xi revealed the essential characteristics of China-Africa unity and cooperation, pointed out the direction of bilateral ties, and outlined the specific paths for the common development of China and Africa. He has greatly improved and innovated the theoretical framework and ideological system of China's policy toward Africa, which has then become an important theoretical innovation of Xi Jinping thought on diplomacy of socialism with Chinese characteristics for a new era and provided a strong political principle and guide for the development of China-Africa relations in the future. This summit marks another milestone in the history of China-Africa relations.

With the vigorous development of China-Africa cooperation, the international community has paid more attention to the bilateral ties. Out of concern over China's growing influence in Africa, Western countries have made up some ridiculous theories to willfully smear and defame China-Africa relations, such as "neo-colonialism" "resource contention" "debt trap", which have disturbed the development of China-Africa relations to a certain extent. In this context, it is increasingly urgent and important for the academic community in China to strengthen its research on Africa and Africa-China relations, timely launch relevant research results, enhance discourse in international relations, demonstrate the fruits of the pragmatic cooperation between China and Africa, reflect the sound development of China-Africa relations objectively and actively, and let the world hear China's voice.

Directed by Xi Jinping Thought on Socialism with Chinese Characteristics for a New Era, the Chinese Academy of Social Sciences has strived to build theoretical fronts of Marxism, serve as a think tank for the decision-making of the Communist Party of China, make new and greater contributions to the construction of the discipline system, academic system and discourse system concerning the philosophy and social sciences with Chinese characteristics, thus constantly enhancing the international influence of Chinese philosophy and social sciences. The Institute of West-Asian and African Studies under the Chinese Academy of Social Sciences is a regional research institute established under the instructions of Chairman Mao Zedong. It has long been committed to studying African issues and China-Africa relations, with equal emphasis on basic research and applied research. It has also published a large number of academic monographs and papers, continuously expanding the influence both at home and abroad. The China-Africa Institute, established in April 2019 with the Institute of West-Asian and African Studies as the main body, is an important measure announced by Xi Jinping, also General Secretary of the Communist Party of China, at the Beijing Summit of the Forum on China-Africa Cooperation to strengthen people-to-people exchanges between China and Africa.

In accordance with the spirit of Xi's letter to congratulate the inauguration of the China-Africa Institute, the institute aims to draw on both sides' academic resources, facilitate mutual learning between China and Africa, strengthen exchanges of experience on governance and development, provide good ideas and advice for China-Africa cooperation as well as the cooperation between the two sides and other parties, enhance understanding and friendship between the Chinese and the

African people, provide intelligence and talents to support China and Africa in jointly promoting cooperation under the Belt and Road Initiative, forging a future-oriented comprehensive strategic and cooperative partnership and building an even closer China-Africa community with a shared future. The China-Africa Institute mainly performs four functions. For starters, it serves as an exchange platform that helps strengthen academic exchanges between China and Africa. It attempts to organize well such activities as Africa Lecture, China Lecture and Ambassador Lecture, and host the conference on dialogue of Chinese and African civilizations. Meanwhile, it will also put into better operation the China-Africa exchange systems and mechanisms of governance, sustainable development, and jointly building the Belt and Road. Secondly, it is a research base focusing on the joint construction of the Belt and Road. Specifically, it will conduct research on China-Africa cooperation, follow up major and hot issues of common concern to China and Africa, and publish research subjects and results on a regular basis. Thirdly, it intends to give full play to the role as a talent highland and train high-end professionals. It will carry out academic qualification and degree education, implement the program of exchange visits between Chinese and African scholars, train young experts, support young scholars and cultivate high-end professionals. Meanwhile, it attempts to popularize the friendly stories between China and Africa as a window of communication. It intends to run well the official Wechat account of the China-Africa Institute as well as the official website in both Chinese and English, and publish *The Journal of China-Africa Studies* in multiple languages.

In order to implement the spirit of Xi Jinping's congratulatory letter, better gather the resources of Chinese and African academic think tanks, unite African scholars, improve the academic level and innovative ability of Chinese researchers on Africa, promote the integrated development of Africa-related disciplines, launch high-quality works and strengthen the construction of academic ethics, the China-Africa Institute, with a keen awareness of national realities and a global vision, has established a library oriented towards all Chinese researchers on Africa. The Library of the China-Africa Institute, adhering to a foundational principle to introduce high-quality works, has set up an editorial board composed of relevant government officials and experts and scholars, which will then select and publish research results on Africa and China-Africa relations. There are five series of books under the library. The academic series cover the systematic and thematic research results of a certain African discipline, such as the development issues and paths of Africa and China-Africa cooperation, aiming to promote the development of disciplines and give advice. The classic translation works are made up by the Chinese version of classic academic works concerning African issues composed by scholars from Africa and other regions. The series focus on revealing comprehensively the academic level and views of African scholars and how they think about their own development issues. The think tank report series mainly study China-Africa ties and also include China-Africa cooperation in various fields, country-specific bilateral relations, China's interaction with other countries in Africa. It aims to reflect the current situation of China-Africa cooperation in an objective, accurate and detailed manner and give advice on the advance of China-Africa ties in the new era. The research paper series involve the innovative academic papers of Chinese experts and scholars on major African issues in politics, economy, security, social development, as well as the international relations of Africa in a context where the international society has witnessed changes and socialism with Chinese characteristics has entered the new era. The series feature multidisciplinary, fundamental, systemic and symbolic research results. The almanac series include a series of information documents, with columns such as Important Documents, Hot Topics, Features, Reviews, Introduction to New Books and Academic Journals, Academic Institutes and Trends, Data and Events of the Year, aiming to collect the new viewpoints, trends and results concerning African studies systematically on a yearly basis.

It is expected that China's studies on Africa and Africa's studies on China will usher in a new chapter at the new historical starting point of the establishment of the China-Africa Institute. The institute will gather domestic research forces, unite experts and scholars from African countries, make pioneering efforts to innovate and promote China's studies on Africa, Africa's studies on China and China-Africa relations research, better serving both sides in jointly building of the Belt and Road and facilitating the all-round and in-depth development of China-Africa friendship and cooperation in the new era.

Vice President of the Chinese Academy of Social Sciences,
Director of the China-Africa Institute
Cai Fang

Abstract: The eradication of poverty, the improvement of people's lives and the gradual realization of common prosperity are the essential requirement of socialism and the important mission of the CPC. Since the 18th CPC National Congress, China has mobilized the forces of the whole Party, whole country and whole society to launch a national compaign against absolute poverty in order to ensure that all poverty-stricken areas and people enter into a moderately prosperous society in all respects by 2020. As one of the main battlefields for poverty alleviation in China for a new era, the Qinling-Bashan contiguous areas with acute difficulties (hereinafter referred to as "Qinling-Bashan mountainous regions") have actively explored the effective paths to poverty alleviation by carrying forward and developing the Marxist anti-poverty thought and implementing the basic strategies of targeted poverty reduction and alleviation, thereby making their due efforts and contributions to the gradual and quality-oriented poverty alleviation. During the process of poverty alleviation in Qinling-Bashan mountainous regions, characteristic industries are developed according to local conditions and have effectively increased local income people's. Targeted relocation, precise implementation and refined management are adopted to ensure that the relocated people, gain stable resettlement, get employed and become rich step by step and solve the difficulty that local lard is too poor for people to live on it. Poverty alleviation, ambition enhancement and intellectual support are combined to fully mobilize the enthusiasm of poverty-stricken areas and people, effectively stimulate the endogenous impetus for poverty alleviation and block the inter-generational transmission of poverty, thus ensuring the high-quality poverty alleviation of poor people in poverty-stricken areas. Guided by the conviction that "lucid waters and lush mountains are invaluable assets", Qinling-Bashan mountainous regions have made full use of local ecological resources, exploited ecological advantages, promoted the sustainable development of local economy through ecological conservation and management and explored the road of poverty alleviation through ecological conservation with local characteristics. Meanwhile, the party, government and military organs, enterprises and public institutions have carried out the designated poverty alleviation compaign, which is part of poverty alleviation movement with Chinese characteristics. With the assistance of the Chinese Academy of Social Sciences, Danfeng County in Shaanxi Province actively explored the effective paths to poverty alleviation in extremely impoverished areas and contributed "Danfeng Experience" for winning the battle against poverty with high quality as scheduled. The practice and result of poverty alleviation in Qinling-Bashan mountainous regions represents a miniature of China's efforts to get rid of absolute poverty. China's experience in poverty alleviation for a new era reflects the development trend of the new era and is thus advanced. Its characteristics and mechanisms are worthy of promotion. After bidding farewell to absolute poverty, China will commit itself to solving the problem of relative poverty and implementing the strategy of rural vitalization so as to ensure the achievements of poverty alleviation can undergo the test of history and the people.

Key words: Qinling-Bashan mountainous regions; poverty alleviation; poverty governance; targeted poverty reduction; targeted poverty alleviation

Contents

Chapter 2
Poverty Alleviation by Supporting the Industry in Contiguous Areas with Acute Difficulties

Chapter 3
Relocation from Inhospitable Areas: Cracking Down on the Problem of Living and Employment

Chapter 4
Endogenous Impetus for Poverty Alleviation through Ambition & Intellectual Enrichment

Conclusion

Introduction
A New Look of Qinling-Bashan Mountainous Regions

Poverty alleviation is the assiduously sought goal of mankind. Chinese President Xi Jinping pointed out that, the eradication of poverty, the improvement of people's lives and the gradual realization of common prosperity are the essential requirement of socialism and the important mission of the CPC. [1] Bettering the lives of the people is a goal for every one of the initiatives of the CPC and the Chinese government. Especially since the 18th CPC National Congress, China has intensified efforts to improve the self-development capability of poverty-stricken areas and the people living under the poverty line by regarding the contiguous areas with acute difficulties as the main battlefields of poverty alleviation. Qinling-Bashan mountainous regions have thus got rid of absolute poverty and taken on a new look.

1. 1 Bidding Farewell to Poverty: Theory and Practice of Poverty Governance

As a big developing country, China has committed itself to poverty reduction and development and made outstanding achievements. Scientific paths and effective experience regarding poverty governance are implied in the anti-poverty practice of the contiguous areas with

---

[1] The CPC Central Party History and Documentation Research Institute, *Xi Jinping's Remarks on Poverty Reduction*, Beijing: The Central Documentation Press, 2018, p. 3.

acute difficulties. When China is about to win a decisive victory in poverty alleviation, it is necessary for us to summarize the country's experience in poverty alleviation and make China's voice widely heard throughout the world. Just as General Secretary Xi Jinping pointed out, "Poverty alleviation should not only be carried out well but made well known to the world. "[1]

1. 1. 1　History of poverty governance in China

Over the past seventy years since the founding of the People's Republic of China ("New China"), China has continuously facilitated poverty governance and realized the fundamental interests of the masses. The history of poverty governance in New China can be roughly divided into the following stages.

First, broad-sense poverty reduction period under the planned economy system (1949 – 1977). Small-scale relief type poverty reduction dominated in China during this period. "Blood transfusion" type relief was provided to the poor whose basic life needs cannot be guaranteed in remote underdeveloped regions, disaster-induced poverty populations and war-disabled populations through the top-to-bottom civil relief system. Also, extensive infrastructure construction was carried out. A basic rural social security system, with community five-guarantee system (childless and old persons are guaranteed food, clothing, medical care, housing and burial expenses by the communes) and relief to extremely poor populations in rural areas as focus, was initially built. Second, large-scale poverty reduction period brought about by the economic system reform (1978 – 1985). When it came to the poverty governance during this period, poverty reduction was realized mainly through reform dividends. By facilitating the rural reform, promoting the dual management system based on household contracting management and in combination with centralization and decentralization, and pushing the deepening of rural economic system reform, China had greatly liberated

---

[1]　Xi Jinping, "Speech at the Symposium on Winning a Decisive Victory in the Battle against Poverty", *People's Daily*, 2020-03-07 (2).

rural productivity, directly driven the growth of agricultural yield, improved the income of rural populations, and effectively eased rural poverty issues. Third, institutionalized regional poverty reduction period characterized by boosting development (1986 – 2000). With social and economic development, the effect of poverty reduction directly through rural reform and production development had tended to slow down. A designated poverty reduction organization was established in China in 1986 to initiate large-scale, institutionalized and regulated poverty reduction work. The organization was originally known as the State Council Leading Group for Economic Development of Poor Areas and was later renamed as the State Council Leading Group of Poverty Alleviation and Development. Poor regions were focused on and the strategy of poverty reduction by boosting development was adopted, with projects as main carriers. The *Seven-year Priority Poverty Reduction Program* was issued by the State in 1994. According to the program, China would strive to provide adequate food and clothing to 80 million rural poverty populations in around seven years. The program made the poverty reduction work more targeted, measures more integrated and capital investment much larger. The goal had been basically achieved by the end of 2000. Fourth, village by village and "two-wheel" driven poverty reduction (2001 – 2012) period. The *Outline for Poverty Reduction and Development of China's Rural Areas (2001 – 2010)* was promulgated. In the middle and western regions of China, 592 key counties for poverty alleviation and development were identified. The focus of poverty reduction was shifted to villages and 150, 000 poor villages were chosen throughout the country. Poverty reduction and development were carried out village by village with emphasis placed on industry development and transfer of labor forces. In 2007, the rural minimum living security system was fully implemented. And the "double-wheel drive" effect brought about by poverty alleviation and development as well as the minimum living security system was enhanced. Fifth, targeted poverty reduction and alleviation period (2013 till now). Since the 18th CPC National Congress, the CPC Central Committee, with Comrade Xi Jinping at its core, has attached great importance to poverty reduction and development, placed poverty reduction and development in an important position of governing the State, and formed a series of new thoughts, ideas and arrangements on poverty governance. A series of unconventional moves have been adopted to ensure the eradication of absolute poverty in all respects by 2020.

1.1.2   Strategic arrangements of the CPC Central Committee and the State Council

Since the founding of the People's Republic of China, especially the reform and opening up, the world has witnessed a continuous improvement in the CPC capability of governing the State as well as the governance system and capability of China, and a sustained rise in economic growth, thus effectively establishing an economic foundation for eradicating absolute poverty. In the 18th CPC National Congress convened in November 2012, the goal of building a moderately prosperous society in all respects by 2020 was proposed. In November 3, 2013, General Secretary Xi Jinping proposed for the first time the concept of "targeted poverty reduction" when inspecting Shibadong Village, Paibi Town, HuaYuan County, Xiangxi Tujia and Miao Autonomous Prefecture. He pointed out that the success of poverty reduction and development lies in precision and made specific demands to accurately identify those to be helped, make precise project arrangements, use funds most effectively, take measures aimed directly at each household, send the right people to each village, and get well-defined results from poverty alleviation. In order to achieve the goal of building a moderately prosperous society in all respects on schedule, the *Decision of the CPC Central Committee and the State Council on Eradicating Poverty in China* was issued by the CPC Central Committee and the State Council in November 2015. According to the Decision, with targeted poverty reduction and alleviation as basic guideline, the concerted efforts of the whole Party and the whole society should be exerted to lift all rural poor populations and counties out of poverty and alleviate regional poverty under the prevailing standards of China by 2020①. At the 19th CPC National Congress held in October 2017, it was emphasized that the people's aspirations to live a better life is our goal and proposed that solid action should be taken in the three critical battles, namely, forestalling and defusing major risks, targeted poverty alleviation, as well as pollution prevention and control. In the *Three-Year Guideline of the CPC Central Committee and the State Council on Winning the Battle against Poverty* issued on June 15, 2018, it was pointed out that more solid and steady efforts should be delivered on schedule to accomplish the task of poverty alleviation and intensified poverty alleviation in extremely impoverished regions was particularly highlighted. From 2015 to March 2020, General Secretary Xi Jinping organized seven thematic meetings on winning the battle against poverty and summoned the comrades in charge of related provinces. Additionally, the strategy of Rural Revitalization was proposed in the Report of the 19th CPC National Congress. The *Opinions of the CPC Central Committee and the State Council on Implementing the Strategy of Rural Vitalization* was issued as the No. 1 Central Document for the year 2018. The No. 1 Central Document for the year 2019 put forward the general policy of prioritizing the development of agriculture and rural areas, thus providing a clear direction for the sustained development of poor areas.

1. 1. 3 Path to implementing the guiding principles of the CPC Central Committee in contiguous areas with acute difficulties

Since the 18th CPC National Congress, China has made remarkable achievements in poverty alleviation. The poor population was reduced from 98. 99 million in the late 2012 to 5. 51 million in the late 2019; the incidence of poverty was cut from the previous 10. 2% to 0. 6% during this period; and a population of more than 10 million was lifted out of

---

① China's poverty alleviation standards for the rural poor in 2015 are as follows: achieving the standards of "two no worries" and "three guarantees", specifically achieving the goal of poverty alleviation so that those who have been living in poverty no longer have to worry about food and clothing and of guaranteeing compulsory education, basic medical treatment and housing security, with annual per capita net income of 2, 855 Yuan as target.

poverty in the seven consecutive years[1]. That was the greatest achievement ever made in China's history of poverty reduction. Such a big success should be attributed to the poverty alleviation in contiguous areas with acute difficulties as the main battlefields. In the *Outline for Poverty Reduction and Development of China's Rural Areas (2011 – 2020)*, the contiguous areas with acute difficulties, including Liupanshan mountainous regions, Qinling-Bashan mountainous regions, Wuling mountainous regions, Wumeng mountainous regions, desertification and rock desertification regions in Yunnan, Guangxi and Guizhou, border mountainous regions of western Yunnan, Daxinganling mountainous regions in the southern foothills, Yanshan-Taihang mountainous regions, Lvliang mountainous regions, Dabie mountainous regions, Luoxiao mountainous regions, as well as such regions where favorable policies are clearly implemented as Tibet, Tibetan areas in Qinghai, Sichuan, Yunnan and Gansu and four prefectures in southern Xinjiang, are considered as main battlefields of poverty alleviation. [2] Big challenges against poverty have been caused to these regions due to factors such as backward social and economic development, high incidence of poverty and natural environment. It is the steady advancement of the poverty alleviation in contiguous areas with acute difficulties that the goal of bidding farewell to absolute poverty can be achieved as scheduled. In this context, it is of great importance to intensify the efforts to summarize and propaganda China's anti-poverty practice, tell Chinese stories better, make the voice of China widely heard throughout the world[3] and contribute China's experience and plans on anti-poverty practice for the poverty governance of the whole world, especially the third world. In particular, it is necessary to tell the stories of the poverty alleviation in contiguous areas with acute difficulties better. Known for the Qinling and Bashan mountains, Qinling-Bashan mountainous regions cover 80 counties (districts, cities) in Gansu,

---

① Xi Jinping, "Speech at the Symposium on Winning a Decisive Victory in the Battle against Poverty", *People's Daily*, 2020-03-07 (2).

② *Outline for Poverty Reduction and Development of China's Rural Areas (2001 – 2020)*.

③ Liu Yongfu, "Resolutely Winning a Victory in the Battle against Poverty under the Guidance of General Secretary Xi Jinping's Remarks on Poverty Reduction", *Administration Reform*, 2019 (5), pp. 4 – 11.

Sichuan, Shaanxi, Henan and Hubei provinces and Chongqing City, and are mainly distributed in the southern region of Shaanxi Province (referred to as the " southern Shaanxi "). In 2010, China's rural populations whose income were below the threshold for poverty reduction, 1, 274 Yuan, numbered 3. 025 million. The incidence of poverty was 9. 9%, 7. 1% higher than the national average. The per capita net income of farmers was only 67. 2% of the national average. [1]

Overall, the path and connotationfor absolute poverty alleviation of Qinling-Bashan mountainous regions can be summarized as follows. During the process of making joint efforts in poverty alleviation and building a moderately prosperous society in all respects, the policies of the CPC Central Committee and the State Council are resolutely implemented; the top-level design of poverty alleviation is paid attention to; and the institutional advantages and the role of policy guidance are brought into full play. The principle of precision is adopted as the outline; the principles of classified governance and targeted implementation of measures are adhered to; and the measures directly aimed at each household are taken. The Party's leadership is regarded as the key and diversified organization and implementation modes including Party Committees' leadership, the governments' direction and multi-party collaboration are implemented. A modern large-scale characteristic, diversified industrial system is built in poverty-stricken areas based on industrial development. With regional resources as support, local advantages are effectively exploited according to local conditions to consolidate the responsibilities of local governments and give full play to the vitality of grassroots organizations. Good rural customs are developed and the self-development capability of poor populations is promoted by simulating the endogenous impetus of the poor. The relationship between ecological conservation and poverty alleviation is smoothened through relocation of the poor, ecological conservation and all-for-one tourism and with regional sustainable development as orientation. Basic public services and social security for the poor are conscientiously offered to the poor with stable poverty alleviation as guarantee, thus effectively

---

[1] *Plan on the Development and Poverty Alleviation of Qinling-Bashan Mountainous Regions (2011 – 2020).*

resisting the risk of returning to poverty. The industrial development, environmental governance, grass-roots governance and health governance in poverty-stricken areas are vigorously promoted; poverty governance is incorporated into the overall governance of these areas; a multi-level, multi-path and multi-participant grand anti-poverty pattern is formed; and the overall social and economic development in extremely poor areas are controlled through poverty alleviation.

1.2   Poverty Reduction and Ecological Conservation in Qinling-Bashan Mountainous Regions

Poverty reduction and ecological conservation are both long-term undertakings that require continuous efforts. Since the adoption of reform and opening up in China, Qinling-Bashan mountainous regions have achieved remarkable results in povertyalleviation, development and ecological conservation. However, challenges remain in ecological conservation and governance in order to effectively win the battle against poverty with high quality as scheduled.

1.2.1   Still Severe situation despite significant anti-poverty effect

Since the adoption of reform and opening up in China, significant poverty reduction effect has been achieved in Qinling-Bashan mountainous regions. According to statistics, for Shangluo City in Shaanxi Province, a city centrally located in Qinling-Bashan mountainous regions, in 1978, the per capita net income of farmers was only 58.2 Yuan and the poor populations numbered approximately 1.7 million; the grain yield was 523,500t, the ratio of economic crops to grain crops was 0.09: 1 and the total output value of agriculture, forestry, animal husbandry and fishery only reached 318 million Yuan. [1]

---

① Statistics Bureau of Shangluo City, "Rural Areas Takes on a New Look in the 40 Years of Reform and Opening Up: A Summary of the Achievements of the Agricultural and Rural Development in Shangluo within the 40 Years of Reform and Opening Up", 2018-08-01, http://tjj. shangluo. gov. cn/ index/ShowArticle. asp?ArticleID = 2910.

For Bazhong City in Sichuan Province, 1978, the per capita net income of farmers was only 119 Yuan; and for Guangyuan City in Sichuan Province, 1978, the per capital disposable income of rural residents was only 78 Yuan. For Shiyan City in Hubei Province, 1978, the total GDP was only 723 million Yuan, with per capita GDP of only 2, 249 Yuan. Backward social and economic development had made the poverty problem obvious. By the year 2000, Qinling-Bashan mountainous regions have basically accomplished the tasks allocated by the State in the *Seven-Year Priority Poverty Alleviation Program*, a program designed to lift 80 million people out of absolute poverty in a period of seven years from 1994 to 2000, basically meeting the food and clothing needs of the poor populations in the regions. Counties and districts in the regions had basically exceeded the threshold for satisfaction of basic food and clothing needs. Since the beginning of the 21st century, the State has paid increasing attention to and made investments in the work related to agriculture, farmers and rural areas, thereby greatly facilitating the poverty reduction and development of Qinling-Bashan mountainous regions and enabling the further significant decrease in poor population. In 2010, the per capita GDP of Qinling-Bashan mountainous regions and the general budgetary revenues of local governments reached 11, 694 Yuan and 455. 2 Yuan respectively, 3. 84 and 4. 4 times that of 2001; the ratio of primary to secondary to tertiary sectors was 21:46:33; the income of rural residents reached 3, 978 Yuan, 2. 8 times that of 2001; and the urbanization rate increased from 16. 7% in 2001 to 30. 4% in 2010. [1]

Despite the remarkable achievements in poverty reduction, Qinling-Bashan mountainous regions remain to face severe situation in completely eradicating poverty and ensuring regional social and economic development. The *Plan on the Development and Poverty Alleviation of Qinling-Bashan Mountainous Regions (2011 – 2020)* shows that the key counties for poverty alleviation at the national and provincial levels accounted for 90% of all the counties in the regions. In 2010, China's rural populations whose income were below the threshold for poverty

---

[1] *Plan on the Development and Poverty Alleviation of Qinling-Bashan Mountainous Regions (2011 – 2020)*.

reduction, 1, 274 Yuan, numbered 3. 025 million. The incidence of poverty was 9. 9%, 7. 1% higher than the national average and 3. 8% higher than the average of western China. The per capita net income of farmers that year was only 67. 2% of the national average. Due to the restrictions of environmental conditions and lagged development in the infrastructure construction of Qinling-Bashan mountainous regions, 40. 2% of the rural households faced varying degrees of difficulties in drinking and 69. 3% still had drinking safety problems. Rural network transformation had not been completed in 24. 7% of the administrative villages there. There were lots of inter-provincial and inter-county dead end roads; there was insufficient coverage of railway network and nine counties and districts of Longnan had no access to expressways. There were even 50. 6% of the administrative villages that had no access to asphalt roads in the regions, which seriously hindered regional development. Also, there were big shortcomings in the basic public services of Qinling-Bashan mountainous regions. In 2010, the per capita education and health expenditure of the regions was only equivalent to 56% of the national average. Among the 45 counties where the Kaschin-Beck disease had not been controlled, 16 ones were located in Qinling-Bashan mountainous regions, with a significant problem of disease-induced poverty. Less than 84% of the administrative villages had established village health clinics and the rate of participation in the new rural cooperative medical care system was less than 90%. Before the start of the battle against poverty, there remained a large poor population in the regions. Take Shangluo City in Shaanxi and Bazhong City in Sichuan for example. In the end of 2015, Shangluo had a total of 490, 200 registered poor residents from 161, 400 households, 15. 5% of the poor populations of Shaanxi Province; and 701 registered poor villages, including 175 extremely poor villages, 36. 3% of the total villages of the Province; [1] and the seven counties (districts) where poor villages were represented key counties (districts) for poverty reduction and development designated by the State and also those facing the most severe tasks in poverty reduction and development of the province. In the

---

① Wang Yongxing, Cui Fuhong, "210,000 people got rid of poverty this year in Shangluo City", 2018-10-13, http: //www. yybnet. net/shangluo/zhenan/201810/8258876. html.

end of 2014, Bazhong had a total of poor populations of 430, 156, with incidence of poverty being 14. 2%, 6. 5% higher than the average level of Sichuan Province. As of the end of the year, Bazhong had a per capita GDP of 13, 756 Yuan, only 29. 6% and 39. 2% of the whole country and Sichuan Province, respectively. What need to be effectively solved in the complete poverty alleviation, high-quality poverty alleviation and steady poverty alleviation of Qinling-Bashan mountainous regions include how to help support resources to better target poor populations, effectively solve the practical difficulties faced by the poor due to different reasons; how to get rid of the development dilemma of "highlands in majority with limited water resources and farmlands", develop a competitive modern poverty reduction industry and ensure the sustainable development of poor villages; and how to stimulate the endogenous impetus of the poor to get rid of poverty and better prevent the poor from falling into or returning to poverty caused by diseases, education and disasters.

1. 2. 2　Challenges against comprehensive ecological conservation and development despite significant ecological improvement

Mostly fragile in ecological environment, contiguous areas with acute difficulties produce a significant ecological effect. The poverty alleviation in these areas holds its key in striking a balance between ecological construction and poverty reduction and development.

With a total area of 225, 000 square kilometers, Qinling-Bashan mountainous regions cross the Qinling and Bashan Mountains. Mostly hills and hilly areas, the regions cross three major river systems including the Yangtze River, Yellow River and Huaihe River and are thesource origin of the Huaihe River, Hanjiang River, Danjiang River, Luohe River and other rivers, with a developed water systems. In the past, many parts of the regions were unsuitable for human inhabitation. Anyhow, disaster victims, refugees and the people that were relocated in a planned way moved to these regions in different historical stages due to disasters, wars caused in dynasty changes and feudal governments' troop stationing and diverting migrants for pioneering. Coupled with the population growth since the founding of New China, ecological conservation had not been paid enough attention to and the ecological bearing capacity of Qinling-Bashan mountainous regions had undergone great pressure for a period of time. As ecological conservation is increasingly attended, these regions are witnessing continued ecological conservation and improved ecological construction. Aerial seeding, returning farmland to forestland, natural forest protection and the construction of ecological projects in natural reserves are regarded as breakthrough points to contribute to the significant improvement in forest coverage rate, sewage treatment rate, harmless domestic garage treatment rate and other indexes.

However, Qinlin-Bashan mountainous regions remain to face huge challenges in comprehensive ecological conservation and development. As one of the six regions with the most frequent occurrences of debris flow in China, these regions are prone to suffer from floods, droughts, landslides and other natural disasters, with severe problems of falling into or returning to poverty. Among the 51 counties severely hit by the Wenchuan earthquake, 20 ones are located in Qinling-Bashan mountainous regions. Also as an important ecologically functional zone that maintains biodiversity and water conservation, the regions undertake major tasks such as water source protection for the mid-line section of the South-to-North Water Diversion Project, biodiversity protection, water source conservation, as well as soil and water conservation. Within the scope of the regions, 85 places are banned for development and 55 counties are classified into key ecologically functional zones restricted by the State for development[1]. It is the legal responsibility of the regions to maintain biodiversity and keep the water here safe and clean. How to ensure effective governance of ecological problems in poverty alleviation, develop ecological resources more scientifically, convert ecological advantages into economic gains, avoid the poverty risked caused by natural disasters and facilitate the development of characteristic tourism still requires the continuous exploration of Qinling-Bashan mountainous regions.

---

① *Plan on the Development and Poverty Alleviation of Qinling-Bashan Mountainous Regions (2011 - 2020).*

1. 3   Latest Achievements and Highlights of Poverty Alleviation in Qinling-Bashan Mountainous Regions

Since 2016, Qinling-Bashan mountainous regions have won a decisive victory in eradicating absolute poverty and achieved remarkable results, which are mainly reflected in the following aspects:

In terms of industrial development, the regions actively explore regional resources, exploit the existing farming and breeding experience and promote the development of large-scale characteristic agriculture featuring branding and technologization. The leading industries with strong market competitiveness and complete industrial chains have been formed in most poor counties and districts. By the end of 2018, 18 modern agricultural industry parks with total area of over 666. 7 hectares and output value of more than one hundred million Yuan each, 97 "one village, one product" standard demonstration parks with an area of 20 to 33. 3 hectares each and more than 23, 000 characteristic mini gardens had been built in Wangcang County, Guangyuan City, Sichuan Province[1]. In the end of 2018, 400, 666. 7 hectares of characteristic industrial bases were developed in Shiyan, Hubei Province, with an output value arising from agroproducts processing of 42. 13 billion Yuan, and 1, 215 cooperatives were developed in 456 poor villages. In Shangluo City, Shaanxi Province, 320 million bags of edible fungi and 375, 000 tons of fresh mushrooms were produced, ranking the city the first in the Shaanxi Province. The city had a total walnut planting area of 227, 933. 3 hectares and output of 165, 000t, the comprehensive output value exceeding 5 billion Yuan. The national walnut price index publishing platform was established in Luonan County, Shangluo City and the online trading platform of the Northwestern China Walnut Trading Center was completed. [2] The development of characteristic industries has

---

[1]   Chang Liqiang, "Opening Up a New Path to Poverty Alleviation in Qinling-Bashan Mountainous Regions", *Farmers Daily*, 2018-11-20, p. 6.

[2]   Zhang Zhiyou, Chen Xin, "Ten Highlights of Shangluo's Walnut Industry in 2019", 2020-02-20, http: //lyj. shangluo. gov. cn/pc/index/article/98098.

effectively enhanced the self-development capability of the mountainous regions and provided a strong support for the poor there to get rid of poverty and become rich.

In terms of immigration and relocation, by adhering to the principles of "targeted relocation, precise measures and refined management" and the goals of "smooth moving out, stable resettlement, getting employed and becoming rich step by step" for relocated poor people, Qinling-Bashan mountainous regions have effectively solved the production and living problems of the poor living in high-risk disaster areas, barren areas in production origin and other areas that are not suitable for human habitation within the scope of Qinling-Bashan mountainous regions and thoroughly eradicated the problem that local residents cannot be supported by the lands on which they live. In January 2017, Comrade Wang Yang, then vice premier of the State Council and head of the State Council Leading Group of Poverty Alleviation and Development, fully recognized the relocation work of Shangzhou District and Danfeng County in Shangluo City when inspecting these areas. In April 2020, General Secretary Xi Jinping gave a recognition and guidance on the anti-poverty work of Laoxian Town, Pingli County, Ankang city, Shaanxi Province, including relocation of local residents. Since the start of the 13th Five-Year Plan Period, 146,400 local residents from 47,000 households have relocated from inhospitable areas and 104,000 local residents from 31,300 households have been relocated accordingly in Hanzhong City, Shaanxi Province. For eight years, a total of 637,400 local residents from 194,600 households have been relocated for the purposes of avoiding disasters and getting rid of poverty, making the urbanization rate of the whole city increase by 10.8%. In the city, 16 provincial "double demonstration" communities, 25 municipal "double demonstration" communities and 114 new community-based factories have been built, allowing 37,000 residents to get jobs near the places of residence. [1] Since 2016, more than 53,000 houses have been built for the people who are relocated from inhospitable areas in Bazhong City, Sichuan Province; 189,000 relocated poor people

---

[1] "A total of 637,400 people relocated in Hanzhong for 8 years", Shaanxi Daily, 2019-01-14, p. 10.

have been registered; the people relocated there have had access to roads, electricity, water, TV and communication facilities; and sports sites, shopping malls, health clinics, cultural stations, garbage collection and transport points have been built, [1] thus effectively guaranteeing the living and production of the relocated people there.

In terms of ecological poverty reduction and environment construction, Qinling-Bashan mountainous regions have vigorously promoted ecological conservation and construction. Through a series of ecological poverty alleviation tasks such as designation of ecological forest rangers, compensation for ecological benefits, returning farmland to forestland, forestry development, engineering and labor services, technical and skills training, the regions have created income sources for the poor and realized the organic combination of ecological conservation and poverty alleviation. The grid management of the part of Qinling Mountains within the jurisdiction of Ankang City is conducted. Within such part of Qinling Mountains, 9 Level II grids, 78 Level III grids and 1, 231 Level IV grids are established, thus eliminating the blind zones for ecological and environmental management of Qinling Mountains[2]. In 2019, the number of national ecological forest rangers exceeded 1, 500 and 567, 000 poor people from 168, 000 households benefited from ecological construction for poverty alleviation[3]. Shangluo promotes all-for-one tourism and has built more than ten scenic spots at or above 4A level with three modes including high-quality scenic spots, characteristic towns and beautiful villages as support. A number of characteristic towns such as Luonan Music Town, Lihua Cultural and Creative Town, and beautiful villages of Qinling Mountains, such as Zhujiawan Village in Zhashui County and Qiandianzi Village in Shanyang County have been developed.

In terms of infrastructure construction and public service, in Longnan City, Gansu Province from the years 2015 to 2018, more than

① Li Junru, "Bazhong solves the 'four difficulties' and vigorously promotes poverty alleviation through relocation", *Bazhong Daily*, 2016-06-13, p. 2.

② Zhang Binfeng, "Ankang gradually builds a long-term mechanism for ecological conservation in the Qinling Mountainous", *Shaanxi Daily*, 2018-10-29.

③ "Ankang receives three consecutive merits", 2020-04-02, http://www.xibujuece.com/chengshi/shaanxi/ankang/2020/0402/66999.html.

12,000 kilometers of village roads were cemented; the drinking safety problem having troubled more than one million rural residents were solved; the houses of more than 100,000 households were transformed; and poor villages had full access to electric power supply and some better administrative villages had full coverage of roads. For the 598.81km village roads in Shangluo, the "asphalt returning to sand" problem was rectified in place. The 444.73km roads to extremely poor villages were completed. 4,971 infrastructure and public service facilities were built in the city[1]. In 2017, 1,886 students from poverty-stricken households were assisted in the city and the funds of 1.023 million Yuan were allocated to achieve the goal of 100% enrollment of school-age children in Wanyuan, 2017.[2] In Hanzhong City, standard village health clinics with collective property rights were built in 1,010 poor villages of Hanzhong and 669,540 poor people participated in the rural cooperative medical care system. 4,977 severely ill patients were all treated in a centralized way and 52,187 patients of chronic diseases such as hypertension, diabetes, tuberculosis and severe mental disorders were entitled to follow-up service provided by contracted family doctors on a quarterly basis.[3] By making up for the shortcomings in basic public services such as basic medical care and compulsory education, the bottlenecks that constrained the development of Qinling-Bashan mountainous regions have been effectively broken through, thus laying a solid foundation for sustainable social and economic development.

Qinling-Bashan mountainous regions have made historic achievements inpoverty alleviation and will get rid of absolute poverty as scheduled. It is of typical characteristics in featured industry development, pro-poor tourism, follow-up support for the relocated people, multi-participant collaboration, motivating the innovation of grassroots organizations, exploiting local resource advantages and

① Guo Shimeng, Ji Xinpeng, "Poverty Alleviation Report from the Deep Qinling Mountains: Highlights of Shangluo's Poverty Alleviation in 2019", *Shaanxi Daily*, 2019-12-25, p. 3.

② "The Wan Yuan Education Bureau vigorously implements education to support poverty alleviation", 2017-11-17, http://www.dz169.net/2017/1117/92600.shtml.

③ Hanzhong, "maintain the bottom line, make up for shortcomings, seek long-term benefits", 2019-10-23, Hanzhong Poverty Alleviation Office, 2019-10.

improving the minimum guarantee system, etc. The regions have accumulated lots of poverty alleviation experience. The experience is worthy of further exploitation, effective refining and wide reference when the regions tell Chinese poverty alleviation stories better.

Chapter 1
History of Poverty Reduction and Development of Qinling-Bashan Mountainous Regions

General Secretary Xi Jinping has pointed out that anti-poverty is a major event in the governance of a country, either in China or the rest of the world, either in the ancient times or the present. The eradication of poverty, the improvement of people's lives and the gradual realization of joint prosperity are an essential demand requirement of socialism and an important mission of the CPC. Before the founding of New China, the CPC led a vast number of peasants in beating local tyrants and dividing lands, aiming to liberate these peasants. Now, the Party led a large number of farmers in getting rid of poverty and building a moderately prosperous society, with a view to helping them lead a happy life. [1] During the process of building a moderately prosperous society in all respects, China faced the most arduous tasks in rural areas, especially in poor areas. Qinling-Bashan mountainous regions, as one of the 14 contiguous areas with acute difficulties, have a long history and unique location and represent an important ecological barrier. It is also one of the most daunting challenges in the process of poverty governance in China.

1.1　The Qinling-Bashan Mountainous Regions with a Long History

Qinling-Bashan mountainous regions cross sixprovinces and cities of

---

[1]　*Selected Important Documents since the 18th CPC National Congress (Part II)*, Beijing: Central Document Publishing House, 2018, p. 31.

China, including Gansu, Sichuan, Shaanxi, Chongqing, Henan and Hubei. Ankang and Hanzhong in Shaanxi, Longnan in Gansu, Nanyang in Henan, Shiyan in Hubei, Guangyuan and Bazhong in Sichuan are key areas for poverty alleviation in the regions. The regions have a profound history. During the thousands of years of history, the regions have gradually grown among repeated challenges due to their important military positions. The beautiful sceneries here have also attracted a lot of writers and poems. During the Period of Democratic Revolution, the regions were ignited by the flames of revolution and a large number of heroes dedicated their lives to the liberation cause of the Chinese nation.

1. 1. 1   Old site of ancestors, birthplace of civilization

Qinling-Bashan mountainous regions have a long history of human inhabitation and are one of the birthplaces of the Chinese nation and the Chinese civilization. According toarchaeological findings, the movements of our ancestors can be seen in Shangluo as early as the Paleolithic Period more than one million years ago. During the Neolithic Period, our ancestors lived and multiplied here along the banks of Luohe River, Danjiang River, Jinqian River, Qianyou River and Xunhe River. The Yangxu Mountain in Luonan County was said to be the place where, Cang Jie, one of the four ancient Chinese saints, created words. According to the *Records of Shangzhou Prefecture in Zhili Province*, "The twenty-eight words in the stone house of the Yangxu Mountain are the remains of Cang Jie. "[1] According to historical records, Shangluo was the initial place for the Shang Clan to establish the Shang Dynasty. The *Records of the Grand Historian: the Shang Dynasty* reads, "The mother of Yin Xie was called Jian Di. There was also a lady surnamed Gu and she was the second concubine of Emperor Ku. " "After Xie grew into an adult, he gained merits by helping Yu the Great control flood. Emperor Shun thus ordered Xie, ' Now, the public did not know how to respect each other. The normal father-son, monarch-subject, husband-wife, young-old relations and those among

---

① "Approaching Shangluo: Introduction of Shangluo Culture", 2016-09-26, https: // www. sohu. com/a/115080967_488428.

friends have been disrupted. You are ordered to offer education on making the five relations smooth. You should learn to be tolerant in offering such education. ' Xie was awarded lands in the place Shang and given the surname Zi. Xie obtained development in the periods of Tang Yao, Yu Shun and Yu the Great, did good deeds for the common people and made remarkable achievements. Thus, the public lived a steady life. "[1] At Longgang Temple Cultural Relics in Nanzheng District, Hanzhong City, the remains of human movements in the Paleolithic and Neolithic Periods have also been found. The "Longgang Man" of the Paleolithic period lived 1.2 million years ago, earlier than the "Lantian Man", "Beijing Man" and "Shandingdong Man". The Neolithic relics of Longgang were left 7,000 to 6,000 years ago. They are the relics of the maternal clan period of the primitive society. It demonstrates that at least six or seven thousand years ago, the ancient civilization of the Hanzhong Basin reached quite a high level. [2] During the long history, many beautiful legends and long-lasting memories have been left to Qinling-Bashan mountainous regions, which have been circulating in the memories of the Chinese for long.

1.1.2   A transportation center that has endured challenges

Qinling-Bashan mountainous regions have always been regarded as a military fortress during the Feudal Age of China. Just due to the reason, they are put under the control of feudal system for a long time. During the Warring States Period, in the thirteenth year of King Huiwen of Qin State or 312 BC, the Qin State started to set Hanzhong County (now Ankang City, which was moved to the present Hanzhong County in the early of the Eastern Han Dynasty). The County started from the Yangping Pass in Mianyang (now Wuhou Town, Mianxian County, Shaanxi Province) in the west and ended till Yunguan (now

---

[1]   Yu Fangping, "Identification of Yin Xie's Initial Fiefs in Shangluo's Local Chronicles", *Journal of Shangluo Teachers College*, 2001(4), pp. 64 – 65 + 68.

[2]   "The Significance of the Old Stone Tools of Longgang Temple", 2019-06-20, http://www.hanzhong.gov.cn/zjhz/lswh/201906/t20190620_587274.html.

Yunxian County in Hubei) and Jingshan, extending for thousands of miles. [1] In the first lunar month of the first year of the Han Dynasty or 206 BC, Xiang Yu named Liu Bang as the King of Han, "The lands of Ba, Shu and Hanzhong were awarded to the king and Danzheng, now Hanzhong City, was used as capital". The Han Dynasty, which lasted more than 400 years and had a profound influence on the Chinese history and culture, was just born here. Due to the geographical location, Qinling-Bashan mountainous regions often accepted people who were relocated here for various reasons, and then the Hubei-Shangluo Trade Channel, Henan-Shangluo Trade Channel and Shangluo-Guanzhong Trade Channel came into being. [2] Especially during the Ming and Qing Dynasties, due to military garrison, population growth and disasters, refugees moved to southern Shaanxi and the feudal governments consciously guided poor peasants through the policies of late levy and less taxation to guide them to cultivate wastelands in southern Shaanxi. That has significantly increased the number of residents in mountainous areas[3], injected vitality into the development of Qinling-Bashan mountainous regions, and also brought huge pressure to ecological environment. The important strategic position also caused Qinling-Bashan mountainous regions to get trapped in wars, causing social unrest. For example, during the Period of the Three Kingdoms, Hanzhong was located between Guanzhong and Bashu. The roads converged and the terrain conditions were dangerous. These regions thus became a strategic center for the fierce competitions between Wei and Shu States. This had also caused a serious impact on the social and economic development of Qinling-Bashan mountainous regions and also made the regions trapped in wars.

---

[1] Song Jie, "The important Impact of Hanzhong on War between Shu and Wei States of the Three Kingdoms Period", *Journal of Capital Normal University (Social Science Edition)*, 2004 (1), pp. 5 – 13.

[2] "Geographical Structure and Others of Migrants from Zhen'an County in Ming and Qing Dynasties Observed from Tablets", *Journal of Shangluo Teachers College*, 2005 (3), pp. 23 – 27.

[3] He Degui, *Research on the Implementation of Relocation Policies for Disaster-Avoiding Migrants in Mountainous Areas: Statements in Southern Shaanxi*, Beijing: People's Publishing House, 2016, pp. 49 – 52.

1. 1. 3　Magnificent Qin State and beautiful Chu State born from cultural landscapes

Qinling-Bashan mountainous regions have two mountains, namely Qinling Mountains and Bashan Mountains. As the watershed between the Yangtze River and the Yellow River, the Qinling Mountains have a total length of about 800 kilometers. Mountains are adjacent and rivers are interlaced with each other here. Named after the ancient Ba Nation and the Bafang State, the Bashan Mountains start from the Jialing River Valley in the west, end till the Wudang Mountains in the east and extend from northwest to southeast for about 300 kilometers. Qinling-Bashan mountainous regions, which combine the magnificence of the Qin State and beautiful sceneries of the Chu State presents asplendid picture of both states. The regions have attracted the writers and scholars of dynasties to write and leave excellent works. For example, Li Bai, a famous poet of Tang Dynasty, wrote " Satrap Pei has immortal temperament, keep away from common people and affairs. Your expressions are shaped like the cloud above the fairyland on the waterside and seem to calmly imagine purple light. You assume your office in Shangzhou, make political achievements with mind at ease. Just go beyond the common world and conscientiously explore the quiet and deep realm"; Bai Juyi, also a poet of Tang Dynasty, said "Birds tweet with fallen flowers, returning to south gratifies your mind. Get accommodation in Qinling Mountains at moon night, or make a tour to Shujiang River in spring"; Huang Tingjian, a poet of Song Dynasty left the following words in his *Across West Mountain*, "Through undeveloped spring leaves, I look far into the west mountain and wonder when they are accessible. With clouds rising in the sky, I recall an old glossy ganoderma picking man who is singing songs. " The beautiful landscape also nourishes the simple character of residents in Qinling-Bashan mountainous regions.

1. 1. 4　Red flags in the old revolutionary base area

Qinling-Bashan mountainous regions have a total of 47 old revolutionary base areas in 58. 8% of the all the counties here. At the beginning of the democratic revolution, the Hubei-Henan-Shaanxi Revolutionary Base Area was born in these regions. During the Period of Great Revolution, two special CPC branches, Shangxian and Longjuzhai, were established in Shangluo. After the failure of the Great Revolution in 1927, a group of CPC members returned to Hanzhong and established the CPC Nanzheng Group for propaganda of Marxism, Leninism and CPC policies. In November 1930, the Southern Shaanxi Special Committee of the CPC or the Hannan Special Committee was formally established. On February 7, 1933, the Provincial Committee of the Sichuan-Shaanxi Border Region of the CPC and the Soviet Government of the Sichuan-Shaanxi Border Region were established in Tongjiang County. In March 1935, the Sichuan-Shaanxi Soviet Area that covered an area of over 200,000 square kilometers and had a population of over 7 million was formed. It covered more than 20 counties, including Daxian, Chengkou, Wanyuan, Zhenba and Xixiang in the east and Wangcang, Guangyuan and Ningqiang in the west. [1] Since the outbreak of the Chinese People's War of Resistance against Japanese Aggression, the people of southern Shaanxi spontaneously established the First People's Anti-Japanese Army of southern Shaanxi. They sought the leadership of the Party and accepted the order to fight against the Japanese by going northward, becoming the sole revolutionary team that joined the Red Army and was incorporated into the system of the Army. During the Revolutionary War, a large number of heroes sacrificed their lives for the revolution and made important contributions to the establishment of the new regime. In June 1985, Li Xiannian, then president of China, inscribed, "The martyrs of the Henan-Hubei-Shaanxi Revolutionary Base Area will be immortal!" The red mark of Qinling-Bashan mountainous regions has become the valuable spiritual wealth of the people in the mountainous regions.

---

[1] "The Red Fourth Army in Hanzhong", 2014-09-23, http://www.hanzhong.gov.cn/zjhz/lswh/201409/t20140923_5246.html.

1. 2   Development of the Qinling-Bashan Mountainous Regions from the Founding of New China to the Adoption of Reform and Opening-up (1949 – 1978)

In the early period of the founding of New China, the people of the Qinling-Bashan mountainous regions actively participated in the production and construction of the regions in the face of the urgent need to improve their lives and the mountainous region economy to be urgently developed. By adhering to the principle of self-reliance, all members were mobilized to make joint efforts, thus significantly improving the living and production conditions of the regions and laying a solid foundation for the subsequent poverty reduction and development.

1. 2. 1   The mountainous region economy be developed

In 1949, China had a per capita industrial and agricultural output value of only 86Yuan, annual per capita national income of only 69. 29 Yuan, annual per capita grain yield of only 209kg, annual per capita oil yield of only 4. 7kg, annual per capital cloth output of only 3. 49m and annual per capital cotton yield of only 0. 82kg. [1] The extremely serious poverty problem was threatening the livelihood and even lives of most Chinese people. In 1949, the annual GDP of major prefecture-level cities within Qinling-Bashan mountainous regions was generally at an extremely low level (see Table 1. 1). In 1949, Hanzhong had a per capital GDP of only 96 Yuan; the absolute income of rural residents of Bazhong, Sichuan was only 3. 1 Yuan and the absolute consumer spending of rural residents in the city was only 3 Yuan; and the annual per capital GDP of Longnan, Gansu was only 39 Yuan. [2]

---

[1]   Data source: *China Economic Yearbook 1981*.

[2]   "An Account of Longnan's New Development Using Numbers", *Gansu Daily*, 2019-10-15 (11).

Table 1. 1   **Annual GDP of major prefecture-level cities of Qinling-**
Bashan mountainous regions in 1949

Province	Prefecture-level City①	GDP in 1949 (in hundred million Yuan)
Shaanxi	Hanzhong	1. 81
	Ankang	1. 4
	Shangluo	0. 4
Sichuan	GuangYuan	0. 47
	Bazhong	0. 87
Gansu	Longnan	0. 5
Henan	Nanyang	2. 59

Source: Party newspapers and websites of Provinces and prefecture-level cities.

Qinling-Bashan mountainous regions, which ushered in liberation after wars, underwent huge challenges in developing production, improving lives and reducing poverty. How to effectively exploit regional resources under the strict constraints of the natural conditions featuring "highlands in majority with limited water resources and farmlands", develop mountainous region economyin line with local conditions, leading the masses in developing production, eliminating the serious impacts of natural disasters on agricultural production and solving the problems of living and production facing the general public. Under the leadership of the Party and the government, the people of Qinling-Bashan mountainous regions started a large-scale production campaign.

1. 2. 2   Mobilization of the general public into production

In the wave of building socialism, a thriving mass movement was launched in Qinling-Bashan mountainous regions, which improved the living and production standards of the masses. The Northern Sichuan[2] Mass Production and the production campaign of "One Liter of Walnuts per Household" in Shangluo were just the representative cases.

---

① For ease of reading, current official names have been adopted for all prefecture-level cities.

② It refers to the northern part of the Sichuan Basin with Guangyuan, Bazhong, and Nanchong as centers, and belongs to the Daba mountainous regions.

1. 2. 2. 1 Mass production launched in northern Sichuan to improve people's lives

Farmland water conservancy projects were vigorously promoted throughout thecounty from February to August, 1950 in order to facilitate agricultural production. During the period, new repairs and restoration projects such as channels, dams, water carts and water wells were used to recover and add a total of 544, 000 hectares of farmlands. Also, annual repairs and consolidation of the lands with an irrigation area of 825. 3 hectares were completed. ① During the construction of water conservancy projects, the projects such as Northern Sichuan Sunzigou Irrigation Project were effectively repaired, which provided a strong support for the agricultural production of northern Sichuan. In June 1951, land reform was completed in 380 towns in the suburbs of Nanchong and under the jurisdiction of six counties in Nanchong, Suining, Nanbu, Langzhong, Santai and Yuechi, and four districts in Daxian, Guangyuan, Bazhong and Jiangyou. The poor farmers, more than 50% of the local rural populations, shared around 0. 067 hectare of land (about 3,000kg grain output per hectare) and a certain amount of RMB. That had greatly stimulated farmers' enthusiasm for production and the rural mass production movement was thriving. According to incomplete statistics, there were more than 24, 000 new and restored ponds and weirs, either big or small, in the regions. They can irrigate more than 33, 564 hectares of lands, reclaim more than 10, 000 hectares of wastelands and more than 50 million plants were grown there. ② In order to solve the problem of selling local products in the southwestern China, officials of the region were sent to major cities of China to investigate the supply and demand of local products, publicize and introduce the local products of the region so as to increase the exports. Also, local product transportation and sales contracts were signed between different provinces of the southwestern China to increase domestic sales.

Also, the masses of northern Sichuan were mobilized to develop health and education undertakings. By adhering to the guideline of

---

① "This Year's Farmland Water Conservancy", *People's Daily*, 1950-8-25 (1).

② "One Heart in the Frontline and Rear Areas: On Mass Production Movement in the Rural Areas of Northern Sichuan", *People's Daily*, 1951-6-18 (2).

"Prevention First", large-scale preventative injections of mixed cholera and typhoid vaccines were given. In 1950, bacterial dysentery was discovered in Zhongjiang in northern Sichuan and was quickly put to an end under the rigorous control of the local governments and health authorities. [1] After land reform and rent reduction in the vast rural areas of northern Sichuan, the local masses used a proportion of their victory fruits obtained from these actions to run schools, build school buildings and buy school furniture. The number of rural primary schools and students witnessed a significant increase. According to the statistics of the Department of Culture and Education of the Northern Sichuan People's Administration then, there were 15, 622 primary schools (including over 13, 900 private ones) and up to 1, 197, 600 students in the whole northern Sichuan in the spring of 1951. [2] In 1978, the per capita disposable income of rural residents of Bazhong was 89 Yuan and the consumer spending by rural residents was 63 Yuan.

1. 2. 2. 2　The masses of Shangluo mobilized to develop the mountainous region industry

The planting of walnuts has a history of more than 2, 000 years in Shangluo City. Since the Tang Dynasty, the walnuts in Shangluo have developed to a large scale. The Shangluo Prefectural Committee of the CPC and the Shangluo Prefectural Administrative Office initiated the campaign of "One Liter of Walnuts for Each Household" by drawing experience from the masses' production and analyzing local production conditions. On September 20, 1957, the decision of "One Liter of Walnuts for Each Household" was finally made at the expanded meeting of the Shangluo Prefectural Committee of the CPC. The local people proactively responded to the call and the mass movement of walnut planning was unfolded in a full swing in the whole prefecture. By the end of the year, the task of "One Liter of Walnuts for Each Household" was over-fulfilled. In 1958, the Shangluo Prefectural Committee of the CPC

---

[1]　"Achievements have been made in southwestern region's summer epidemic prevention work this year, without serious epidemic and infectious diseases", *People's Daily*, 1950-9-11 (3).

[2]　"Farmers in northern Sichuan established a large number of primary schools", *People's Daily*, 1951-6-19 (3).

called on each household to plant two more liters of walnuts. According to statistics, 93, 000 liters of walnuts were planted in the entire prefecture and nearly three liters were planted by each household as per the 32, 000 households then. ① On January 31, 1958, Chairman Mao Zedong instructed in the *Sixty Working Methods of the Communist Party of China*, "the experience that one liter of walnuts was planted by each household in Shangluo Prefecture is worth to be studied by other places of China. The experience may be extended to the planting of fruit trees, mulberry, oak, tea, varnish, oil trees and other economic forests after it is discussed and obtains the consent of the masses. " On February 26, 1958, the Shaanxi Provincial Party Committee of the CPC issued the *Notice on Promoting the Experience of "One Liter of Walnuts for Each Household" of Shangluo Prefecture* in the whole province. It called on the people of the whole province to take actions and actively learn and promote the advanced experience of Shangluo. In September of the same year, the Walnut Production Site Meeting was held on the Bayi Forest Farm, Wuguan Commune, Danfeng County, Shangluo Prefecture and was attended by representatives from 16 provinces and municipalities throughout the country. At the meeting, the participants were encouraged to promote the experience of Shangluo Prefecture in the areas which is suitable for planting walnuts throughout the country. ② In 1962, there were more than eight million walnut trees in Shangluo Prefecture, nearly 24 times more than that prior to the year 1957. ③ On May 20, 1962, the People's Daily gave a long account of the story titled *Down-to-earth Steps: Before and After the Campaign of "One Liter of Walnuts for Each Household" in Shangluo Prefecture*. By the end of 1970s, Shangluo had become an export base famous for walnut trading and the exports of walnuts reached one sixth of those of the whole country.

---

①   Wang Genxian, "The Documentary of the ' One Liter of Walnuts for Each Household' Campaign in Shangluo Prefecture", *Shaanxi Forestry*, 1994 (1), pp. 20 – 21.

②   Ibid.

③   Liu Ye, Huang Zhi, "Practical Steps: On the Success and Failure of the ' One Liter of Walnuts for Each Household' Campaign in Shangluo District", *People's Daily*, 1962-05-20.

1. 2. 3 Characteristics and quality of development and construction during the period of socialist exploration

The years 1949 to 1978 were a period of exploring path to the Chinese socialism. Under the leadership of the CPC, the masses of Qinling-Bashan mountainous regions got engaged in production by relying on themselves to improve production and living conditions. The poverty reduction practice is of the following important characteristics.

1. 2. 3. 1 Desiring to work hard rather than enduring hard days

At that time, Qinling-Bashan mountainous regions were faced with an environment with extremely backward infrastructure facilities and serious shortage of production conditions. In the face of difficulties, the masses fought against poverty with firm determination and built large-scale water conservancy facilities and schools. They worked hard to improve production conditions, find a way out for the development of the mountainous areas. It was the spirit and strong will of "desiring to work hard rather than enduring hard days" that provided a momentum for the development of the extremely barren and backward Qinling-Bashan mountainous regions and made the desire of the masses to improve their lives realized step by step. The firm determination to fight against poverty is what should be insisted on in the poverty reduction practice of any period.

1. 2. 3. 2 Self-reliance, active explorations

The action that each household in Shangluo planted one liter of walnuts was taken after the officials of Shangluo Prefecture inspected villages had in-depth conversations with the masses of the mountainous areas and obtained an understanding towards the development of economy in the mountainous areas. It demonstrated their effective understanding of Shangluo's foundation for the existing walnut planting. The agency sales of local products in southwestern China were also a good solution to the sales problem that was discovered through active explorations and by continuously accumulating experience and lessons. In the face of lots of difficulties encountered in production, the masses of Qinling-Bashan mountainous regions exploited the resources and production foundation that can be relied on in the local through self-reliance and continuously explored effective ways and experience, which represent important weapons for overcoming practical problems in poverty reduction.

1. 2. 3. 3 All the masses mobilized to deliver joint efforts

The success in the great production of northern Sichuan and the planting of walnuts in Shangluo should be attributed to the joint participation and concerted efforts of the masses. Infrastructure construction and the control of infectious diseases cannot do without the strong support from the masses. Faced with huge challenges and difficulties, we must uphold the dominant position of the masses, firmly and resolutely mobilize, organize and reply on the masses. Only by rallying the joint efforts of the masses can we overcome difficulties one after another.

1. 3 Poverty Reduction and Development of Qinling-Bashan Mountainous Regions from the Third Plenary Session of the 11th Central Committee to the 18th CPC National Congress (1978 to 2012)

The Third Plenary Session of the 11th Central Committee of the CPC held in December 1978 opened a new chapter for China's reform and opening up. From the Third Plenary Session of the 11th Central Committee to the 18th CPC National Congress, the poverty reduction and development of Qinling-Bashan mountainous regions entered a new phase and lots of poverty reduction experience was explored.

1. 3. 1 Initiation of institutionalized poverty reduction

In the end of 1978, the rural poverty incidence rate reached 97. 5%. Taking the rural population with permanent residence for general projection, the rural poor population was 770 million. [1] The great decision of reform and opening up made at the third Plenary of the 11th Central Committee of the CPC initiated a new process of rural reform. Economic construction directly lifted a large number of rural poor people out of poverty and made them rich. Anyhow, as economic construction was gradually pushed, the effect of economic growth in directly getting the poor out of poverty became weakened. Due to the insufficient development foundations, resources and conditions and the existence of complicated causes for poverty, some contiguous areas with acute difficulties including Qinling-Bashan mountainous regions remained to encounter concentrated and extreme poverty problems when economic construction was gradually pushed. These problems thus became the most daunting challenges. In order to facilitate poverty reduction and realize joint prosperity, China officially launched a large-scale institutionalized poverty alleviation and development program in 1986.

1. 3. 2　Institutionalized poverty alleviation based on local conditions in multiple measures

1. 3. 2. 1　Industry orientation, integrated efforts

Qinling-Bashan mountainous regions actively promoted industrial development and improved the income level of the poor through industries, trying to achieve sustainable livelihoods. In 1986, the households and people who earned an income of less than 150 Yuan each in Longnan Prefecture of Gansu accounted for 34. 2% and 49. 8% of the total rural households and populations there. Based on local reality, the Longnan Prefectural Committee of the CPC and the Longnan Prefectural Administrative Office proposed the poverty reduction projects to be intensified in poverty reduction and encouraged the poverty reduction

---

[1]　"Achievements in poverty reduction and development have attracted worldwide attention, and decisive progress has been made in the fight against poverty: report series V on the social and economic development achievements in the 40 years of reform and opening up", 2018-09-03, http://www. gov. cn/xinwen/2018-09/03/content_5318888. htm.

measuring featuring "four-one". ① Through one and a half year of practice, 3,933.3 hectares of terraced fields were built in the entire Longnan. Coupled with the original terraced fields, 115,000 rural households got 0.067 hectare of basic farmland per person. Longnan Prefecture allocated special funds to support the development of economic forests in difficult areas. Through the "national investment in providing seedlings and commune members in providing labor service", the area of trees planted in two years reached 116,000 hectares, enabling 56,400 households to get 0.067 hectare of orchard each. In order to achieve the goal of one household selling one big livestock per year, the prefecture have identified 599 aquaculture projects, built 29 improved breeding sites and 50 feed processing plants to promote the development of farmers' household aquaculture. With the advancement of reform and opening up, the poor people are actively raising their income by providing labor services, and many farmers have started to get rid of the traditional concept of "never going out, regardless of poverty or death" and go out for work. In 1986, 62,000 people went out to work and earned a total income of more than 19 million Yuan. ②

1.3.2.2　Extensive mobilization, public participation

Poverty reduction requires the participation of all poor people. Effective ways to encourage public participation were explored in all places of Qinling-Bashan mountainous regions. In Shiyan City, Hubei Province, poverty-stricken villages were encouraged to decide on poverty alleviation projects through "bean voting"③. The decision-making power was handed over to farmers based on the thought that farmers shall have the right to formulate plans, decide on ideas, select projects, use funds

---

① The supported will, within two to three years, get 0.067 hectare of basic farmland per person and 0.067 hectare of orchard, sell one big livestock each year per household (equivalent to the number of pigs or sheep), and provide labor services per person each household.

② "Achievements are steadily made in the poverty reduction of Longnan Prefecture: getting 0.067 hectare of basic farmland per person and 0.067 hectare of orchard, selling one big livestock each year per household (equivalent to the number of pigs or sheep), and ensuring the provision of labor services per person each household", *People's Daily*, 1987-7-27 (2).

③ Villagers voted in a democratic way on poverty reduction projects. One bean represents one vote. The project winning more "beans" in the voting will be implemented.

and seek markets. The determination of all poverty reduction projects, determination of the supported and utilization of poverty reduction funds shall be submitted to the Villagers' Assembly for voting. The government did not issue any official document on any specific poverty reduction project so that the masses select their own ways to get rich. In Yindongshan Village, Tuguanya Town, Danjiangkou City, the masses chose the anti-poverty projects of "pigs, marsh, oranges, tea and roads" in the simplest and most primitive democratic way, "throwing corn grains". When the government investment was less than 1 million Yuan, the people there raised over 3 million Yuan by themselves to develop more than 66. 67 hectares of high-quality tea fields and "King Orange 121" ordered lands, and build over 30 new fish ponds, more than 100 biogas digesters and more than 20 "Happy Farmhouses" with ecological homes as themes. They were awarded by the State Council Leading Group Office of Poverty Alleviation and Development as a "Model Village in Integrated Development. "[1]

In order to develop the infrastructure facilities necessary for production, the Ankang Military Subarea intensified efforts and exploited its overall strength to organize the militias in organic units to participate in poverty reduction. During the period from 1991 to 1996, more than one thousand militias were mobilized in organic units to fight against poverty in over 110 key projects; over 200, 000 grassroots militias were organized in aggregate and more than 20 million man days were invested. As a result, 19, 333. 3 hectares of farmlands were developed in the Qinling and Bashan Mountains. The per capita arable land area in the rural areas of Ankang, which featured highlands in majority with limited water resources and farmlands, was added by 0. 018 hectare. More than 900 kilometers of water channels and more than 120 ponds were built, turning dry fields on the over 20, 333. 3 hectares of mountains into high-yield fields where stable yields can be ensured despite drought or excessive rain. More than 1, 200km highways were built and widened, ending the history of carriage by shoulder in 80% of villages in these regions. More than 33, 333. 3 hectares of trees were

---

[1]   "Shiyan, Hubei handed over the decision-making power to farmers: villager's ' bean voting' poverty reduction project", *People's Daily*, 2006-4-23 (7).

planted and over 6, 666. 7 hectares bases of special trees such as mulberry, chestnut, orange and paint were built, laying an important foundation for poverty alleviation in the old revolutionary base areas. ①

1. 3. 2. 3   Active innovation, arborous explorations

In the poverty reduction, the local governments in Qinling-Bashan mountainous regions actively drew effective experience from other regions and accumulated the good experience and practices that can solve practical problems. For example, during the period of the implementation of the *Seven-Year Priority Poverty Alleviation Program*, the rural bank poverty reduction model adopted by Bangladesh was introduced into Shangluo City. The door-to-door poverty alleviation work mode with Shangluo characteristics, with micro-credit at its core, was explored and promoted. Project development was implemented in each household; poverty reduction through science and technology was applied in each household; the living and production standards of villages and households were improved; and social assistance was offered to each household. A total of 20 township poverty reduction branches, poverty alleviation centers and 21, 995 joint guarantee groups were established in the whole prefecture. ② During the same period, 383 million Yuan of micro-credit poverty alleviation funds were allocated to each household and to support poor households to develop income-increase projects. The food and clothing needs of over 700, 000 poor populations were satisfied. ③ In Shangluo, the poverty reduction experience aligning the rural minimum subsistence allowance system to the poverty reduction and development policies were also explored. Related tasks were strictly performed in four stages namely, early preparation, recognition and

---

① "By giving play to the overall operational advantages, adapting to the requirements of the market economy, the Ankang militias have achieved good results in poverty alleviation", *People's Daily*, 1996-12-23.

② Cui Bo, "Priority in the development of human resources: a strategic choice for poverty reduction and development in the early 21st century: A special survey report in Shangluo, Shaanxi Province", *Poor Areas in China*, 2000 (08), pp. 4 - 8.

③ "Poverty Reduction in Shangluo: Creating a New Brilliance with New Ideas: ' A Probe into Shangluo that Makes Breakthroughs in Development ' Report Series ", 2008-10-11, http://www. shangluo. gov. cn/info/1054/11010. htm.

identification, file registration and implementation of policies. Eight standard operation procedures were followed, including identification and recognition of indexes, establishment of a review group, householder's application, door-to-door identification, democratic review, examination and approval, registration and entry, formation and implementation of policies. The combination with reality was highlighted in the actual work. The low-income household ranking method by which villagers' representatives were ranked in an ascending order according to whether they earned lower or higher income so as to determine low-income households. Also, the " six-not-included " method was implemented. [1] In August 2011, the on-site meeting on the effective linkage of the two systems [2] was held in Shangluo and the "Shangluo experience" was thus promoted throughout the country.

From the reform and opening up till the 18th CPC National Congress, Qinling-Bashan mountainous regions achieved remarkable results in poverty reduction and development with institutionalized poverty reduction practices as support. The poor population of the regions decreased significantly, and infrastructure construction, industrial development and basic public service coverage improved a lot. According to the data for the year 2010, the per capita GDP and the general budgetary revenues of local governments in the regions were 11, 694 Yuan and 455. 2 Yuan; and the income of urban and rural residents reached 13, 155 Yuan and 3, 978 Yuan respectively. In the regions, 82% of the students received nine-year compulsory education and the average length of education received by local residents was 8 years. The rate of participation in the new rural medical care system reached 89. 3% and the people living on minimum subsistence allowances were basically supported. The urbanization rate reached 30. 4%; the rate of access to

---

[1]　Six-not-included households: Households living in multi-storey buildings or purchasing commercial houses, households with motor vehicles and large agricultural machinery, households with fixed work and stable income, households supported by fiscal expenditure, households whose daily spending is obviously higher than the local average, households who engage employees for a long time to get engaged in production and business activities.

[2]　"The effective linkage of the two systems in our city has become the national poverty reduction experience", website of Shangluo Municipal People's Government, http: // www. shangluo. gov. cn/info/ 1054/3949. htm, August 19, 2011.

asphalt (cement) roads in administrative villages arrived at 49. 4% and the rate of access to electricity in natural villages was 73. 7% . ① All these had laid a solid foundation for the complete eradication of absolute poverty.

(Yuan)

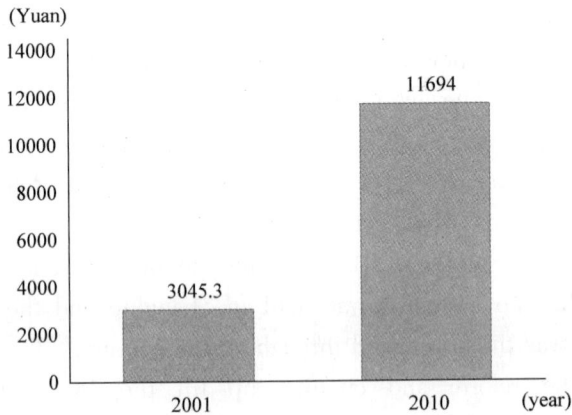

Figure 1. 1　Per capita GDP of Qinling-Bashan mountainous regions in 2000 to 2010②

(Yuan)

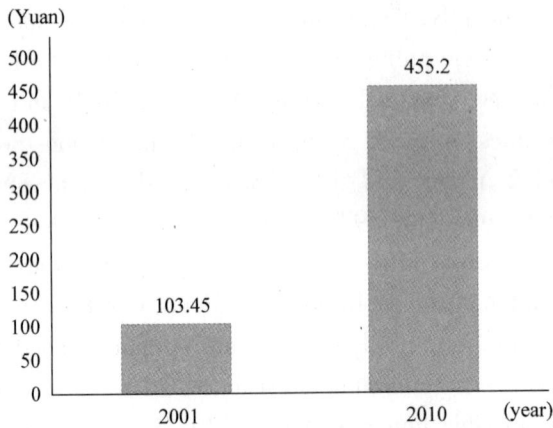

Figure 1. 2　Per capita fiscal revenues of Qinling-Bashan mountainous regions in 2000 to 2010③

---

　　① Data source: *Plan on the Development and Poverty Alleviation of Qinling-Bashan Mountainous Regions* (*2011 – 2020*) .

　　② Ibid.

　　③ Ibid.

1.4   Endeavor to Get Rid of Poverty and Build a Moderately Prosperous Society in Qinling-Bashan Mountainous Regions since the 18th CPC National Congress

On November 29, 2015, the CPC Central Committee and the State Council promulgated the *Decision on Winning the Battle against Poverty* to launch a general attack on absolute poverty so as to ensure poverty-stricken areas and poor people to get rid of poverty as scheduled by 2020. Qinling-Bashan mountainous regions won a complete victory in poverty alleviation through the practices of industry orientation, blood transfusion type poverty alleviation, prioritized poverty alleviation, overall development, social security orientation and prevention of returning to poverty.

1.4.1   Challenges against Qinling-Bashan Mountainous Regions before the anti-poverty campaign

1.4.1.1   Backward infrastructure facilities, obvious traffic restrictions

Before 2012, Qinling-Bashan mountainous regions were restricted by the natural geographical environment and there was still a big gap in infrastructure facilities conditions. The*Plan on the Development and Poverty Alleviation of Qinling-Bashan Mountainous Regions (2011 – 2020)* shows that the regions are faced with a serious problem of water shortage; the effective irrigation area of basic farmlands only accounts for 37.5% of the total area; 69.3% of the farmers here are still troubled by drinking safety issues; and 24.7% of the administrative villages have not completed their rural network transformation. Especially in terms of transportation, there are lots of inter-provincial and inter- County dead end roads and there is an insufficient coverage of railway network. In the regions, 4.5% of the Towns and 50.6% of the administrative villages here have no access to asphalt (cement) roads. In 2014, the total mileage of the highway network in Qinling-Bashan mountainous regions exceeded 180,000km; the density of road network and populations in the regions was 83. 4km per 100 square kilometers and 51. 3km per 10, 000 persons; and 97% of the Towns had access to asphalt (concrete) roads. However, national and provincial trunk highways occupied only a small share, with a total mileage of only 14,000km, not less than 8% of the total mileage of the entire highway network. Also, the highways in Qinling-Bashan mountainous regions were low in class and the total mileage of Class I and II highways only accounted for around 6% of the total mileage of the highway network. The number of villages with asphalt (cement) roads in villages accounted for less than 50% of the total villages; the number of Towns with graded passenger stations was only around 47% of the total Towns; and only 16% of the administrative villages had simply-built stations, flag stops or shelter signs. [1] Backward infrastructure facilities had constrained the living and production of the masses and the development of Qinling-Bashan mountainous regions.

1.4.1.2   Insufficient industrial scale and efficiency, weak ability to make the poor become rich

Qinlin-Bashan mountainous regions still lagged behind in industrial development. In terms of agricultural industry, poor households had little production experience, weak agricultural planting technology, less ability to withstand market risks, less desire and ability to grow economic crops. And their agricultural income was still at a low level. Also, a large number of villages had no collective economy yet. Take the major economic crops in Qinling-Bashan mountainous regions as example:

Chinese herbal medicines in Longnan City. In 2010, the planting area of Chinese herbal medicines in Longnan reached 59,900 hectares, with 116, 500t excavated. However, the Chinese herbal medicine industry was insufficiently invested in and weak in technical strength. It remained at the stage when revenues were increased through increased planting area and yield accumulation and its technical strength was still at the lowest level. Due to excessive mining and digging, some famous

---

Chinese herbal medicines, such as phellodendron amurense and acanthopanax root in Kangxian and Wenxcian Counties and magnolia officinalis in Wenxian County, were faced with the possibilities of resource shrinkage and variety extinction. The Chinese herbal medicines in Longnan were mainly planted by farmers and purchased by vendors; there were a small number of small-scale processing enterprises that focused on rough processing; and there was no perfect large-scale Chinese herbal medicine wholesales market. [1]

Konjac in southern Shaanxi. In 2009, there were more than 20 konjac fine and micro powder processing enterprises in southern Shaanxi, with an annual processing capacity of over 8, 000t; and five konjac food processing enterprises, with an annual processing capacity of over 4, 500t. However, improved breeding were insufficient and most breeding planted were seriously susceptible to major diseases such as soft rot and sclerotium rolfsii. Also, due to the backward education background of farmers and their less understanding of konjac planting technology, extensive operation was carried out after artificial planting on farmlands and less technical content was involved in production. Due to the impacts of years and market, the purchase price of fresh konjac products fluctuated greatly. Konjac processing enterprises' inability to respond to market shock due to their small scale, low level and weak effect of radiation still existed. [2]

Tea industry in southern Shaanxi. In 2011, more than 3 million employees were engaged in the tea industry of southern Shaanxi and the planting area reached nearly 70, 000 hectares. However, due to the low yield of tea from each hectare of tea garden and low degree of industrialization of tea, many enterprises remained at a low level in the modernization of production and processing. Due to the lack of brand building system for tea producers, regional brands of the tea industry in southern Shaanxi had not been formed. At the same time, due to the lack

① Yang Yan, Pan Shuizhan, Zhang Jie, "Problems and Countermeasures Regarding the Development of Chinese Herbal Medicine Industry in Longnan Mountainous Regions", *Modern Agricultural Science and Technology*, 2011 (18), pp. 374 – 375.

② Chen Xueyan, Zhang Yu, Yang Peijun, et al., "Development Status, Problems and Countermeasures of Konjac Industry in Southern Shaanxi", *Shaanxi Journal of Agricultural Sciences*, 2009 (6), pp. 100 – 101.

of funds, research and development units, distribution enterprises, processing enterprises and farmers were short of funds, which hampered the development of the industry. [1]

In general, Qinling-Bashan mountainous regions remained at a low level in the secondary and tertiary industries. In terms of the ratio of primary to secondary to tertiary industries in 2010, the ratio in Shaanxi was 21. 0: 39. 9: 39. 1 and that in southern Shaanxi (including Hanzhong, Ankang and Shangluo cities) was 31. 90: 35. 65: 32. 45. The share of the secondary industry in southern Shaanxi was nearly 20% higher than the average of Shaanxi Province[2]. In the major prefecture-level cities of Qinling-Bashan mountainous regions, the added value of the primary industry over the total GDP was higher than the average of the Province but that of the secondary industry over total GDP was lower than the average of the Province (see Table 1. 2). The lagged development of the secondary industry, especially the labor-intensive industries that were highly capable of driving the poor to become rich, had led to the insufficient driving effect of non-agricultural industries the over the poor.

Table 1. 2 **Share of added values of three industries in major prefecture-level cities and Provinces of Qinling-Bashan mountainous regions in 2012**

Province or prefecture-level city	Share of added value of primary, secondary and tertiary industries in total GDP
Hanzhong	20. 65 : 43:78 : 35. 57
Ankang	15. 8 : 50. 6 : 33. 6
Shangluo	18. 1 : 48. 0 : 33. 9
Bazhong	23. 8 : 42:9 : 33. 3
GuangYuan	19. 6 : 47. 0 : 33. 4
Longnan	25. 4 : 30. 6 : 44. 0
Sichuan Province	13. 8 : 51. 7 : 34. 5

① Zhang Peng, "Problems and Countermeasures for the Sustainable Development of Tea Industry in Southern Shaanxi", *Reform and Strategy*, 2014 (07), pp. 110 – 113.

② Zhang Zhonghua, Zhang Pei, Sun Haijun, "Research on the Population Transfer Model of Ecologically Sensitive Areas in Western Mountainous Region under the Background of Unified Urban-Rural Planning", *Planner*, 2012 (10), pp. 86 – 91.

Cont.

Province or prefecture-level city	Share of added value of primary, secondary and tertiary industries in total GDP
Shaanxi Province	9. 5 : 55. 8 : 34. 7
Gansu Province	7. 45 : 55. 82 : 36. 73

Source: statistical yearbooks of Provinces, statistic communiqués of national economy and social development of prefecture-level cities.

1. 4. 1. 3   Large differences within the regions and difficulty in producing the radiation effect

There is a large gap of development in the areas of Qinling-Bashan mountainous regions. In 2010, the level of the counties with the lowest per capital general budgetary revenues of local governments and per capita pure net income of farmers was only 23. 2% and 45. 7% of the average of the regions. The economic characteristics of the enclave formed in the construction of the "three lines" in the regions were obvious and the contradiction between urban and rural dual structures was prominent[1]. There was a large gap in the per capital annual income of rural residents from that of urban residents in Qinling-Bashan mountainous regions, with the former being only 20% to 30% of the latter (see Table 1. 3) . Also, Qinling-Bashan mountainous regions are characterized by unreasonable distribution of cities, small urban scale and weak driving effect. Most Towns in southern Shaanxi are distributed along Hanjiang River, Danjiang River, Jialing River and their tributaries, in low-lying hilly areas and plain areas. The Towns in the plain area are densely populated while there are few Towns in the low- and medium-mountain areas. They are unevenly distributed and the scale hierarchy is complicated. In terms of spatial structure, the three prefecture-level cities, Ankang, Shangluo, and Hanzhong, are weakly connected to each other, and the central cities and Towns are separated

---

① Data source: *Plan on the Development and Poverty Alleviation of Qinling-Bashan Mountainous Regions* (2011 – 2020) .

from their hinterlands. [1] As a result, there is less radiating effect produced by the regional central cities on the surrounding radiation. Also, it cannot facilitate poverty-stricken villages to get rid of poverty.

Table 1. 3 **Comparisons of per capita income of urban and rural residents at major prefecture-level cities of Qinlin-Bashan mountainous regions in 2012**

Prefecture-level city	Per capita income of urban residents (Yuan)	Per capita income of rural residents (Yuan)	Ratio of per capita income of rural residents to per capita income of urban residents
Hanzhong	19827	6181	31. 2%
Ankang	20300	5815	28. 6%
Shangluo	19998	5425	27. 1%
Bazhong	16999	5387	31. 7%
GuangYuan	17012	5649	33. 2%
Longnan	14077	3088	21. 9%

Source: sorted and calculated according to thestatistical yearbooks of Provinces, statistic communiqués of national economy and social development of Longnan City in 2012.

1. 4. 1. 4   Serious disaster-induced poverty or problem of returning to poverty

Qinling-Bashan mountainous regions were faced with serious disaster-induced poverty or problem of returning to poverty. More than half of the lands in southern Shaanxi were areas highly susceptible to medium-and large-scale geological disasters and more than ten thousand of households were threatened by geological disasters (see Table 1. 4) . Especially, in July 2010, the southern Shaanxi suffered from two rounds of once-in-a-century heavy rainfall caused disasters to ecological construction and also brought about torrential floods, landslides, debris flows and other disasters. As a result, the number of people affected in the whole Shaanxi Province reached 4. 61 million and 813, 000 people were relocated in emergency (mainly in southern Shaanxi). Huge personnel and poverty losses and major damage to public infrastructures

---

[1]   Zhang Zhonghua, Zhang Pei, Hu Zhen, "Local Mechanisms and Models for Integrated Urban-Rural development in the Underdeveloped Mountainous Areas of Western China: Case Study of Qinling regions in southern Shaanxi", *Urban Studies*, 2014 (1), pp. 90 – 95.

were caused.

Table 1. 4   **Distribution and threats of geological disasters**
in southern Shaanxi, 2013

Region	Area of high susceptible zone (km²)	Percentage (%)	Area of susceptible zone (km²)	Percentage (%)	Area of high and middle susceptible zones (km²)	Percentage over total land area (%)	Number of places with potential geological disasters	Number of households threatened	Number of people threatened
Ankang	6724. 12	28. 59	8582. 63	36. 48	15306. 75	65. 05	3848	23319	114289
Shangluo	3794. 50	19. 70	6683. 50	34. 60	10478. 00	54. 30	1670	13211	68039
Hanzhong	9321. 00	33. 80	7456. 00	27. 40	16687. 00	61. 20	2090	18234	96990

Source: quoted from He Degui, *Research on the Implementation of the Relocation Policy for Refugees from Mountainous Disasters: Statements of Southern Shaanxi*, People's Press, 2016, p. 53.

The Wenchuan earthquake that occurred in May 12, 2008 also caused severe damage to the social and economic construction of Qinling-Bashan mountainous regions. Twenty counties severely and seriously affected by the earthquake were located in Qinling-Bashan mountainous regions and were faced with arduous post-earthquake revitalization and development tasks. For example, in Bazhong, Sichuan, 44, 985 farm houses from 11, 925 households, with a total area of 870, 800 square meters, collapsed; 403, 368 farm houses from 127, 857 households, with a total area of 8, 189, 600 square meters, were damaged; the direct losses of rural areas caused due to the earthquake in the whole city reached 792, 019, 100 Yuan. [1] Also, Qinling-Bashan mountainous regions play huge ecological functions in water conservation and the maintaining of biodiversity. In the regions, 42 counties are located within the water source conservancy zone of the South-to-North Water Diversion Project. So, ecological conservation and construction have imposed restrictions on social and economic development.

---

[1]   Wang Li, "New Chapter of Scientific Reconstruction: Review on Bazhong City's Acceleration of Post-Disaster Reconstruction", *Bazhong Daily*, 2010-05-12.

1. 4. 1. 5   Poverty gap resulted from lack of basic public services

The lack of basic public services such as medical and health services has always been an important challenge against extremely poor areas. In 2010, the administrative villages with health clinics and village doctors in western China accounted for 80. 8% and 79. 1% of the total villages there. In 2010, the per capita health and education expenditure in Qinling-Bashan mountainous regions was only 56% of the national average. These regions had a shortage of grassroots health talents and serious shortage of general practitioners. The number of health technicians per 1, 000 persons in most prefecture-level cities was significantly lower than the average of the correspondingProvince (Table 1. 5). The grassroots medical and health services failed to satisfy needs and there were still shortcomings in the prevention and control of endemic and infectious diseases. Among 45 counties whose Kaschin-Beck disease was uncontrolled in the country, 16 counties were within the regions, 35. 6% of the counties with the Kaschin-Beck disease uncontrolled. Due to the lack of basic medical services, disease-induced poverty and returning to poverty became prominent. Also, the problem of education for the poor has not been completely solved and there remained some students who became poor due to receiving education or dropping out of school due to poverty. Due to the extreme poverty, the incidence of poverty in many areas was still about 20% to 40% around 2012, and even in some prefecture-level cities, the figure reached 50% (Table 1. 6). Some poor people had insufficient endogenous motivation to escape poverty.

Table 1. 5   **Number of health technicians per thousand persons in major prefecture-level cities of Qinling-Bashan mountainous regions in 2012**

Province or city	Number of permanent residents (0,000)	Number of health technicians	Number of health technicians per thousand person
Shaanxi	3753. 09	216304	5. 76
Hanzhong	341. 84	17619	5. 15

Cont.

Province or city	Number of permanent residents (0,000)	Number of health technicians	Number of health technicians per thousand person
Ankang	263. 36	11754	4. 46
Shangluo	234. 19	9879	4. 22
Sichuan	8076. 2	389001	4. 81
Bazhong	330. 79	11777	3. 56
GuangYuan	253. 00	12811	5. 06
Gansu	2577. 55	111907	4. 34
Longnan	256. 95	8486	3. 30

Source: sorted and calculated according to statistical yearbooks of Provinces.

1. 4. 2　Winning the battle against poverty, building a moderately prosperous society

As one of the main battlefields against poverty, Qinling-Bashan mountainous regions are striving to realize complete poverty alleviation with the determination and actions of catching up and surpassing others in the era of building a moderately prosperous society in all respects. In April 2020, General Secretary Xi Jinping inspected Jinmi Village, XiaolingTown, Zhashui County in Shangluo, Laoxian Town, Pingli County in Ankang City and other places and gave a recognition and guidance on the work of poverty alleviation there. [①]

1. 4. 2. 1　Industry orientation, blood transfusion type poverty alleviation

Industrial development is a fundamental strategy for stimulating the endogenous impetus of the poor people and achieving sustainable development of poverty-stricken areas. The counties and districts in Qinling-Bashan mountainous regions actively develop leading characteristic industries. In Guangyuan City, Sichuan Province,

---

① "Xi Jinping emphasized steady fulfillment of the 'six stability' work and 'six-guarantees' tasks when inspecting Shaanxi: striving for a new chapter in Shaanxi's new era to catch up and surpass others", *Shaanxi Daily*, 2020-04-24 (2).

characteristic competitive industries are developed; major industry leaders produce a driving effect and e-comments are encouraged to sell poverty reduction products. In the city, 100 modern agricultural parks, 1,857 characteristic village industry demonstration parks (covering 739 poor villages) and 18,600 household-owned characteristic industrial parks (including 56,000 poor households) have been completed. In September 2019, the National Industry Poverty Alleviation Promotion Conference was held in Guangyuan, Sichuan Province. In order to stimulate the enthusiasm of poor people to get engaged in production, rural civilization building has been carried out in Qinling-Bashan mountainous regions. Since December 2017, Ankang in Shaanxi has fully promoted the building of the "Love shops" for earning fork customs points in accordance with the principles of "Points change bad habits; diligence improves life; good environment refreshes people and all public build villages". As of the end of 2019, 1,185 "Love Shops" had been completed and put into operation. At 1,883 villages (communities) in the entire city, village conventions and villagers' agreements have been revised and updated; mass organizations for rural civilization building at the village level, mainly consisting of moral review committees, marriage and funeral affairs councils, village affairs councils as well as anti-drug and anti-gambling committees, have been established and perfected. Review activities are held on a quarterly basis. ① "Mass comments, discussions on rural sages and public announcements" review activities are organized to make a large number of positive models in poverty alleviation to play an even bigger positive effect and significantly improve rural customs. The Ankang Group Office for New Folk Customs Construction has won the Chinese Poverty Alleviation Organization Innovation Award for 2019.

---

① Zhang Tingming, "Guangyuan pays close attention to poverty alleviation by supporting industry and relies on industry to promote the income increase of 174,900 poor households", *Sichuan Daily*, 2019-08-30 (1). "Fresh Air for Qinling-Bashan Mountainous Regions—An Overview of the New Folk Customs Construction in Ankang City", 2019-01-26, Http://www. shaanxi. gov. cn/sxxw/xwtt/df/132913. htm.

1. 4. 2. 2　　Prioritizing ecological conservation, pursing the development of the whole regions

Qinling-Bashan mountainous areas are an important water conserving area for the South-to-North Water Diversion Project. In order to ensure ecological conservation and green development, it is extremely important to strike a balance between ecological conservation and poverty alleviation. In Shangluo City, Shaanxi Province, poverty alleviation through ecological conservation, such as designation of ecological rangers, compensation for ecological benefits, returning farmland to forestland, forestry development, engineering and labor services, technical and skills training, has been steadily promoted. Also, by perfecting "tourism + " top-level design and with three carriers of high-quality scenic spots, characteristic towns and beautiful villages as focus, Shangluo has built more than ten scenic spots at the level of 4A or above and a number of beautiful villages so as to make the tourism industry an important driver for ecological conservation and poverty alleviation. In order to solve the problem that local residents cannot be supported by the lands on which they live, the poverty alleviation through relocation is steadily promoted in Qinling-Bashan mountainous regions. The relocation and reemployment of the masses have been better solved by identifying the supporting infrastructure facilities at the points of resettlement and of basic public services and promoting the construction of community factories, anti-poverty workshops and agricultural park construction, thus better achieving the goals of smooth moving out, stable resettlement and becoming rich. The relocation and poverty alleviation model represented by the "Community Factory" in Pingli County, Ankang City was rated as one of the Top Ten National Experience in Targeted Poverty Alleviation and Top Ten Cases of China's Reform in 2017. ①

1. 4. 2. 3　　Social security orientation, prevention of returning to poverty

Prevention of returning to poverty is the key to high-quality poverty alleviation. Qinling-Bashan mountainous regions have made great efforts

---

① "People relocated from southern Shaanxi have achieved remarkable results in poverty alleviation", 2018-09-13, http: //gtzyt. shaanxi. gov. cn/info/1038/39994. htm.

to compensate for the shortcomings of the poor in basic public service, steadily promoted poverty reduction through education and healthcare, with social security as basic guarantee, so as to solve the problems of poverty due to education and diseases and life difficulties of the poor, block inter-generational transmission of poverty and resist the risks of induced poverty and returning to poverty. Hanzhong City is vigorously promoting the 4 + X multiple security system, mainly basic medical insurance, critical illness insurance, civil relief, special government relief and other methods. The first municipal health consortium of the whole province has also been established here. According to statistics, as of October 2017, 41, 000 of the supported in the whole city were hospitalized, with a total hospitalization expenditure of 243 million Yuan and actual reimbursement percentage of 92. 3% [1]. In order to implement the central government's policy requirements of family doctors contracting services for chronically impoverished people [2], Hanzhong has explored a "2 + 2 + 1" family doctors contracting service model to promote the effective implementation of basic public health services for the poor. Shangluo has further improved the effectivealignment between the minimum subsistence allowance system and the poverty reduction and development policy, and included all satisfactory registered poor people in the scope of rural minimum living security, and further built a safety network for the poor.

1. 4. 3   Pursuing and surpassing to build new countryside

All poor counties of Qinling-Bashan mountainous regions within the jurisdiction of Shaanxi, Hubei, Henan and Chongqing have been lifted out of poverty. The three poor counties in Longnan, Gansu that have not been out of poverty are make efforts so as to ensure complete poverty alleviation as scheduled. Qinling-Bashan mountainous regions have made great achievements in poverty alleviation (Table 1. 6). Located in the

---

[1]   Gong Shijian, Zhang Jingbo, "Hanzhong: Healthy Poverty Alleviation Drives ' Three Tigers' Away", *People's Daily*, 2017-12-15 (13).

[2]   One village doctor, one village health and family planning specialist, one Township health clinic doctor, one Township public health specialist, and one County-level instructor.

Table 1.6   **PA effect of major prefecture-level cities in Qinling-Bashan mountainous regions**

Prefecture-level city	Number of agricultural poor populations (0,000)		Poverty incidence in rural areas (%)		Annual per capita disposable income of rural areas (Yuan)		GDP (hundred million Yuan)		Enrollment rate of junior school-year students		Number of health technicians		Milleage of highways (km)		Number of Poor villages out of poverty	Number of persons relocated in PA (0,000)
	2012	2019	2012	2019	2012	2019	2012	2019	2012	2019	2012	2019	2012	2018		
Hanzhong, Shaanxi	103.72	2.63	34.5	0.9	6181	11098	754.57	1547.59	98.64	100	17619	26735	17935	20533	—	14.64
Ankang, Shaanxi	100.5	3.34	40.7	1.3	5815	10475	496.91	1182.06	99.99	99.99 (2018)	11754	18877 (2018)	22182	24501	1010	33.52
Shangluo, Shaanxi	49.02 (2015)	1.53	35.3 (2015)	1.3	5425	10025	423.31	837.21			9879	16131	12988	13886		19.83
GuangYuan, Sichuan	63.19 (2010)		26.62	0.06	5649	13127	468.66	941.85			12811	19136	17206	20033 (2019)	739	
Bazhong, Sichuan	57.59	0.19	16.3 (2014)	0.06	5387	13232	390.40	754.29	99.9	100	11777	17714	16070	18525 (2019)	598 (2018)	18.9
Longnan, Gansu	130.46 (2011)	3.69	53 (2011)	1.56	3088	7734.2	226.0	379.2 (2018)	86.9 (2014)	99.9 (2018)	7647	13602 (2018)	15404	17137		18.5 (2018)
Shiyan, Hubei	83.3 (2014)	0.38	37.2 (2014)	0.17	4566	11378	955.7	2012.7	99.9		21633	28452	22036.5		456	35.5
Nanyang, Henan	110 (2011)	6.53	12.3 (2011)	1.88 (2018)	7752	15166	2367.2	3814.98			29900	76900				4.88

Cont.

Prefecture-level city	Number of agricultural poor populations (0,000)		Poverty incidence in rural areas (%)		Annual per capita disposable income of rural areas (Yuan)		GDP (hundred million Yuan)		Enrollment rate of junior school-year students		Number of health technicians		Milleage of highways (km)		Number of Poor villages out of poverty	Number of persons relocated in PA (0,000)
	2012	2019	2012	2019	2012	2019	2012	2019	2012	2019	2012	2019	2012	2018		
Hanzhong, Shaanxi	103.72	2.63	34.5	0.9	6181	11098	754.57	1547.59	98.64	100	17619	26735	17935	20533	—	14.64
Ankang, Shaanxi	100.5	3.34	40.7	1.3	5815	10475	496.91	1182.06	99.99	99.99 (2018)	11754	18877 (2018)	22182	24501		33.52
Shangluo, Shaanxi	49.02 (2015)	1.53	35.3 (2015)	1.3	5425	10025	423.31	837.21			9879	16131	12988	13886		19.83
GuangYuan, Sichuan	63.19 (2010)		26.62 (2010)		5649	13127	468.66	941.85			12811	19136	17206	20033 (2019)	739	
Bazhong, Sichuan	57.59	0.19		0.06	5387	13232	390.40	754.29	99.9	100	11777	17714	16070	18525 (2019)	598 (2018)	18.9
Longnan, Gansu	130.46 (2011)	3.69	53 (2011)	1.56	3088	7734.2	226.0	379.2 (2018)	86.9 (2014)	99.9 (2018)	7647	13602 (2018)	15404	17137		18.5 (2018)
Shiyan, Hubei ·	83.3 (2014)	0.38	37.2 (2014)	0.17	4566	11378	955.7	2012.7	99.9		21633	28452	22036.5		456	35.5
Nanyang, Henan	110 (2011)	6.53	12.3 (2011)	1.88 (2018)	7752	15166	2367.2	3814.98			29900	76900				4.88

Source: prepared by the authors according to provincial and prefecture-level statistical yearbooks of Qinling-Bashan mountainous regions, statistic communiqués of national economy and social development of prefecture-level cities, annual reports on the work of governments of prefecture-level cities, websites of people's governments at all levels as well as reports from central and provincial authority media.

Note: All the data above refers to year-end data or annual data of the current year.

central part of China, these regions enjoy the unique advantages of connecting east and west and running through north to south. It is estimated that after the goal of poverty alleviation is achieved in 2020, the overall industrialization and urbanization level of the region will remain low compared to other regions but the region plays an important role in the national ecological security system. The endeavor to achieve a more balanced and sustainable high-quality development of regional ecological environment and economic society will be another important strategic task following poverty alleviation. [1] As the socialism with Chinese characteristics enters a new era, Qinling-Bashan mountainous regions are effectively consolidating the fruits of poverty alleviation, intensifying the new achievements with the determination and actions to pursue and surpass and striving for better life of the people under the guidance promoting the comprehensive revitalization of the countryside and supporting the prioritized development of agriculture and rural areas. The Qinling-Bashan mountainous regions in the new era are constantly moving forward.

---

[1]   Lu Hang, "Make Poverty Alleviation Withstand the Test of History", *China Social Science Journal*, 2020-04-24 (1).

Chapter 2
Poverty Alleviation by Supporting the Industry in Contiguous Areas with Acute Difficulties

On February 12, 2018, General Secretary Xi Jinping pointed out at the Symposium on Eliminating Poverty in a Targeted Manner that, "poverty alleviation by supporting industry is the fundamental strategy for making the poverty alleviation work stable. However, short cycle, small investment and high efficiency rather than long-term benefits and stable income increase are emphasized in the poverty alleviation by supporting the industries in most regions. It is hard for these measures to produce a long-lasting effect. How to consolidate the effect of poverty alleviation and ensure its sustainability are the important issues to be seriously considered and solved in the battle against poverty". [1] In the contiguous areas with acute difficulties of Qinling-Bashan mountainous regions, effective paths to targeted poverty alleviation are explored according to local conditions to help the poor develop sustainable industries. Also, modern agricultural development, beautiful village construction, poverty reduction and development are combined in an organized manner, which do not only help to win the battle against poverty but also enable stronger agriculture, richer life and more beautiful villages.

---

[1] the CPC Central Party History and Documentation Research Institute, *Xi Jinping's Remarks on Poverty Reduction*, Beijing: The Central Documentation Press, 2018, p. 3.

2. 1   Anti-poverty Effect and Enlightenment from the "Qinling Herbal Medicine Storehouse"

A characteristic industry is an industry or industrial cluster developed by a region based on its unique resources, culture, environment, technology and other aspects, with a high degree of recognition. Compared with any common industry, the characteristic industry can better bring the regional advantages into full play and enjoys higher market competitiveness and economic benefits. In 2014, the General Office of the CPC Central Committee and the General Office of the State Council issued the *Opinions on promoting Rural Poverty Reduction and Development through the Innovation Mechanism.* It was clearly stated that the income increase by supporting characteristic industries is one of the top ten tasks for poverty reduction and development in the new era. Located in the central part of the Qinling Mountains, Shangluo is one of the areas that are most suitable for the growth of Chinese herbal medicines. It has been traditionally known as a natural herbal medicine storehouse of Qinling Mountains. Among the 2, 002 types of Chinese herbal medicines included in the *Collection of Chinese Herbal Medicines*, 1, 192 ones are produced in Shangluo. However, for a long period of time in the past, there was no way for the advantages of Shangluo in herbal medicines to be converted into economic strength. In the context of the tough battle against poverty, Shangluo is vigorously promoting poverty alleviation by supporting the Chinese herbal medicine industry in the face of the opportunities of the State's poverty reduction and development in the contiguous areas with acute difficulties and by supporting the industry. The brand of "Shangluo herbal medicine" has become a representative work of Shangluo in economic growth and the Chinese herbal medicine industry has become a driver to push poverty alleviation in the city.

2. 1. 1   Practice of developing Chinese herbal medicines in Shangluo

Shangluo attaches great importance to the development of the

Chinese herbal medicine industry. The government takes the lead in integrating supporting the poor in poverty alleviation with industry operation by following the development model of " enterprises (cooperatives, associations) + bases + farmers ", thus practically implementing the "blood transfusion" type poverty reduction.

2. 1. 1. 1   Giving full play to geographical advantages, increasing policy support

The unique ecological environment constitutes the basis for developing the Chinese herbal medicine industry. In recent years, with the State's promulgation of a series of policies in support of the traditional Chinese medicine (TCM) healthcare industry, the Chinese herbal medicine market in China has become popular and brought vitality to the development of poor mountainous areas in Shangluo. The following actions have been taken. (1) Establishing a leading group. In order to seize the opportunity of poverty alleviation by supporting the industry, the leading group for the development of Chinese herbal medicines has been established in Shangzhou District, Shangluo City to scientifically plan the development of the local Chinese herbal medicine industry. In order to stimulate the enthusiasm of the poor households for planting Chinese herbal medicines, the poor households who plant common herbal medicines will be granted with a subsidy of 7,500 Yuan per hectare and who plant precious herbal medicines will be granted with a subsidy of 75, 000 Yuan per hectare. (2) Organizing technical training. In order to ensure the production of high-quality Chinese herbal medicines, the Shangluo Municipal People's Government has invited professional talents, including experts from Northwest Agriculture and Forestry University and Shaanxi University of Chinese Medicine, to give 140 technical training to 8, 302 heads from herbal medicine planting enterprises and specialized cooperatives, major Chinese herbal medicine planters, technical cadres and common herbal medicine farmers. The government fully exploited the natural and ecological advantages of Qinling-Bashan mountainous regions, selected and appointed technical cadres for key herbal medicine planting villages in a targeted way so as to help farmers solve the technical problems met in planting Chinese herbal medicines and train the new professional farmers who understand management and technologies in the new era. (3) Establishing a special fund. In order to achieve the goal of building a "66. 7-hectare Chinese herbal medicine demonstration base", the special fund for the development of the Chinese herbal medicine industry, with 5 million Yuan allocated each year, is established in Zhashui County for the rewarding, R&D, protection, development and base construction of the Chinese herbal medicine industry. The poverty reduction funds are used in practice to improve the poverty reduction benefits of the Chinese herbal medicine industry.

2. 1. 1. 2 Highlighting the benefits from the poverty alleviation by supporting industry, establishing the binding model

Only by ensuring the collaborative development of poverty reduction and characteristic industries can we achieve sustainable poverty alleviation. In order to find a characteristic industry and bring the local people to become rich, Shangluo actively responds to national policies, implements the strategy of "making the County and its people rich by developing Chinese herbal medicines" by exploiting the local rich Chinese herbal medicine resources, and practically regards the development of Chinese herbal medicine industry as a leading industry for restructuring rural industry and accelerating farmers' pace in getting rid of poverty and becoming rich. (1) Creating more job opportunities. By focusing on the goal of building a modern Chinese herbal medicine industry, the city develops Chinese herbal medicine processing enterprises, absorbs tens of thousands of poor households to get jobs, solves the problem of the reemployment of surplus labor forces by creating more jobs, encourages poor people to get rid of poverty with their hands, and help poor households to get stable income sources. (2) Introducing the "Three-transfer" mechanism. Shangnan County is one of the poorest counties in Shangluo. By integrating poverty alleviation and industrial development in an organic way, the county lists the Chinese herbal medicine industry as a key industry for poverty alleviation, implements the "Three-transfer reform" in rural areas, mainly "transfer resources into equity, funds into dividends, and farmers into equity owners", encourages township offices to introduce the "three-transfer" mechanism, converts the funds, lands and other resources of poor households into dividends and invest them in Chinese herbal medicine cooperatives or companies, and allocate dividends to the participating households, thus getting poor households out of poverty. (3) Encouraging planting. Zhashui County is known as "Hundred-mile Valley of Medicine". According to the layout on the whole river valley and the whole river system, the county adopts the development model of "leading enterprises + agricultural cooperatives + farmers (poor households) + orders ", actively promotes the regional arrangement, large-scale development, standard production and industrial development for Chinese herbal medicine industry, allows poor households to actively participate in the planting of Chinese herbal medicines, links the interests of poor households to the planting of Chinese herbal medicines, realizes the blood transfusion type poverty reduction for the Chinese herbal medicine industry, gradually establishing the whole chain model for the Chinese herbal medicine industry that covers seedling selection, planting, processing and sales.

2. 1. 1. 3　Highlighting industrial transformation and upgrading, promoting scale development

The Chinese herbal medicine industry is an important pillar for agriculture and an industry to get rural areas out of poverty in Shangluo. In order to make the Chinese herbal medicine industry bigger and stronger and improve the level of transformation of Chinese herbal medicines towards industrialization, the Chinese herbal medicine enterprises in Shangluo has taken the path to industrial development featuring "companies (cooperatives) + bases + rural households" under the support of the government and formed a TCM healthcare industry chain that integrates production, purchase and sales. (1) Establishing associations of Chinese herbal medicines. In order to promote the "Shangluo herbal medicine" brand to the outside, 16 specialized cooperatives and associations for Chinese herbal medicines were established in Shangzhou District. More than 5, 000 people have been attracted to join the associations. As a result, the whole district witnesses increased Chinese herbal medicine planting area and realizes scaled, mechanical and standard planting. (2) Establishing a planting base for Chinese herbal medicine industry. It is crucial to seize the development opportunity of the Chinese herbal medicine industry and realize the scaled development of the industry. In order to achieve the goal of building a modern Chinese herbal medicine industry base, Shangzhou District has developed Chinese herbal medicine processing enterprises and absorbed nearly one thousand poor households for reemployment. In 2018, a new 2, 333. 3-hectare Chinese herbal medicine base was established in Shangnan. In combination with poverty alleviation campaign, the construction of the Chinese herbal medicine demonstration base was facilitated by designating special technical personnel to sites and adopting other forms. Additionally, specialized cooperatives engaged in purchase, sales, processing and planting of Chinese herbal medicines were established in many areas of Shangluo, thus forming a one-stop industrial chain of Chinese herbal medicines. (3) Established industrial parks. It is an effective approach to ensuring large-scale development of Chinese herbal medicines by integrating modern agriculture and the Chinese herbal medicine industry. In Zhashui County, five medical parks including Panlong Ecological Industrial Park, Fengbeihe Schisandra Technology Demonstration Park, and Caoping Isatis Root Ecological Industry Park have been established, 29 enterprises and 37 industrial projects have been introduced, and 10, 997 poor people from 3, 093 households have got their jobs.

2. 1. 2 Effect of poverty alleviation by developing the Chinese herbal medicine industry

While facilitating the development of Chinese herbal medicine industry, Shangluo has realized the coordinated development of industrial integration, poverty alleviation and rural governance, forming a virtuous circle of poverty reduction, income increase, favorable ecology and active economic growth.

2. 1. 2. 1 Industry scale developed and expanded in poor areas

By focusing on the ideas of developing bases, highlighting processing, promoting marketing and creating brands, Shangluo gives full play to the advantages of local Chinese herbal medicines, develops business entities in an innovative way, accelerates the development of the Chinese herbal medicine industry, and gives a big push topoverty alleviation. As of the end of 2019, the total area of Chinese herbal medicines in the whole city has reached 162, 840 hectares; the annual output reached 868, 300t and the Chinese herbal medicine industry has had an output value of 15. 492 billion Yuan. The city adopted the "government guidance, market promotion, enterprise dominance, mass participation" approaches and actively promoted the "three drives + one innovation" development model, namely driving by leading enterprises, cooperatives and major planters, innovation of poverty alleviation through finance. It also implemented the "three-transfer" reform, adhered to the development path of " enterprises (cooperatives) + bases + rural households + orders", and actively guided enterprises, cooperatives and large-scale farmers through land transfer, land escrowing, share participation with lands and other methods to promote contract farming, vigorously develop large-scale standard herbal medicine bases. Large-scale development of the Chinese herbal medicine industry has been realized in the city.

2. 1. 2. 2　The economic market of less developed counties activated

In 2018, Shangluo ranked top among all prefecture-level cities of Shaanxi in terms of Chinese herbal medicine planting area and yield and was also listed as a standard planting base for Chinese herbal medicines. Industrial parks and clusters, with pharmaceutical manufacturers as the core, have been formed in Shangzhou, Shanyang and Zhashui. And the Chinese herbal medicine industry has become the one that dominates the local industry at the county level. The leading enterprises that are engaged in the processing and circulation of Chinese herbal medicines have obtained a rapid development. A large number of leading Chinese herbal medicine processing enterprises, including Tasly, Xiangju and Sciphar in Shangzhou, Bicon, Tianzhirun and Chongbentang in Shanyang, Panlong and Ouke in Zhashui, Ruiqi and Hongfa in Zhen'an, are gradually growing. Currently, there have been 15 large-scale Chinese herbal medicine processing enterprises in Shangluo. Among them, Bicon Pharmaceutical and Panlong Pharmaceutical have been successfully listed as key leading Chinese herbal medicine manufacturers in the city. The Chinese herbal medicine industry of the city is witnessing a strong momentum.

2. 1. 2. 3　The increased impetus for rural farmers to get rid of poverty

By fully linking the development of Chinese herbal medicine industry and targeted poverty alleviation for the poor, Shangluo has vigorously promoted the business models such as "companies + bases + poor households" and "leading enterprises + cooperatives + poor households", established an interest linking mechanism, promoted the Chinese herbal medicine industry to move towards regional arrangement and large-scale, standard production and industrialized development, enabled poor households to actively get involved in the planting of Chinese herbal medicines, linked the interests of poor households to the modern pharmaceutical industry chain, realized poverty alleviation by supporting the Chinese herbal medicine industry in a blood transfusion way, thus building the industry into a truly leading one that promotes the economic growth of the whole city. Up to now, more than half of the farmers in the city have planted Chinese herbal medicines and 127, 800 poor people from 34, 800 households in the city have earned an additional income of more than 4, 800 Yuan on average, 1, 319 Yuan per capita. For the American Ginseng Industrial Base in Longtan village, Luoyuan Town, Luonan County, more than 2. 67 hectares of American Ginseng lands were transferred in three years. Poor households may earn income from land transfer costs and by working at the base. During the years 2018 to 2019, a total of more than 50, 000 Yuan was paid as wages and some people earned an annual average income of over 3, 000 Yuan purely by working at the base. Zhang Tao, a major planter in Longtan Village, transferred 4. 067 acres of land to plant codonopsis pilosula. The planting area of codonopsis pilosula in the whole village reached more than 10. 67 acres, enabling 61 households including 44 poor households to participate. The Chinese herbal medicine industry has become a pillar industry for poverty alleviation in Shangluo City.

2. 1. 2. 4　"Shangluo herbal medicine" brand established and promoted

In 2007, Shangluo proposed the focus of "top ten Chinese herbal medicines of Shangluo" as the goal of promoting the income increase from Chinese herbal medicines of Shangluo. It constructed the Shangluo Chinese herbal medicine industry park and made efforts to build the brand of "Shangluo herbal medicine". Currently, Shangluo ranked the top in Shaanxi in terms of scale, quality and benefits of the Chinese herbal medicine industry, making the Shangluo herbal medicine brand more widely heard. Shangluo salviae miltiorrhizae was successfully included in the top ten Chinese herbal medicines of Shaanxi; the Salviae Miltiorrhizae Planting Base of Tasly in Shangluo, the Schisandra Chinensis Planting Base in Zhashui, the Forsythia Planting Base in Luonan and the Medical Dogwood Planting Base in Danfeng were successfully listed among "Top Ten Model bases for Chinese Herbal Medicine Planting". And Shangluo Linlian Biotech Co., Ltd. won the honorary title of "National Quality Agricultural Base in 2018" as the sole Chinese herbal medicine production base in Shaanxi Province.

2. 1. 3　Enlightenment from anti-poverty practice in Shangluo

2. 1. 3. 1　Making full use of factor endowments to build a regional leading industry

Shangluo is unique in Chinese herbal medicine resources. How to shift the resource advantage to economicbenefits is to be considered and solved by each poor region. It is necessary to take suitable measures according to local conditions, attach great importance to the local competitive industry and regard the regional competitive leading industry as the one to adjust rural industry structure and accelerate the pace of getting farmers out of poverty. As the core for the growth of the entire regional economy, the leading industry dominates the development direction of regional industry structure and contributes to regional development a lot by driving the development of other industries through the chain effect. To help poor regions out of poverty, it is necessary for us to make great efforts in the leading industry, take measures according to local conditions, regard differential and characteristic development as a main approach to accelerated development and strive to convert potential advantages into practical economic advantages.

2.1.3.2 Improving the linking mechanism for scaled industrial development

The key to the development of the Chinese herbal medicine industry is to follow the ideas of scaled development, standardization, industrialization and branding. Chinese herbal medicine is a special industry and its planting and processing are closely linked. The modernization of Chinese herbal medicines particularly requires comprehensive arrangement and unified planning. Thus, it is necessary to build a linking mechanism for industrial development, accelerate the building of Chinese herbal medicine warehousing and logistics systems, intensify the efforts to develop leading enterprises, and introduce the famous Chinese herbal medicine groups with strong capital, advanced and mature technologies. Local rich Chinese herbal medicine resources are developed by building factories through sole investment, cooperation and reorganization with the current enterprises and other approaches. It is essential to strengthen the comprehensive development and utilization of Chinese herbal medicines, highlight Chinese herbal medicines, actively develop related industries such as TCM-related foods, diet supplements, organic chemistry, fertilizers and other related industries, extend the chains of Chinese herbal medicines and develop new growth points for the Chinese herbal medicine industry, thus allowing the industry to gain a strong momentum for development and a rapid growth in overall benefits.

2.1.3.3 Intensifying the efforts on technological innovation and improving industrial development level

Technological innovation is the key to further sustainable development of the Chinese herbal medicine industry. In order to improve the development of the industry, four private Chinese herbal medicine research institutes, including Chinese Herbal Medicine GAP Research Project Center, Qinling-Bashan Improved breeding Cultivation and Development Center, Shaanxi Solid Chinese Herbal Medicine Preparation and Improved breeding Screening Engineering Technology Research Center, and Shaanxi Orthopedics and Tumor Engineering Technology Center, have been established in Shangluo. Also, specialized Chinese herbal medicine research centers and product R&D centers have been established in leading enterprises, with over 100 R&D technicians involved. Only by forming a comparatively complete technology support system and supporting service system following the completion of research centers can we greatly improve the local standards for the production of Chinese herbal medicines.

2. 1. 3. 4   Improving the benefits of poverty reduction through funds and policy support

In view of regional resources and the reality of economic growth, the government has taken measures such as favorable policies and capital investment to promote the prioritized and rapid growth of characteristic industries, thus promoting the economic growth of the entire region. Rapid and successful development of the Chinese herbal medicine industry in Shangluo demonstrates that in order to make the modern Chinese herbal medicine industry bigger and stronger, the government should provide vigorous, favorable support for the industry, increase capital investment and integrate the agriculture-related development funds towards the Chinese herbal medicine industry so as to provide reliable capital support for the development of the industry. Also, a diversified investment and financing mechanism for the development of Chinese herbal medicines should be established. Some special development funds for the Chinese herbal medicine industry should be preserved from provincial fiscal expenditure and be mainly used for improved breeding screening, planting base construction, new product development, new technology promotion and application. Also, supporting funds should be preserved from municipal and County fiscal expenditure. Financial institutions should be encouraged to provide credit support to the development of the Chinese herbal medicine industry, expand corporate financing channels and develop the Chinese herbal medicine industry in a coordinated way.

2. 2   Walnuts as a Major Anti-poverty Industry in Shangluo City

As the region faced with the most arduous task of poverty alleviation in Shaanxi Province, Shangluo insists on the principle of "pursing

overall social and economic development through poverty alleviation",
makes the greatest efforts, sends the most capable cadres, adopts the
most rigorous measures, focuses on the goals of "two no worries and
three guarantees"[1] Shangluo is one of the areas that are most suitable for
walnut growth and also a famous walnut production area in China.
" Walnut slopes, walnut grooves, walnut needles and walnut
roads. Walnut trees can be seen everywhere and may be within the reach
of height", this ballad is a true portrayal of the development history of
Shangluo's walnuts. Based on the unique advantages of the walnut
industry, Shangluo has always regarded walnuts as the primary industry
for poverty alleviation of the whole city, promote walnut industry
development and get poor households out of poverty by integrating
resources, making intensified investments, implementing poverty
alleviation at each point, creating benefits for each household and
pursing comprehensive development. As of the end of 2019, the total
area of walnuts in the city had reached 227,733. 3 hectares and the yield
surpassed 158,000t. The comprehensive output value exceeded 5 billion
Yuan, which lifted 255,000 people from 73,000 poor households out of
poverty.

2.2.1 Prioritizing the industry and making it bigger

By focusing on the idea of establishing a big industry with the little
walnuts, the Shangluo Municipal Party Committee and Municipal
Government always regard the walnut industry as an important
breakthrough point and carrier of poverty alleviation and firmly grasp the
important goal of improving both quality and efficiency of the walnut
industry and increasing the income of farmers. Shangluo has proposed the
idea of building the strategic position of "Shangluo walnut" as another
fruit industry brand of Shaanxi following Weibei apple. A leading group
for walnut industry development has been built in Shangluo. The walnut
industry development has been studied and the working meetings on the

---

[1]   The "two no-worries" refer to achieving the goal of poverty alleviation so that those who have
been living in poverty no longer have to worry about food and clothing. And the "three guarantees" refer to
achieving the goal of guaranteeing compulsory education, basic medical treatment and housing security.

quality and efficiency improvement of the walnut industry held several times been held several times. A series of policy measures regarding the acceleration of walnut industry development has been issued, such as *Opinions on Accelerating the Quality and Efficiency Improvement of the Walnut Industry*, *Implementing Opinions on Encouraging and Supporting the Development of the Walnut Industry (Trial)* and *Implementing Plan on the Activities of Walnut Industry Demonstration Points Under the "Three-General-Secretary &Three-Head" Accountability System (Trial)*. In Shangluo, County or district leaders and heads have been organized more than ten times to inspect the scientific management of walnuts on site. And the walnut exhibition and promotion conferences, project contract signing conferences, themed exhibitions and high-end forums, etc. have been held in Beijing, Xi' an, Yangling and other places. The city also signed a framework agreement with the Shaanxi Forest and Grassland Bureau and the Northwest A&F University to jointly build a model city in walnut industry and deepen walnut industry technology cooperation to strongly promote the development of walnut industry. The Shangluo Walnut Industry Development Office at the deputy County level has been established, with staffing increased and personnel identified. In each County, a walnut industry management and service organization has been built and an industrial poverty alleviation organization system have been established and improved.

2. 2. 2 Identifying goals and envisioning the road-map for getting rich

As a "gold key" to the door of poverty alleviation in Shangluo, the walnut industry helps the masses live a happy life as early as possible during the process of building a moderately prosperous society in all respects. Based on the industrial foundation of massive walnuts and their driving effect, the city has scientifically formulated the "13th Five-Year Plan" for walnut industry development and identified objectives, tasks, priorities and guarantee measures. It is planned that 23, 333. 3 hectares of new standard walnut orchards and 66, 666. 7 hectares of standard management demonstration and foundation orchards will be built; 33, 333. 3 hectares of fine walnut breeding will be improved and purified;

500 new business entities and 6. 67 hectares of three-dimensional walnut ecology demonstration orchards will be developed. Two hundred specialized walnut cooperation organizations will be developed and 2, 000 walnut technology service personnel will be trained, thus allowing 200, 000 people from 100, 000 households to get engaged in the development of walnut industry. Currently, the area of Shangluo Walnut Base keeps stable at 226, 666. 7 hectares and the coverage rate of comprehensive scientific management reaches 80% or above. The yield of the fruit-growing walnut orchard per hectare reaches 1, 800kg. The per capita walnut income of farmers in the city reaches 4, 000 Yuan, 25% of the per capita net income of farmers in the city. The walnut industry has become the most important income-increase project for the poor people in Shangluo. Since 2016, Shangluo has exerted targeted efforts and witnessed significant improvement in both quality and efficiency of the walnut industry. In 2016 alone, the city achieved an increase in walnut yield of 40, 900t, with an income increase of 810 million Yuan and annual yield increase of 61. 3%.

2. 2. 3   Implementing pilot projects at designated points to guide income increase

In Shangluo, general secretaries at the municipal, county and township levels as well as heads of the city, counties and towns are in charge of the activities of walnut industry demonstration points. The chief leaders take the initiative in managing the scientific walnut demonstration points, provide the masses with walnut fertilizers, pruning tools, pesticides and instruments, and organize comprehensive scientific walnut management, including careful reclamation and expansion, fertilization and irrigation, shaping and pruning, and pest control. The area of the scientific walnut management demonstration points each municipal leader is responsible for shall not be less than 66. 67 hectares; the area of the scientific walnut management demonstration points each county or district leader is responsible for shall not be less than 53. 33 hectares and that each Township leader is responsible for shall not be less than 20 hectares. The management responsibility campaign will last five years, from January 2016 to the end of December 2020. Also, the management mode will keep changed in five years once determined and no demonstration points will be changed when personnel are replaced so as to ensure the continuity and effect of the management work. The municipal leaders inspects the scientific walnut management in each key month of spring and autumn, gives scores to all demonstration points upon the end of each inspection, and announces the inspection results throughout the city. Shangluo has two national leading forestry enterprises, five national walnut demonstration bases and three provincial walnut demonstration bases. As of the end of 2018, the city had identified 228 scientific management responsibility demonstration points in charge of by three general secretaries and three heads and the area of the total pilot points reached 11, 333. 3 hectares. New operation mechanisms and technologies are piloted in demonstration points to guide the sustained, rapid growth of the walnut industry in the whole city.

2.2.4   Intensifying moves and accelerating the pace of poverty alleviation

Intensifying moves is mainly reflected in the following two aspects. The first is intensifying support policies. The Shangluo Municipal Party Committee and Municipal People's Government have issued the *Measures on Industry Support in Poverty Alleviation* to make the supporting policies for walnut industry development clear. In 2016 alone, the municipal walnut industry policy bonus of 24. 2 million Yuan was awarded to the leading countries in quality and efficiency improvement, 10 demonstration township offices, thirty "three-general secretary, three-head" fine demonstration points, 35 specialized walnut production villages, 30 model walnut planters, ten leading enterprises in running walnut bases first and 25 preliminary processing demonstration points. The second is intensifying capital investment. A 10 million Yuan walnut industry development fund is established each year at the municipal level. Ten million Yuan and five million Yuan walnut industry development funds have been established in four major walnut-producing counties including Shangzhou, Luonan, Danfeng and Shanyan and three walnut base counties including Shangnan, Zhen'an and Zhashui. Also, each department actively finances projects, uses the funds of related industry projects in a binding way and prioritizes the funds for walnut industry development. For example, in 2017, Shangluo coordinated and identified the walnut industry development fund of 180 million Yuan, built 6,000 hectares new orchards and placed 192,666. 7 hectares under comprehensive scientific management. Additionally, the walnut industry development is also included in the indicators of annual target responsibility assessment on party committees, governments and departments. Year-beginning deployment, phased inspections, half-year implementation, year-end assessment, public announcements, awarding of mobile flags, final accountability and other measures are taken to better facilitate the development of walnut industry.

2. 2. 5　Innovating mechanisms and optimizing anti-poverty models

Shangluo City actively explores new industrial development mechanisms and models, makes efforts to tackle the bottlenecks constraining the walnut industry development mechanism, effectively integrates and drives the development of poor households. The development model featuring enterprise-driven, specialized cooperative operation, guidance by major industry household and carrying of industrial parks is established. A five-in-one new poverty alleviation model that integrates market, enterprises, cooperatives, bases and rural households is established. Also, a large number of leading enterprises, such as Luonan Tianyu, Shaanxi Zhiyuan, Xi'an Shuangcheng, Yilong Agriculture and Animal Husbandry, Shengda Agriculture and Sideline Products, Tianyu Runze Agricultural Ecology, etc. , are encouraged and supported to establish a new mechanism of linkage between enterprises and walnut planting bases and facilitate rural households to get rid of poverty and become rich by means of land transfer, ordered production, borrowing seedlings and returning fruits[1]. In 2017 alone, enterprises

---

　① Borrowing seedlings and returning fruits: Leading enterprises, cooperatives and other entities provide seedlings to planters at cost prices and provide relevant planting technique services for free. After the fruits are mature, enterprises and cooperatives will recover fruits at the agreed price and deduct seedling costs. The linkage among enterprises, cooperatives and poor households can effectively solve the problems that poor households wish to develop industries but have no funds to bear the cost of seedlings and no sales channels after planting, thus increasing the poor households' enthusiasm for planting and ability to resist risks.

transferred 4, 333. 3 hectares of walnut bases, drove 18 demonstration bases and enabled more than 300, 000 rural households to increase income through land transfer and working at industry parks. For example, Shaanxi ZhiYuan Food Co. , Ltd. is a joint-stock enterprise based in Shangluo that integrates scientific research, production and trade. It is mainly engaged in the development and production of walnut product series and also deals with other forestry related products. It has five Chinese leading production lines for producing walnut product series, with an annual output of 2, 500t. In 2014, the company integrated various project funds of 8 million Yuan according to the development model of "enterprises + bases + rural households", signed with 300 rural households the letters of intent on land use and had 66. 67 hectares of farmlands. Also, in combination with the reality of villages and based on transfer management, it actively explores the model of joint construction and joint management. With the consent of rural households, it signs with rural households the joint construction and joint management agreement with villager group as unit. In the first ten years, the company formulates a unified management plan to provide rural households with free seedlings, fertilizers, pesticides and other materials and farmers work for the company and obtain subsidies. Both parties build 66. 67 hectares of improved seeding orchards together. Ten years later, the company continues to provide technical service and allocate dividends according to benefits. By means of transfer management, joint construction and management as well as cooperative operation, etc. , a total of 275. 3 hectares of walnut demonstration bases have been completed, with Liangchakou Village, Faguan Town, Shanyang County as the center. As a result, hundreds of farmers are reemployed and the per capita walnut income of fruit farmers has reached 2, 000 or above.

　　With respect to the development of specialized cooperative operation, specialized walnut cooperatives with villages as units are established in Shanyang County and Shangzhou District. Rotary tillers, fertilizers, weeding machines, pest control vehicles, etc. are purchased in a unified manner. Through paid services, the unified management of one orchard, one village and one area is promoted to improve operating performance and increase the income of poor households. In terms of the development led by major planters, Wang Jianhang, a major planter of Shangzhou District, has led 62 poor households of Renjia Village, Yangyuhe Town in managing 22. 13 hectares of walnut orchards, with added per capita income of over 1, 850 Yuan. Zhang Daoming, a major walnut planter in Zhashui County, has supported 28 poor households through mentoring, assistance, education and guidance and assisted the village in developing 160 hectares of improved walnut orchards. In 2016, there were 33 major walnut planting households whose development income exceeded 50, 000 Yuan in the whole village. In counties such as Danfeng and Luonan, preferential policies are formulated to encourage 137 major planting households who understand technologies and management to undertake contracted operations. Management houses, irrigation facilities, production roads and other facilities have been built in a centralized manner. In terms of the bearing of industrial parks, the Minle Modern Agricultural Park in Danfeng has absorbed 350 poor households to get jobs and start business in the park by relying on facility agriculture, walnut shell activated carbon processing, etc. Shaanxi Tianyu Runze Company has transferred 86. 67 hectares of walnut orchards and established a walnut theme park and built the industry park into a tourist park and picking garden, etc. Industrial development is driven through scientific walnut management and leisure tourism. Poor households achieve stable income growth through land transfer and by working in parks. Currently, the whole city has 1, 268 walnut orchards with an area of 3. 33 hectares or above each, with the total area exceeding 56, 666. 7 hectares, which has greatly promoted the deep integration of primary, secondary and tertiary industries and led the development of the industry.

2. 2. 6　Brand promotion and capability building for poverty alleviation

The walnut industry of Shangluo has covered 98 towns (sub-districts) and more than 98% of the farmers in the city. It has become the green anti-poverty industry with the largest coverage and most obvious advantages in the city. Shangluo actively develops the commodity distribution market by relying on commercial enterprises, industrial businesses and e-commerce platforms. Once walnuts become mature, merchants from all places of the country will rush here to purchase. The original walnut fruit and walnut shell upon initial processing are actively traded. In Luonan, Shangzhou and Danfeng, etc. , distributing trading markets have gradually become influential centers for circulation and trading of original walnut products in Shaanxi and even in the entire northwestern China. Based on the traditional processing enterprises, nearly 20 processing enterprises have been established to process 20 product series in Shangluo. The products mainly include amber walnut, refined walnut oil, walnut jelly, walnut crisp candy, walnut milk and walnut sauce. With the development of a number of emerging leading enterprises such as Shaanxi Junwei, Zhiyuan, Jiajin, Tianyu and the integration and optimization of existing processing enterprises, the production, processing and marketing levels of Shangluo walnuts have been improved. Also, the city highlights walnut quality supervision and brand building, guides fruit farmers to establish brand awareness, actively promotes the green organic cultivation model, make timely harvesting, develops primary mechanical processing, timely removes shells, cleans and dries walnuts so as to increase goods value. Also, the city gradually regulates the order of walnut market, protects the image of Shangluo's walnut brand and continuously increases the quality and economic strength and PA capability of the walnut industry.

Through industry guidance, Shangluo relies on industrial development to enable the masses to obtain fixed income sources. It makes efforts on the walnut industry, helps the poor to participate in industry development for long-lasting poverty alleviation and intensifies efforts to make poverty alleviation by supporting the industry as an important breakthrough point for PA.

2.3   "Little Edible Fungus, Big Industry": Zhashui Path to Poverty Alleviation

Zhashui, Shaanxi Province is a mountainous County featuring highlands in majority with limited water resources and farmlands. As one of the 11 extremely poor counties in Shaanxi, it has 32,400 poor people from 10, 800 households, with poverty incidence of up to 34. 9%; and 79 villages (communities) in the County and 51 poor villages, 62. 9% of the total in the County. Among these villages, there are 24 extremely poor ones, with incidence of extreme poverty of 30. 4% . Increasing industry income is the main approach and long-term strategy against poverty. The development of large-scale characteristic industries and the cultivation of leading industries are the important breakthrough points for building long-term industries. Zhashui County is named for having the most suitable tree species for mass production of edible fungus, "Zha Tree". Covered by 75% vegetation, the city is a city of forest worthy of its name and has been a major origin of black fungus. By relying on such strength, Zhashui follows the principle of promoting development with industry and relying on edible fungus for poverty reduction. It makes efforts to build the quality "Zhashui edible fungus", supports the edible fungus production base and helps villages get rid of poverty and become rich.

2. 3. 1　Main practice of developing "Zhashui Edible Fungus"

Zhashui County has created an edible fungus-led industry through guaranteeing fund demand, establishing a connection mechanism, providing technical support, developing cooperative organizations, and stimulating development vitality, thus achieving an advanced road along which a big national brand grows out of a small County.

2. 3. 1. 1　Guaranteeing the demand of basic fund for industrial development

The participation of multiple parties and the guarantee of development funds are the most basic elements for developing characteristic leading industries. Zhashui County was firm in taking the edible fungus industry as the leading industry for poverty alleviation, guiding, encouraging and mobilizing enterprises and people to take an active part in developing the edible fungus industry. More than 80% of the financial funds related to agriculture were used for the poverty alleviation industries. A total of 365 million Yuan was allocated as special funds for poverty alleviation and various funds for supporting agriculture. The county coordinated 32 industrial loans of a total of 15.02 million Yuan to invest in the edible fungus industry. The county launched the "1153" program for the edible fungus industry, that is, to plant 1000 Mu (66.67 ha.) of edible fungus, which will produce 100 million bags of edible fungus with 5,000 tons of output, and the output value of 300 million Yuan and eight major actions for promoting distinctive industries. It has built 5 production lines for packing 10 million bags of fungus, 1,000 edible fungus hanging bag sheds, and 42 demonstration bases of million bags of edible fungus, thus forming a development pattern of large scale, facility, and industrialization for edible fungus industry. Today, Zhashui edible fungus has developed into a leading industry for local people to get rid of poverty, become better off and generate income, and has gradually formed a new model of benign development of "industrial development, collective income increase, and farmers becoming better off".

2.3.1.2　Establishing an interest pooling mechanism for the anti-poverty industries

In order to realize the long-term development of theedible fungus industry, Zhashui County has established an interest pooling mechanism for poverty alleviation, that is, "six types of connection, distribution by a three-seven proportion, and joint promotion by two shares". By "six types of connection", it means six forms in which poor households are embedded in economic entities such as collective economy, that is, "connecting shares for earning share capital, connecting leasing for earning rental, connecting adoption of industries for earning interests, connecting contracting for earning benefits, connecting labors for earning wages and connecting services for income increase". By "distribution by a three-seven proportion", it means to evaluate the project assets formed by poverty alleviation funds in terms of money, quantify 70% of the total converted assets as preferred equity shares for poor households, and 30% as collective asset equity shares for villages (communities), and then register the equity allocation, issue stock certificates, and pay dividends according to shares. In terms of profit distribution, 10% of the total net income is reserved as provident funds, 10% as public welfare funds, and 10% as risk funds for the development of the villages' collective undertakings, and the remaining 70% is used for the dividend from the income of collective assets. [1] This mechanism ensures that each poor household can be embedded in the industry chain and tied up in the interest chain. According to the own conditions of poor households, a variety of flexible access to the industry chain can help people to earn money in five aspects. The poverty-stricken households of the whole County have joined the collective economic organization. Among them, 7,053 poverty-stricken households have established a stable relationship of interest with 149 market entities, thus achieving bonding of shares, interests and hearts among the business entities, poor households and collective economies in a real sense. Furthermore, through the "multiple shares into one", the idea of "joint promotion by two shares" is innovated, so that poverty-stricken households benefit from the conversion of "resources" into asset shares and industrial funds into equity shares. In 2018, Zhashui County developed soil-based edible fungus, producing a total of 50 million bags of edible fungus with an output value of 150 million Yuan and a profit of 20 million Yuan. The 486. 87 ha. of land quantified through conversion of shares in the County produced a dividend of 6. 25 million Yuan. The 7, 140 poverty-stricken households in the County are embedded in the whole industry chain integrating R&D, production, processing and sales, making small edible fungus truly a big industry for poor people to increase income and become better off.

2. 3. 1. 3   Connecting the outside for technology support

Based on the "1153" plan of the edible fungus industry and using technology as its support, Zhashui County launched in April 2017 the construction of special towns featuring edible fungus. The Shaanxi Academy of Sciences established a center for edible fungus technology research and development locally and introduced Academician Li Yu and his team of Jilin Agricultural University and the research team of the School of Big Data and Food Science of Northwest University, setting up projects and winning more than 50 million Yuan in related national

---

[1]   "Zhashui's New Mechanism for Innovation in Poverty Alleviation and Benefiting Poverty", 2019-02-26, http://www. shangluo. gov. cn/info/1057/80720. htm.

projects, mobilized social enterprises to invest more than 50 million Yuan, and jointly developed strains to overcome the key technologies in cultivation methods, humidity, temperature, and picking timing control in the development of edible fungus industry. At the same time, the project for building Zhashui edible fungus Big Data Center was approved, which further reduced the labor cost of developing the edible fungus industry. The establishment of a production and marketing information network platform and mobile media client terminal improved the management level of the edible fungus base and product quality, and sales information, thus realizing the healthy and rapid development of the edible fungus industry. In addition, Zhashui County actively cooperates with colleges and universities in training edible fungus technology professionals, conducted popularization of edible fungus science in Townships, and organized more than 160 sessions of training in edible fungus production technology, providing scientific and technological support for the development of the edible fungus industry.

2. 3. 1. 4 Developing various types of cooperative organizations

Zhashui County has done more to support cooperative organizations. It has successively issued various incentive policies on encouraging the development of economic cooperation organizations. It grants a discount loan of 100, 000 Yuan to each family farm that leads more than 3 poor households and a discount loan of 500, 000 Yuan to each professional farmers' cooperative that leads more than 10 poor households. It has also coordinated financial institutions to develop 32 "industrial loans" of 15. 02 million Yuan to various business entities, and encouraged capable households with technology, venues and equipment to develop edible fungus sheds, acquisition and processing, logistics and transportation and other cooperative organizations. It has developed 303 professional cooperatives and 40 family farms, providing strong support for the scale management of the edible fungus industry. At the same time, it has also vigorously promoted the development model of "borrowing bags and repaying in edible fungus" and "borrowing sheds and repaying in edible fungus", by which poor households may participate in industrial development without investing capital. 809 poor households in the County have produced 7. 223 million bags of edible fungus through "borrowing bags and repaying in edible fungus"[1], achieving income increase by 2000 Yuan per household. 230 households contracted edible fungus sheds through "borrowing sheds and repaying in edible fungus", achieving income increase by 5000 Yuan per household.

2. 3. 1. 5　Stimulating the vitality of industrial scale development

In order to meet the needs of industrial development, Zhashui County has gradually formed a large-scale development trend with state-owned companies as the leader, non-public economy as the support, and cooperative organizations as the auxiliary. These three platforms work together to ensure the development of the edible fungus industry. Zhashui County has set up four state-owned enterprises, namely Travel Investment, Poverty-alleviation Investment, Technology Investment and Forestry Investment, each of which is responsible for building an edible fungus bag production line with an annual production capacity of 20 million bags. They supply raw materials to major edible fungus production bases in the County at cost prices to ensure sufficient supply and low cost of edible fungus raw materials, and have gradually formed a whole-chain industrial development model from production end to recovery end. It is not enough to only have state-owned enterprises. Zhashui County has successively introduced non-public enterprises such as Shaanxi Zhongbo, Shaanxi Origforest, Shaanxi Qinfeng and Shaanxi Xintiandi to participate in the production and operation such as production of edible fungus bag materials, cold chain storage, supporting product development, packaging and marketing, which have stimulated the vitality of the whole industry.

---

① Borrowing bags and repaying in edible fungus: The village collective economic organization and the enterprise sign a contract for borrowing bags. The farmers and the village collective economic organization sign a "borrowing bags repaying in edible fungus" agreement. The village collective economy provides edible fungus bags for free. After each season of edible fungus is harvested, farmers will hand over the finished edible fungus to the village collective for unified sales. The village collective economic organization will deduct the cost of borrowing the bags from the sales funds and return the rest to the poor households. In this way, the poor households can participate in the edible fungus industry without the need to invest money. For details, please refer to "Double Borrowing and Double Repayment for Mutual Benefit and Win-Win and Diversified Income Increase, Zhashui Innovation Model Enhances Ability to Eradicate Poverty and Benefit the Poor ", http://eslrb. slrbs. com/tbarticle. do? epaper = viewarticle&AutoID = 258543.

Today, the new industrial development model of "Zhashui edible fungus" across the whole county has been favored nationwide. A series of preferential support policies combine to greatly mobilize the enthusiasm of the poor households in developing the edible fungus industry, which has catalyzed the endogenous momentum of industrial development. The edible fungus industry in Zhashui has grown rapidly. In 2018, Zhashui County developed a total of 72 million bags of edible fungus. The 2,500 tons of edible fungus produced were sold out, producing the output value of 210 million Yuan. It led 10,000 poor people. In 2019, the edible fungus industry covered 44 villages in 9 towns across the county, with the growing scale up to 7,500 bags, an annual output of 3,440 tons of dry edible fungus and an output value of nearly 225 million Yuan. 6,944 poor households have got rid of poverty by relying on the edible fungus industry. The hard work of the poor people was repaid in real money. The edible fungus industry, as the leading industry in poverty alleviation in the county, has been recognized as a national geographic mark and geographical indication product of agricultural products. The brand of "Zhashui edible fungus" is well-known throughout the country and its social influence continues to grow.

2.3.2　Achievements in poverty reduction by edible fungus industry

Guided by the idea of "government-leading, enterprise-participating, three-transfer targeted, and three-level advancement", Zhashui County has focused on the theme of "relying on industry to promote development and relying on edible fungus to help shake off poverty" and united relevant departments to take multiple measures to develop the edible fungus industry into a leading industry that can overcome impoverished fortresses, and go all out to build the whole industry chain integrating R&D, production, processing and sales of edible fungus, which has achieved significant economic and social benefits. Jinmi Village, Xiaoling Town, Zhashui County, once an extremely poor village, has now been lifted out of poverty in recent years by developing industries such as edible fungus, Chinese medicinal materials and tourism. On the afternoon of April 20, 2020, General Secretary Xi Jinping inspected in Jinmi Village, understanding the variety and planting process of edible fungus, and asking about the price of edible fungus, sales, and income of villagers. General Secretary Xi Jinping praised them for they developed the little edible fungus fungi into a big business.

2. 3. 2. 1　Stabilizing the foundation for industrial development

Zhashui County has carried out edible fungus technical training for relevant planters so that they may increase their knowledge and understanding of edible fungus planting and production technology, and master the essentials of edible fungus planting and production technology, providing strong technical support to promote the development of the leading poverty alleviation industry of "one main industry and two advantageous industries" and guarantee that poor households may steadily increase their income and get rid of poverty. In the first half of 2019, Zhashui County conducted special edible fungus production and technology training for members of the "four teams" of towns (sub-districts) involved in the development of the edible fungus industry, legal persons of village collective economic organizations, households engaged in edible fungus cultivation, and poor people. The county specially invited experts from Northwest A&F University to give on-site lectures to explain the current status and development trend of edible fungi industry such as edible fungus, preparation and production of fungus, high-quality and efficient cultivation technology of edible fungus, quality safety and management of agricultural products, as well as marketing and brand management of edible fungus such as edible fungus, etc. ; it also organized learners to go to the edible fungus base in Xichuan Village, Xialiang Town for intuitive lectures, field technical guidance, and conducted training to learners on field management and production of edible fungus, large-scale cultivation of edible fungi and the marketing of edible fungi, mainly edible fungus, so that more farmers will join the edible fungus industry, which will help maintain the long-term stability of the edible fungus industry.

2. 3. 2. 2　Extending the industrial development chain

Through the support of the special projects of the Central Committee for guiding local science and technology development, Zhashui County constructed the R&D base for edible fungus deep-processing products to conduct R&D of edible fungus deep-processing products in an all-round manner. Now it has developed a variety of products including edible fungus slice, edible fungus ice cream, edible fungus submicron powder, and edible fungus tea. It also cooperates with a Taiwan enterprise in researching a series of edible fungus beverages, comprehensively enhancing the added value and core market competitiveness of Zhashui edible fungus products. At present, a whole industry chain covering the breeding, planting, processing, financial and industry intermediary services, technology support of edible fungus and other edible fungi has been formed, and related supporting policies for R&D, production and sales has been strengthened. The industry departments, associations and the market have strengthened the coordination among the upstream and downstream industry chain. The overall competitiveness of the industry is continuously enhanced, and the benefits are significantly improved.

2. 3. 2. 3 Stimulating the vitality of industrial development

Zhashui County innovates the model of "Party branch + three-transfer reform + collective economy + poor households" and adopts the method by which the village collective holds controlling interest, party members and cadres take the lead in shareholding, and poor households voluntarily participate so as to develop village-level collective economy to promote mutual benefit and win-win between the collective economy and poor people. Six income-increasing "packages", that is, three-investment shares, leasing subcontracting, industrial adoption, labor services, product orders, and service development are launched and one or more connection bonds rationally chosen according to the different situations of poor people to achieve connecting shares for earning share capital, connecting leasing for earning rental, connecting adoption of industries for earning interests, connecting contracting for earning benefits, connecting labors for earning wages and connecting services for income increase. In terms of interests distribution, evaluation the project assets formed by poverty alleviation funds in terms of money and distribution of the total discount by a three-seven proportion are used as preferred equity shares for poor households and collective asset equity shares for villages (communities). This has stimulated the enthusiasm of the people for innovation and entrepreneurship, and promoted the poverty-stricken people to actively participate in industrial development and rely on labor to increase income and become better off.

2.3.2.4 Improving the efficiency of poverty alleviation by developing industries

The edible fungus has become one of the key industries for poverty alleviation via industrial development in Zhashui County. Poor households with certain economic strength directly invest in the edible fungus industry. Most of the poor people with working ability can work in enterprises and cooperatives for a long time to ensure that the poor households have a long-term income increase and get rid of poverty. The edible fungus industry has driven more than 10,000 poor households in Zhashui County to realize an annual per capita income increase of 1,000 Yuan. The 486.87 hectares of quantified land produce a dividend of 6.25 million Yuan; more than 3,600 people work seasonally, and the per capita labor income reaches 7,000 Yuan. The operation income from village-level collective economies reach 6.41 million Yuan, and the preferred stock income for poverty-stricken households is 4.487 million Yuan, leading 31,260 people from 9,381 poor households. The poverty alleviation through industries has produced obvious effects.

2.3.3 Experience and enlightenment of the "Zhashui Practice" in the poverty alleviation via industrial development

Characteristic industries are the advantages for a place to develop. Zhashui has embarked a distinctive path of poverty alleviation and prosperity pursuing by ensuring fund demand, establishing connection mechanisms, providing technological support, supporting cooperative organizations, and stimulating development vitality, providing useful reference to poverty alleviation and development in other similar areas.

2.3.3.1　Guarantee funds

The guarantee funds are insurance funds for developing poverty alleviation industries. Only by guaranteeing the investment of development funds in poverty alleviation industries, giving moderate priority to characteristic industries, following the policy of "developing one industry in onecounty", and striving for more development funds can we prevent the unprovoked interruption of industrial development chain, make the poverty alleviation industries continue, further strengthen the infrastructure construction, build more large-scale production bases, and provide insurance for the developing the industries, so that the subsequent development can be better carried out.

2. 3. 3. 2　**Mechanism innovation**

Mechanism innovation is a booster for developing poverty-alleviation industries. Only by exploring the establishment of institutional mechanisms and pursuing scientific operation and standardized management can we make the industry develop in a sustained, stable and healthy manner. General Secretary Xi Jinping points out that the focus of developing the poverty alleviation industries lies in benefiting the people and the difficulty lies in keeping stable development. It is necessary to extend the industry chain, improve the ability to resist risks, and establish a more stable mechanism for connecting interests. In this way, the poor people can increase their income in a continuous and steady manner. [1] Through mechanism innovations such as establishing interest connection, converting assets and capital into shares to achieve the bundling of the interests of the people, we can achieve bonding of shares and connection of interests among the business entities, poor households and collective economies in a real sense, thus making the characteristic industries truly become a big industry for national income increase.

2. 3. 3. 3　**Technological support as the driving force**

Technological support is the source of impetus for developing

---

[1]　During his inspection in Shaanxi, Xi Jinping emphasized to effectively keep employment, the financial sector, foreign trade, foreign and domestic investments, and expectations stable, ensure the employment of residents, the basic livelihood of the people, the market entities, food and energy security, stability of industry chain supply chain, and grass-roots operation, and strive to write a new chapter for Shaanxi to catch up and surpass in a new era, 2020-04-24(2).

industries for poverty alleviation. Only by continuously promoting technological innovation and transformation of scientific achievements and applying them to the production of actual industries can we achieve tangible results. The innovation and reform of industrial development must be achieved by connecting high-tech production areas such as agriculture and forestry colleges and universities, scientific research institutes, and introducing new varieties, new technologies, and new methods, etc. The agricultural technology promotion teams at grassroots level must continuously expand its impact and achieve a wider transformation and promotion of scientific achievements.

2. 3. 3. 4 Scale development as the trend

Scale development is the main trend in developing poverty alleviation industries. We must give full play to the driving role of leading enterprises, non-public economies and cooperative organizations, give high policy preferences, and promote the industrialization of characteristic industries to drive more poor groups. Only in this way can we effectively connect decentralized small production and unified large markets, meet the needs for farmers to participate in the market competition and transition to market operation, improve farmers' organization and achieve transition to modern agriculture.

2. 4 Poverty Alleviation via E-commerce in Shanyang County

Shanyang County is located in Shangluo city, Shaanxi Province. Within the County are Liuling Mountain in the north, Juanling Mountain in the middle, Yunling Mountain in the south, and two rivers running among them. Shanyang County is rich in resources, but the relatively poor geographical conditions and location deep in the mountains make it nearly isolated from other places. Therefore, despite its a great number of characteristic quality agricultural products such as walnuts, shiitake mushrooms and edible fungus, the people in the county still find it difficult to become better off relying on the natural products. In addition, the county's economy is slow in development, leading to low development level on a whole. Relying on the internet to develop e-commerce and promote poverty alleviation through e-commerce is an effective way to solve this dilemma. As General Secretary Xi pointed out, "e-commerce, as an emerging business, can not only promote sales of agricultural and sideline products, help the people get rid of poverty and become better off, but also drive forward rural revitalization. E-commerce is promising. "[1] Since 2016, Shanyang County has been focusing on the goal of "getting rid of poverty and becoming better off" and the online marketing mechanism of e-commerce for poverty alleviation, taken the internet plus initiative as an opportunity, based itself on the reality of the county, and promoted the three-dimensional development of e-commerce, initially forming an e-commerce poverty alleviation development model with local geographical features.

2.4.1　Main practice

The poverty alleviation by e-commerce is to, driven by local governments, guide and encourage third-party e-commerce enterprises to establish e-commerce service platforms, focus on the upward movement of agricultural products, promote the circulation of commodities, continuously improve the ability of the poor to use e-commerce for entrepreneurship and employment, and broaden the channels of sale for the characteristic and high-quality agricultural and sideline products in poor areas and ways for poor people to increase income and shake off poverty, so that the development results of the Internet will benefit more poverty-stricken areas and poor population. "[2] Poverty alleviation by e-commerce makes up for the shortcomings of traditional circulation channels, so that farmers in poor areas face the market directly, thus reducing intermediate circulation links, lowering circulation costs, and increasing the space for farmers' benefits.

---

[1]　"The poverty alleviation strategies behind Xi Jinping's investigation of small towns in Shaanxi", 2020-04-03, http://cpc. people. com. cn/n1/2020/0422/c164113-31683730. html.

[2]　*Guiding Opinions of the General Office of the State Council on Accelerating the Development of Rural Electronic Commerce* (Guo Ban Fa [2015] No. 78) .

2. 4. 1. 1   Strengthening infrastructure construction and increasing policy support

As an authentic agricultural County, Shanyang County is not short of unique agricultural products. However, the scattered, small and complicated agricultural industry makes it impossible for local high-quality products to form a brand effect. Many agricultural products with local characteristics are limited within the County, making production come apart from sales. E-commerce allows them to break the space constraints and connect to a vast market. (1) Improving basic conditions for e-commerce development. Shanyang County has actively responded to the national call on poverty alleviation. Taking advantage of the Internet plus and based on the actual situation of the County, it has built the roads, the Internet, logistics and other infrastructure within the County, strengthened the sharing and connection of rural logistic infrastructure including transportation, commerce, supply and marketing, and post, and improved the basic conditions for developing e-commerce in poor areas. (2) Setting up a special fund for poverty alleviation by e-commerce. Every year, Shanyang County allocated a special fund of 10 million Yuan for developing the e-commerce poverty alleviation industry. It has introduced a number of support policies including office space, housing, training and financial credit, logistics and distribution, publicity and marketing. In combination with plans for poor villages and households to shake off poverty, it has established characteristic industries and leading products, focusing on promoting and creating e-commerce brand enterprises and brand products, so as to promote the online marketing of rural products.

2. 4. 1. 2   Building a "Three-level Platform" and innovating "Three Major Models"

As one of the important means of targeted poverty alleviation, poverty alleviation by e-commerce makes poor groups with poor competitiveness in the traditional market environment have opportunities to shake off poverty and increase income. Shanyang County uses the e-commerce platform to create a rural e-commerce poverty alleviation model that fits the local conditions. First, building a "Three-level Platform". In order to unblock internet marketing channels, Shanyang

County has built a "three-level platform". It has built 18 Town-level e-commerce service stations and 98 village-level e-commerce service points, of which 59 poor villages have successively built "Great Qinling Agricultural Specialty E-commerce (Shanyang) Exhibition Experience Pavilion", e-commerce incubation service center, online goods control sorting and packaging supply center, and rural Taobao operation center in the County seat. JD. com specialty Shanyang Pavilion is online for operation, and agricultural and sideline products trading center is under construction. All these have provided strong support for online sale of agricultural products. Second, innovating " Three Major Models ". Shanyang County has innovated "three major models" and led farmers to increase their income. Establishing the "e-commerce plus orders plus farmers" model, by which e-commerce enterprises are guided to cooperate with farmers and sign order purchase agreements so that farmers can grow according to orders; establishing "e-commerce plus cooperatives (companies) plus farmers" model, by which e-commerce enterprises are guided to cooperate with planting and breeding cooperatives and sign production and sales purchase agreements so that the cooperatives may produce according to the agreement; establishing an "e-commerce plus service station plus agency operation" model, by which e-commerce enterprises are guided to cooperate with village-level e-commerce service stations, and entrust service stations to collect various agricultural and sideline products and sell through agents all types of products produced by enterprises. These three models have radiated and led the people and poor households to participate in the e-commerce industry chain, thus improving the rural e-commerce logistics distribution system, building the flag domain rural e-commerce public service system, and effectively solving the farmers' difficulty in "purchase and sale".

2. 4. 1. 3　Improving the supporting service system to train e-commerce talents

Shanyang County has incorporated e-commerce into its poverty alleviation work system. It has made every effort to promote the construction of Town and village e-commerce service stations integrating purchase and sale by agents, express delivery, information services, and basic finance, improve logistics supporting facilities and speed up training of e-commerce talents. First, setting up Town-level Taobao service sites in the countryside. In 2016, 32 town-level rural Taobao service sites in Shanyang County started business simultaneously, opening a new era of rural e-commerce development in Shanyang and becoming one of the standard counties in the northwest region with eight Taobao service sites in the countryside. The opening of these service sites not only solves villagers' difficulty in buying and selling, but also builds a green channel for entry of industrial products into villages and of agricultural products into cities, which greatly facilitates the villagers' shopping while allowing the various agricultural products to be sold to big cities through the Internet, thus breaking the space constraints, promoting local economic development, and improving the living standards of villagers. Second, integrating courier companies. Relying on China Post, Shanyang County has integrated 15 private courier companies including STO Express, YTO Express, ZTO Express, Best Express and Yunda Express, extending logistics express delivery to 18 Townships and offices and three major scenic spots in the County. According to the standardized process and requirements, it allows the delivery person to use his own vehicle. In this way, the rural deliverymen become courier deliverymen, to such an extent that the logistics express covers 190 villages in the County, with the coverage rate reaching 80% . Third, cooperating with SYW①. In 2018, the government of Shanyang County and SYW under China CO-OP Group signed the *Cooperative Agreement on the Construction of Upward Movement Supply Chain System of Agricultural Products* in Shanyang County. In light of the local existing problems, SYW Shanyang Project Team worked with the township governments and relevant enterprises to make exploration and research and finally formulated a set of practical solutions to effectively integrating agricultural market resources through the construction of agricultural product e-commerce upward system, agricultural product circulation big data system, agricultural product

---

① SYW is an agricultural Internet ecological platform that comprehensively serves large agricultural households in line with the national development strategies and requirements for the work on agriculture, rural areas and rural people and based on modern information technology.

brand building and promotion system, e-commerce talent training, service sites and other projects, thus effectively solving farmers' problem with sales of agricultural products. As a result, the local Chinese medicinal materials, edible fungi and forest fruits are able to go out of the mountain through SYW Internet platform of bulk agricultural products. Fourth, cooperation between enterprises and colleges to organize technical training. In order to ensure sufficient reserves of professional talents for the county e-commerce poverty alleviation industry, Shanyang County attaches importance to training local e-commerce talents as the "talent cohesion" project. By adopting the measures of "going global" and "welcoming in", Shanyang County conducts cooperation with Northwest University, Nanjing Dianshi E-Commerce Company and other colleges and enterprises in regularly selecting e-commerce enterprises to go out for learning and inviting experts to Shanyang to conduct training. In this way, Shanyang County has trained a group of professionals who understand information technology, can operate e-commerce and lead the development of e-commerce. At present, a total of 3,500 person-times have been trained, which has led more than 680 poor people in starting business and finding employment in the e-commerce sector.

2.4.2　Main results achieved

2.4.2.1　Promoting the transformation and upgrading of traditional industries to drive the development of county economy

Since the comprehensive demonstration of e-commerce in rural areas began in Shanyang County, more and more traditional enterprises have actively embraced the internet and used e-commerce channels to purchase and sell products and services. A group of traditional leading enterprises such as Jiajin Trade Company, Zhiyuan Food Company, Guangyuan Food Company, Tianzhuyuan Tea Company, Ruijun Ecological Company, etc. , have been active in using the online platform to conduct sales and opening up new market channels so as to add vitality to and drive the development of the county economy. In 2018, Shanyang County had 13 e-commerce enterprises above designated size, 158 agricultural enterprises (cooperatives, family farms), and 23 logistics and courier enterprises, with the e-commerce network covering 18 Townships and offices, 3 key scenic spots and 160 villages (communities), with an e-commerce transaction value of 590 million Yuan. Shanyang County has been rated as a national-level integrated demonstration county for entry of e-commerce into countrysides, provincial-level e-commerce demonstration county, and agricultural product e-commerce demonstration county. Shanyang County ranks fourth in Shaanxi Province and first in Shangluo City in the "Internet plus" social poverty alleviation work.

2. 4. 2. 2 Promoting the "Shanyang Agricultural Products" brand to drive the scale development of the industry

Shanyang County deeply develops self-operated products such as "Eight Major Articles of Qinling Mountain" and "Shanyang Four Treasures" to build a "mountain agricultural product" brand and create the specialty agricultural product brands including "South Shaanxi Ecological Black Pig", "Qinling Mountain Broiler Chicken", "Shanyang Walnut", "Shanyang Tea" and "Shanyang Nine Eye Lotus", driving the brand development of agricultural products. At the same time, it cooperates with well-known e-commerce platforms such as Alibaba and JD. com to promote the entry of Shanyang's special agricultural products into the large markets. Relying on Shanyang Gaungjiwang E-commerce Company, Shanyang County has cultivated a number of subdivision e-commerce platforms such as housekeeping, industrial products, tourism cultural products, famous agricultural products, handicrafts, etc. , to drive the transformation and upgrading of rural economy, and promote the e-commercialization of rural industrial products, tourism and service products.

2. 4. 2. 3 E-commerce entrepreneurship and employment

The e-commerce talent training program has greatly changed the ideology of local rural youth. A large number of rural youths, college students and migrant workers have returned to their hometown for e-commerce business, stimulating the vitality of innovation and entrepreneurship and boosting the industry development. This has relieved the phenomenon of "left-behind children", "empty nesters", "hollow villages" and so on, producing good social effects. In 2018, the e-commerce industry chain in Shanyang County spurred more than 2,000 entrepreneurial jobs, the number of netizens in the County reached 316,000, and there were more than 1,100 personal online stores and micro-stores.

2.4.2.4 Leading poor people to increase income and become better-off

Developing rural e-commerce is an important part of helping the poor in rural areas, especially in the western rural areas, with poverty alleviation. In 2018 alone, Shanyang County trained 2,966 person-times of the poor through e-commerce, spurring 500 people in entrepreneurship and employment. E-commerce service covered 22,000 poor people, and the products worth of 5 million Yuan from poverty-stricken households were sold online. The product sales, labor employment, and share dividends and other forms benefited more than 1,200 households with over 4,300 people, helping them increase income and combat the poverty and solidly prospering farmers through the e-commerce industry chain. At the same time, developing e-commerce has also effectively promoted poverty alleviation through consumption, that is, all sectors of society can help poor people increase income and alleviate poverty by consuming products and services from poor areas and poor people. [1] The labor union and related enterprises in Nanjing Liuhe District, a pairing assistance entity for Shanyang County, reached a cooperative agreement on supply and marketing of agricultural products with Shanyang County. In 2018, the Liuhe District organized entities within its jurisdiction to purchase agricultural and characteristic products worth 1.2 million Yuan. Before the Spring Festival in 2019, Liuhe District mobilized cadres and staff members of government organs, institutions, and employees of enterprises to place orders worth more than 2 million Yuan for characteristic products from Shanyang. Social forces have effectively increased the income of the poor by purchasing

---

[1] *Guiding Opinions of the General Office of the State Council on Deepening Poverty Alleviation through Consumption and Helping to Win the Poverty Alleviation Campaign* (Guo Ban Fa [2018] No. 129).

products and boosted the enthusiasm of the poor to participate in production.

2. 4. 3　Experiences and enlightenment

2. 4. 3. 1　New opportunities for county-level e-commerce brought by policy inclination

Governments, platforms, online merchants, service providers, traditional enterprises, rural business entities, and poor households are the six important and indispensable participating forces for e-commerce poverty alleviation. The government is the leading force and establishes with major platforms, online merchants and service providers a coordinated mechanism for e-commerce poverty alleviation that conducts effective collaboration and form a joint force to drive traditional enterprises, rural business entities and poor households to participate in the e-commerce industry chain and guide all parties to participate, so as to further improve the efficiency of e-commerce poverty alleviation. Local governments, in particular, shall play a coordinating role in improving the e-commerce development environment in terms of various aspects such as funds, systems, ideas, and guide all parties to unite as one.

2. 4. 3. 2　Creating a characteristics industry brand of e-commerce

The standardization of agricultural product commodities is a necessary prerequisite for rural e-commerce to promote targeted poverty alleviation. Although most rural agricultural products have a number of varieties, they are of small scale industry, low degree of standardization, and low product quality, which is far from the high standards of e-commerce. To effectively implement targeted poverty alleviation through rural e-commerce, it is necessary to promote large-scale and quality farming of agricultural products, strengthen the brand building of special agricultural products, create regional unique brands, and take advantage of natural endowments in poor areas to promote marketing on the Internet platform, raise their profile, and build a distinctive agricultural product brand.

2. 4. 3. 3   Whole industry chain development driven by e-commerce

Rural e-commerce is the integration of online and offline business. Poverty alleviation by e-commerce is not simply to connect e-commerce to rural poverty-stricken areas, but to adapt to local conditions and rely on e-commerce platforms to expand sales channels and urge efforts to make production layout, so that the rural e-commerce development may drive social capital to the countryside, promote the agglomeration and development of production, logistics, design, packaging and other industries in the upstream and downstream of the industry chain, enhance the endogenous momentum of development in rural areas, and enhance the attractiveness of rural areas to production factors including funds and talents. This is the core of developing rural e-commerce.

2. 5   Exploration of a Comprehensive Approach to Poverty Alleviation via Industrial Development in Chenggu County

Chenggu County in the middle of the Hanzhong Basin in southern Shaanxi is a contiguous impoverished agricultural county in the Qinling-Bashan mountainous regions and a county in the Sichuan-Shaanxi Old Revolutionary Base Area. It administrates 15 towns, 2 street offices, 232 administrative villages and 40 communities, a total population of 543, 000 including the agricultural population of 446, 000. At the end of the "Twelfth Five-Year Plan" period, there were 101 registered poverty-stricken villages in the county, and 23, 576 poor households with 63, 441 poor people. The poverty incidence rate was 14. 29% . Since 2016, Chenggu County has vigorously implemented poverty alleviation via industrial development, and delivered utmost efforts and taken comprehensive measures to promote all-around rural reform, develop modern agriculture, promote industrial integration and development, and help the poor increase income, contributing remarkably to poverty alleviation.

2.5.1 Remarkable achievements in poverty alleviation by developing the industry

2.5.1.1 New development of characteristic superior industries

Industries in Chenggu have three main characteristics: First, it has obvious advantages in scale operation. Among the eight leading industries of grain, oil, fruit, animal husbandry, vegetables, and Chinese medicinal materials, the scale of animal husbandry, vegetables, Chinese medicinal materials, and salamander industry ranks above 20th in Shaanxi Province; the output of Yuanhu (rhizoma corydalis) accounts for 70% of the total output in China, making it a veritable hometown of Chinese Yuanhu. Second, new industries are booming. In recent years, new industries such as kiwi, raspberry, photovoltaic power generation, etc. , which were not previously available, have grown stronger. Some new industries have begun to grow and become new growth points that drive poor households out of poverty. For example, the Hehe Group's kiwifruit industrial base of 373. 33 ha. greatly mobilizes more than 100 impoverished households in Dongyuangong Village and Xinyuan Village of Yuangong Town to increase their income from land and labor. The annual income of per household increases by over 3100 Yuan. Third, the modern agriculture improves its quality and performance. The county pursues product structure adjustment, and bulk agricultural products aim at "high-quality famous products", and other agricultural products aim at "characteristic advantages" to improve quality and performance. The special industries such as animal husbandry, fruit, tea, and vegetables have gradually matured and the degree of industrialization has continued to improve.

2.5.1.2 New look of business entities cultivation

First is actively introducing well-known and leading enterprises both at home and abroad to provide a strong driving force. Chenggu County has successfully introduced a number of well-known enterprises such as New Zealand-based Zespri Group, Beijing Shunxin Group, Shaanxi Fruit Industry Group, Universal-PC Technology and Huani Biology by strengthening investment in agricultural industrialization. All these have driven the development of characteristic industries such as fruits, pigs and Chinese medicinal materials. Second is focusing on fostering local leading companies for strong demonstration. The county has cultivated 11 provincial-level leading enterprises of industrialization in agriculture and 20 municipal-level leading enterprises, which has formed a good demonstration effect and become a new force and a main force in poverty alleviation. Third, vigorously developing farmers' cooperatives for strong leading role. At present, 896 professional farmers' cooperatives have been established in the County (among them: 2 national-level demonstration cooperatives, 2 top 10 cooperatives at provincial level, 14 demonstration cooperatives at municipal level, and 10 demonstration cooperatives at provincial level), and 166 family farms (among them: 32 provincial-level demonstration farms and 37 at municipal level). Various market players have driven 13, 800 poor households, covering 27, 000 poor people.

2. 5. 1. 3   Establishment of interest connection mechanism

First is on the diversification of poverty alleviation models. Through various forms such as income from contract production, labor income, leaseback and subcontract income, income from poverty alleviation by asset, and share dividend income, Chenggu County constantly improves the interest connection mechanism and finds ways to allow poor households to participate in production and get employed. Through learning while working, they are able to enhance their development capacity, increase income steadily, and achieve the goal of getting rid of poverty and becoming better off. Second is about precise goal of poverty alleviation via industrial development. Chenggu County has adopted a series of policies and regulations to promote poverty alleviation via industrial development. For example, the business entities supported by the poverty alleviation fund projects must give priority to the poor households for labor and employment; the share dividends from poverty alleviation fund must make sure that the poverty-stricken households have links and shares in the industry chain and the interest chain, and the income of poverty-stricken households must account for more than 70%. These specific regulations can ensure that each household has an income-increasing project and that everyone has a way out of poverty, so that more poor households can increase income and shake off poverty in the industrial development.

2. 5. 1. 4　Economic and social Development to a new level

Since 2011, Chenggu County has been ranked excellent for seven consecutive years in the annual comprehensive assessment in Hanzhong City. The County economy ranks from 27th in 2011 to 9th in 2017, continuing to raise 18 places in six years, and it has been ranked among the "Top Ten Counties for Economic and Social Development in Shaanxi Province", becoming the only (for the first time) county (district) in the southern area of Shaanxi to enter "Top Ten Counties". At the same time, it was also ranked among the 10 "Advanced Counties for Poverty Alleviation" in Shaanxi Province, and was awarded by the provincial leading group for poverty alleviation. In the catch-up and surpass review evaluation in Shaanxi Province in the first half of 2018, Chenggu once again ranked seventh in the monitoring of 77 county-level economic development in the province, and ranked first in the comprehensive ranking of 11 counties (districts) in Hanzhong City.

2. 5. 2　Exploration on poverty alleviation via industrial development in Chenggu County

Chenggu County regards poverty alleviation via industrial development as the top priority, key move and fundamental policy for poverty alleviation. Based on its own resource advantages, it has constantly clarified development ideas, formulated support policies and measures, innovated industrial development models, and promoted poverty alleviation development from "blood transmission" to "blood creation", thus enabling the county's industry to develop well and achieve remarkable results in targeted poverty alleviation. The practice of poverty alleviation via industrial development in Chenggu County is reflected in the aspects as follows:

2. 5. 2. 1　Industries suitable for poverty alleviation based on resources endowment

In order to plan and strengthen the industry for poverty alleviation according to local conditions, Chenggu County firmly works on the "five highlights" as follows: First, highlight the overall plan. In terms of development planning, it pursues the guidance of the new development philosophy, focuses on building a modern industrial system that integrates the development of the primary, secondary and tertiary industries; in terms of spatial layout, it highlights town-based cluster development, forming a rich format, close interest connection, and a new development pattern of integration and coordination of industry and city. In terms of policy guarantees, it has compiled the *Plan of Chenggu County on Poverty Alleviation via Agricultural Industry* (2017 – 2020), the *Three-Year Action Plan to Win the Poverty Alleviation* and 13 sub-plans and annual plans, which have formed a planning system of "three-level linkage, complementary advantages and coverage to households" in the county, towns and villages. It has established and improved the fiscal and taxation, land and other policy guarantee system that promotes the integration of rural primary, secondary and tertiary industries to strengthen security and promotion. Second, highlight selection of industries. It has made efforts to achieve accurate selection of projects for poverty alleviation via industrial development, and, according to resource conditions and market needs, choose agriculture, industry, business, tourism, or forest as conditions permit. In these years, the focus is to create the "eight major industries for poverty alleviation" and promote the formation of the pattern for poverty alleviation via industrial development in which tea grows in the south, fruits in the north and rice and oil plants along the rivers, vegetables grow in suburban and fungi in the mountains and large-scale breeding and medicine along the rivers. Third, highlight the integration of the three industries. Efforts have been made to promote the integrated development of the rural primary, secondary and tertiary industries, and form a joint force for poverty alleviation via industrial development. Firstly, non-agricultural enterprises have increased efforts in targeted poverty alleviation. The county actively organizes nearly 60 industrial and commercial enterprises to directly help 950 impoverished households to increase their income and shake off poverty through the assistance models including labor-employment, raw material purchase, share-dividend, and entrepreneurial incubation. Secondly, accelerating the development of new momentum for industrial development. It pursues the transformation and upgrading of agriculture through adjusting and optimizing the structure, promotes the connection of the secondary and tertiary industries in the rural areas, extend the industry chain, enhance the functions of agricultural leisure and tourism, agricultural experience, cultural inheritance, etc. , and cultivate and develop a number of new modes of agriculture, especially the highlights of leisure agriculture. The county currently has 10 key villages for poverty alleviation via development of tourism, 13 leisure agricultural parks of various types, and 87 farmhouse tourist spots, which have helped 1, 340 poor households shake off poverty. Thirdly, increasing the poverty alleviation via the photovoltaic industry. A total of 9. 45 MW of photovoltaic projects for poverty alleviation have been implemented, directly or indirectly driving more than 900 households to increase their income and become better off. Fourth, highlight the belt development of industries. A citrus industrial belt of 15, 333. 34 ha. has been built along the hillside Towns and villages of the southern slope of the Qinling Mountains in the county, and a kiwifruit industrial belt of 2, 666. 67 ha. has been built along the banks of the Xushui River, the Hanjiang River, the Wenchuan River, the Nansha River, and the Yangou River. Shangyuanguan, Dongjiaying, Sanhe and Shaheying have built 6, 000 ha. of Yuanhu industrial belt along the banks of the Hanjiang River, and 8, 000 ha. of tea industrial belt in the southern mountainous area has been built. Along the banks of the Xushui River to the Hanjiang River, Sanhe, Bowang, Shaheying, Liulin and Shangyuanguan have built a "C"-type vegetables industrial belt of 12, 666. 67 ha. The scale of production, the standardization of quality, and the networking of marketing have made Chenggu County's characteristic industries develop better and better. Fifth, highlight targeted poverty alleviation. By advancing the development of characteristic advantageous industries and characteristic products, a number of leading industries with strong radiation driving ability and good effect of increasing farmers' income has been formed in the county. Through land transfer, Shaheying Town has accelerated the construction of the pastoral complex projects of more than 333. 33 ha. for high-standard kiwifruit, driving the Town's poverty-stricken households to increase income through land transfer and work in the park. On September 27, 2018, a total of nearly one million Yuan was distributed to 328 poor households and 9 village collectives. It has become the leading project in the town to get rid of poverty and become better off. Yuangong Town strives to build more than 53. 33 ha. of toadstool production bases, and the produced toadstool has good market, which directly drives 211 poor households to increase income in a steady manner. Sanhe Town allocates part of the agriculture-related special poverty alleviation funds to set up an industrial development fund, and invests the funds in leading enterprises such as cooperatives and Chinese herbal medicine processing, ensuring that poor villages and households have a stable source of income. The town has raised a total of 2. 59 million Yuan for investment so that the poor can get dividends, which has driven 493 poor households to increase their income steadily.

2. 5. 2. 2　Cultivating a new type of business entity, focusing on the leading and driving role

Chenggu County comprehensively promotes the model for poverty alleviation via industrial development, and strives to deepen the driving of the park, the entities, and the self-cultivating and self-supporting. It continuously improves the ability of the parks and entities to get rid of poverty, and effectively stimulates the endogenous power of the poor, striving to help the poor to continuously increase income and shake off poverty alleviation in a stable manner. First, deepening the driving role of the parks. It actively promotes the poverty alleviation model of "agricultural parks plus poor households" and "large parks plus small business owners " and establishes demonstration parks of poverty alleviation via industrial development so that poor households who work in the parks may get rid of poverty and become better off. With this model, Chenggu County continues to increase investment in agricultural parks, and strives to build modern agricultural parks into a major platform for supporting capital investment, an important support for village collective economy and the poor to increase income, and a core demonstration area for the development of leading industries for targeted poverty alleviation. At the same time, it strengthens the assessment of the 34 established modern agricultural parks at the provincial, municipal, and county levels, highlighting the situation of lifting poverty-stricken villages and poor households out of poverty as an important assessment indicator. Through the assessment, the leading role of agricultural parks has been continuously deepened. Second, deepening the driving role of business entities. It actively introduces, nurtures and develops leading enterprises, farmer cooperatives, and capable households (family farms) , and uses the "enterprise plus base plus poor households" and other forms of cooperation to attract poor households to participate in industrial development, making it a "locomotive" to shake off poverty. At present, the county has 723 various business entities including a number of well-known enterprises such as Qifeng Fruit Industry, Hehe Group, Dahongmen, and Hanzhong Jiahui (among them are 12 leading enterprises, 75 companies, 99 professional cooperatives, 260 poverty alleviation cooperatives, 109 village (stock) economic cooperatives, 3 land stock cooperatives, 136 mutual aid associations, and 29 other business entities) participating in poverty alleviation and connecting with poor villages and poor households, driving more than 13, 800 poor households to develop industries, sell products, take jobs, and receive dividends. Poor households of industrial development type and leading entities have achieved full coverage. Third, deepening assistance in self-growing and self-breeding. It pursues the combination of poverty alleviation and assistance in ambition, employment and skills and continues to strengthen and stimulate the endogenous motivation for poverty alleviation. One is to deepen assistance in ambition. Through organizing and mobilizing the township sages, it is necessary to educate and guide the poor to remove the idea of "waiting for, relying on and requesting", inspire the endogenous impetus to shake off poverty and become better off, strengthen their enthusiasm for and confidence in changing the poverty situation, and drives more qualified poor households to carry out self-growing and self-breeding for self-reliance; The second is to strengthen incentives. By stepping up industrial development awards and rewards, we will better incentivize, guide, and support poor households to develop animal-rearing industries, and actively open the way to prosperity. The third is to focus on supporting technology. It follows the principle of "on-site, practical, and effective", vigorously carries out targeted, "menu-style" practical technical training on special cultivation and breeding, upgrades skills, strengthens skills, so as to drive poor households to take the initiative in poverty alleviation.

2. 5. 2. 3   Strengthening the support of key elements to ensure the healthy development of poverty alleviation industries

Poverty alleviation via industrial development is inseparable from financial support. How tocombat the capital bottleneck? Chenggu County pursues "three increase's": First, increasing the investment of fiscal poverty alleviation funds. Chenggu County continues to give priority to poverty alleviation industry in new funds, projects, and measures. Every year, the county government sets up 50 million Yuan as a special fund for industrial development to support the development of characteristic industries. It has invested more than 30 million Yuan in building the e-commerce industrial park, realizing full coverage of the Town and village e-commerce networks. It has become one of the national demonstration counties for entry of e-commerce into rural areas. It promotes the coordination and integration of agriculture-related fiscal funds, and pursues the centralized use of the special poverty alleviation funds and agriculture-related funds for industrial development. So far, the county has integrated a total of 689 million Yuan of agriculture-related fiscal funds, and built a number of characteristic product processing and service bases with high participation of the poor and strong ability to help poverty-stricken households shake off poverty. The poor people has also significantly enhanced their self-development capacity. Second, increasing financial investment in poverty alleviation. In response to the problem that the poor rural households are hard to get loans, Chenggu County government raised 28 million Yuan to set up a micro-credit guarantee fund, raised 8 million Yuan to set up a micro-credit risk compensation fund, and promptly launched a mortgage-free, guarantee-free, financial discount "micro-credit for poverty alleviation". The cumulative granted small-amount loans for poverty alleviation reached 190 million Yuan, the industrial loans for small and micro enterprises reached 94. 7 million Yuan, and the village-level mutual aid funds granted loans up to 27. 602 million Yuan. Each poor household has a maximum credit line of 50, 000 Yuan, and enjoys government's full discounts for 3 years. At the same time, it also coordinates the commercial banks to innovatively launch financial products such as "enterprise plus farmers", "photovoltaic loans" and "Yuanhu loans", effectively solving the problem of insufficient investment of poverty alleviation funds in industrial development. Third, increasing efforts to attract investment in the bases. The County introduces Sirui and Jiuxin Animal Husbandry Co. , Ltd. to build a base capable of breeding ten thousand head of pigs in Tianming Township; introducing Zhongsheng Group and Parkson Company to establish a base of 66. 67 hectares for growing toadstool in Tianshizi Village and Yuangong Village of Yuangong Town; introducing Zhejiang Mortian Technology Company to build a base of 133. 33 hectares for growing mountainous kiwifruit in Dapan Village and Xiaopan Village of Erli Town; introducing Haoda Biological Company to transfer 100 ha. of land in Shuangjing Village of Laozhuang Town to build a raspberry leisure and sightseeing park; and planning to build the project for Jiangsu-Shaanxi Collaborative Green Food and Drug Industrial Park. The completion of the above-mentioned bases and parks will directly support and indirectly lead more than 2, 100 registered poor households to get rid of poverty and become better off, and lead 21 poor villages in industrial development.

2. 5. 2. 4　Establishing an interest connection mechanism to ensure the poor increase income and shake off poverty

To achieve effective results in poverty alleviation via industrial development, it is necessary to establish and improve a mechanism for connecting the poor people with the interests of enterprises. Chenggu County has its primary goal to make the poor people precisely benefit from the poverty alleviation via industrial development, and to change "simple support to households" into "benefits to households". First, focusing on the goal of poverty alleviation and establishing a connection mechanism. Around targeted poverty alleviation via industrial development, Chenggu scientifically determines the industry, accurately designs the project, clearly drives the entities, precisely connects the poor villages and poor households so as to ensure the accurate connection with the industry, and realize full coverage of the poor people with working ability and effective integration of assistance resources. In accordance with the requirements of "focusing on poor households and driving ordinary households", it tries to make the interests connection between village-level mutual aid cooperatives for poverty alleviation and the cooperatives, industry associations, and industrial parks fully cover the poor people and poor households. It organizes and guides 260 village-level mutual aid cooperatives for poverty alleviation, more than 140 industrial parks (scenic areas), and more than 490 professional farmers' cooperatives to organize the poor people in joint production, joint ventures and joint industries in a variety of forms so that the poor households may directly integrate into the industrial development chain and share dividends from industry operation. Second, focusing on poverty alleviation quality and innovating connection models. In recent years, Chenggu County has conscientiously summarized six typical driving models for poverty alleviation: the work-oriented driving model represented by Shanhua, Yongji, Hehe, CHINWE, and Qincheng companies; the circulating fund payment-based driving model represented by Yuansheng and Shunxin; order-purchasing-driven model represented by Longyan, Zhenwang, and Tianfeng Rice Industry; the share-dividend-driven model represented by Hualv, HeYuan, and Hongtai; the borrowed-purchase-driven model represented by Kunpeng and Baolin Beef Cattle Breeding; and the cooperative assistance-driven model represented by Yulu women's vegetable and fruit professional cooperatives. These models have enabled enterprises and poor households to establish a close interest connection mechanism and form a community of interests, so that the poor households can share the fruits of industrial development and obtain the ability to continue their income increase.

2.5.2.5　Deepening reforms in key areas to foster new momentum for industrial development

Chenggu County has a profound understanding in practice that only by continuously deepening reforms can it inject new momentum into industrial development. To this end, Chenggu County focuses its efforts on the following three moves:

First, deepening the structural reform on the agricultural supply side. Chenggu County pursues the characteristics of poor villages such as pollution-free, ecologically beautiful and high-quality agricultural products and follows market demand to accelerate the industrialization of agriculture and the in-depth development of special industries. First of all, increasing the level of agricultural industrialization. It is necessary to implement special industries to improve the quality and performance of the project, and make better and stronger the "eight major" characteristic leading industries including citrus, kiwi, Yuanhu, and tea. At the same time, eight "novel, strange, and special" new products such as toadstool and golden edible fungus with regional characteristics have been introduced, which has cultivated new growth points and made it a major industry that helps farmers to increase income. The county achieved a total agricultural output value of 8.19 billion Yuan in 2017, ranking third in Shaanxi Province. Next, comprehensively improving the quality of agricultural products. Chenggu County pursues revitalization of agriculture through quality, and helps farmers increase income by improving the quality of agricultural products. It makes efforts to highlight high-quality, safe, and green orientation, support new-type agricultural business entities in applying for certification of "Three-products and One Brand" (three products: pollution-free agricultural products, green food, organic agricultural products and geographical indicative agricultural products) and standardization base construction, and comprehensively improve the quality of agricultural products. It has successively carried out "Three-Products" certification in 18 poverty-stricken villages, and the certification base area is 1,533.33 hectares, helping 764 poor households increase income. After Guojiashan Village obtained the green certification for its citrus, the price of oranges is raised 0.4 Yuan per kilogram higher than that in surrounding villages, with a very promising and attractive market prospect. Finally, creating special brand of agricultural products. On the basis of continuously expanding the scale of leading industries with special features, Chenggu County is firmly committed to creating pollution-free, green, organic agricultural products and regional shared brands to increase product awareness and market share. At present, the county has obtained 18 "Three-products" certification, and Chenggu Citrus and Chenggu Yuanhu have obtained geographical indication certification respectively. In addition, Chenggu Qifeng Xuxiang Kiwi was the first to break through zero export qualifications to the EU in China.

Second, deepening the rural "Three-Transfer" reform. The "Three Transfer (Resources are transferred to equity, capital to share capital, and farmers to shareholders)" reform in rural areas has provided new ideas and new approaches for targeted poverty alleviation, development of the village-level collective economy and improvement in using financial poverty alleviation funds. Chenggu County has actively and steadily promoted the "Three-Transfer" reform. One, advancing according to local conditions. In view of the current situation that most villages in the county do not have all factors for overall promotion, Chenggu County puts forward the "1 plus N" working idea of layered setting, point-by-point advancement, and progressive coverage. "1" means the top level, that is, the establishment of village economic cooperatives or stock economic cooperatives for unified management and operation of village collective assets; "N" means the multi-level under the top level, that is, the operation of various professional cooperatives, companies or family farms and other business entities under the village economic cooperatives or stock economic cooperatives. Through the share operation of each business entity, the farmers, especially poor households will become "1" or "N" shareholders through land or funds, thus building an interest connection mechanism by which "benefits are shared and risks are jointly shouldered". Two, advancement led by models. It summarizes and promotes the five development models for the "Three-Transfer" reform, that is, the suburban comprehensive type of Lianhuachi Village, the industry-driven type of Chenjiawan Village, the regional radiation type of Liuye Village, the fund leveraging type of Huangniuzui Village, and the tourism development type of Xiaobei Village. The pilot work for the "Three-Transfer" reform has been launched in 61 villages. Three, the reform has achieved remarkable results. At present, 95 village (stock) economic cooperatives and 260 village-level poverty alleviation cooperatives have been established, with 14, 300 members, of which 10, 100 are poor. More than 24, 960 households have shared the "Three Transfer" reform dividends of more than 43 million Yuan, and the village collectives have gained more than 41 million Yuan.

Third, deepening the pattern of poverty alleviation via large industries. Chenggu County has innovated and optimized the 110 technology service model, and established a unified and efficient technical resource scheduling and service working mechanism in the inter-department of agriculture, forestry, water conservancy and fruit, thus effectively forming a pattern of poverty alleviation via large industries. Through the implementation of a series measures including connection between technical service performance of poverty alleviation via industrial development and title, the county has always been at the forefront of Shaanxi Province in terms of poverty alleviation via industrial development and technology assistance model and effectiveness. It operates steadily in accordance with the workflows and mechanism including formulation of plans, issuance of instructions, technical services, and linkage operation to comprehensively create an efficient command system for technical services for poverty alleviation via industrial development of "completing dispatch within 1 hour, completing service within 2 days, full coverage, and precise targeting". In 2018, the accumulative targeted service reached 17, 980 person-times, which played a role of technological support in poverty alleviation via industrial development.

2.5.3   Experiences and enlightenment in poverty alleviation via industrial development in Chenggu County

2.5.3.1   Precisely choosing projects for poverty alleviation via industrial development

Poverty alleviation depends on industry, and choosing the right industry is the first step. In terms of selecting characteristic industries, the first thing that Chenggu County has done in recent years is to focus on, according to resource conditions and market demand, creating "eight industries for poverty alleviation", and promoted the formation of the development pattern for poverty alleviation via industrial development in which tea grows in the south, fruits in the north and rice and oil plants along the rivers, vegetables grow in suburban and fungi in the mountains and large-scale breeding and medicine along the rivers, so as to counter market risks with scale; the second thing is to upgrade old industries, and develop new industries based on local farming habits and industrial bases in industrial selection; and the third thing is to vigorously develop the characteristics leading industry with high participation of and great benefit to poor households so as to help farmers increase income. Practice has proved that only by closely focusing on the goal of helping the poor increase income and shake off poverty, adapting to local conditions and seizing the trend, accurately selecting projects for poverty alleviation development, accelerating the cultivation of a number of characteristic advantageous industries, and accurately driving more people to shake off poverty and become better off in a steady manner can a new path of poverty alleviation via industrial development be achieved, provide decisive support to fight against poverty and secure a victory in building a moderately prosperous society in all respects.

2. 5. 3. 2   Strengthening the cultivation of new business entities

The industrial development for poverty alleviation in poor areas must rely on various new types of agricultural business entities with strong market capabilities, high technical level, and sufficient motivation. Through them, they may bring poor households into the industry chain and create stable employment for the poor households, thereby enhancing the ability of the poor to increase income and become better off. On the basis of selecting the right industry, Chenggu County pays close attention to the cultivation of new business entities. One, based on local cultivation. Through the introduction of incentive policies, the county increases support and actively cultivates and develops multi-type and multi-level leading enterprise economic organizations. Two, increasing efforts to attract investment. The county formulates and implements more preferential support policies, targetedly introduces a group of leading enterprises with large operating scale, wide radiation, big influence and strong driving force, and uses the "company plus farmers" and other forms of cooperation to attract poor households to participate in Industrial development. They have played a radiating and driving role of leading enterprises. Three, focusing on "building nests to attract phoenixes". By creating a good entrepreneurial environment, the county has attracted local migrant workers, university graduates, retired cadres and employees, veterans and other capable people to return to their hometown to start businesses, which has promoted the economic development in the county. Practice has proved that a leading enterprise can bring up an industry, and an industry can support the economic development of one place. In poverty alleviation via industrial development, it is necessary to increase support for various types of new business entities. Whatever ownership or type of business entity has a relatively stable and reasonable interest connection with the poor households, can drive the poor households and production bases, and make the poor households really benefit should be treated equally without discrimination. In this way, the poverty alleviation via industrial development can be won.

2.5.3.3 Closely bonding the industry with poor households

Poverty alleviation via industrial development is different from developing industries in poor areas. An important principle is to allow industries and poor households to form a close interest bond. The establishment of an interest connection mechanism between poor households and enterprises can connect the small production of thousands of households and the ever-changing large market together to achieve income increase and poverty alleviation in a stable manner. In the poverty alleviation via industrial development, Chenggu County attaches great importance to establishing and improving a scientific and rational mechanism with standardized operation and mutually beneficial and win-win connection. It not only pays attention to the connection between leading enterprises and poor households, markets and cooperatives, but also handles the relationship between leading enterprises and poor households. It also fully respects the production and operation rights of leading enterprises and poor people and follow the law of market economy so that the new-type business entities and poor households may achieve a win-win cooperation situation. Establishing an interest connection mechanism between industry and poor households is the core of poverty alleviation via industrial development. To this end, it is necessary to further improve the interest connection mechanism of poverty alleviation via industrial development, and effectively improve the participation and benefit of the poor people in developing poverty alleviation industries. It is necessary to pursue the building of a community of interests. Only by ensuring that the poor people fully benefit, increase income and shake off poverty and at the same time by ensuring the legal benefits of various new business entities can a virtuous circle of poverty alleviation via industrial development be realized.

2. 5. 3. 4   Coordination of "organization, branding and e-commerce" to guarantee the efficiency of poverty alleviation via industrial development

In order to improve the efficiency of the targeted poverty alleviation via industrial development, Chenggu County pursues the coordination of "organization, branding and e-commerce" to promote the development of industrialization in agriculture. In coordinating "organization, branding and e-commerce", organization takes the leading position. In the process of increasing the development of farmer cooperatives, Chenggu County focuses on the absorption and assistance of poor households by cooperatives, and through giving play to the function of socialized service of cooperatives, it can help solve the production and management problem that single poor household cannot solve, or not worth solving, so that poor farmers can integrate into the modern agricultural development track as soon as possible. In coordinating "organization, branding and e-commerce", branding is the support. On the basis of industrial organization, Chenggu County attaches great importance to the construction of regional public brands of agricultural products, and combines industrial characterization and product branding to enhance the market influence and premium capacity of agricultural products within the county. In coordinating "organization, branding and e-commerce", e-commerce is the link. Chenggu County firmly seizes the opportunity of entry of the Internet into the countryside, accelerates the development of rural e-commerce, broadens the sales channels of agricultural products, reduces circulation links, reduces circulation costs, and enables Chenggu's agricultural products and new business forms to enter the market faster, thus, effectively helping farmers increase income. Practice has proved that only with the coordination of agricultural organization, agricultural branding, and agricultural e-commerce as the focus to lead the development of the agricultural industry can we improve the efficiency of targeted poverty alleviation via industrial development and promote breakthrough progress in poverty alleviation via industrial development.

2. 6   Practice in Combating Industry & Capital Predicament in Hanyin County

Developing the industry is the fundamental strategy to achieve poverty alleviation, and financial integration is the source of the blood to activate the industry. Under the background of government-led poverty alleviation, the key to poverty alleviation via industrial development lies in correctly positioning the government's functions in industrial development, realizing the effective connection of market demand and production factors, enhancing farmers' participation, and stimulating endogenous power. Hanyin County, Ankang City, Shaanxi Province has made every effort to break the trap of backward industrial development in poor areas and lack of funds for farmers' development. Since 2017, Hanyin County has taken a number of measures to this end. First, through the "Town and Park Industry Alliance" model, it has made the government return to the role of platform, media and service, thus exploring an industrial development path that effectively combines modern agricultural development needs with rural decentralized factors, and promotes the organic integration of small farmers with modern agriculture; second, the county has started full coverage of mutual aid funds in poverty-stricken villages, forming an operating mechanism in which financial funds dominate the supply, the village cooperatives organize the implementation and operation, the farmers' joint guarantee and mutual aid for supervision, and the external professional services provide assistance, thus creating "the small bank accessible to farmers" which provides convenient and efficient capital loan services for farmers. The combination of the two forces has achieved remarkable results in promoting industrial development and lifting poor farmers out of poverty.

2. 6. 1   Exploration of the mechanism for poverty alleviation via industrial development

Hanyin County, one of the poorest counties which are the main targets of national poverty alleviation and development work, faces a double predicament of the industry and capital. First, Hanyin County is located in the Qinling-Bashan mountainous regions, and most of the villages in the County are remote, with highly fragmented land and low level of agricultural mechanization. It has many, miscellaneous, complete and small agricultural products with high cost of agricultural production. It is hard to improve its efficiency of agricultural production and poor households lack ways to increase their income. In addition, the county does not have clear leading industry. All these predicaments are hard to crack down. Second, the county has over 10 towns and 141 administrative villages with a total population of 313, 900 within its jurisdiction. As of March 2018, there had remained 64 poor villages, 15, 749 households with 41, 475 people in poverty. The poverty incidence rate was 14. 88%, with wide coverage and seriousness of poverty. To a great extent, farmers generally lack start-up capital or working capital for production development. In the process of poverty alleviation via industrial development, the "Town and Park Industry Alliance" of Hanyin County is like a "locomotive", leading the overall layout of the agricultural industry, and mutual aid poverty alleviation funds are like "fuels" to solve the shortage of production funds for the poor.

2. 6. 1. 1   Building a "Town and Park Industry Alliance", starting the engine for industry development

At the end of 2017, Hanyin County established a "Town and Park Industry Alliance" platform to realize the interconnection of new business entities such as parks, leading enterprises, and cooperatives with poverty-stricken villages within the county to share in real time market demand and industrial development information. By building bridges between the Towns and the parks for poverty alleviation via industrial development, we can solve the prominent contradictions, such as "poor villages and farmers' difficulty in what industry to choose and where to sell agricultural products" versus "agricultural parks' lack of information on where the park base can be constructed", versus "the processing enterprises' difficulty in where to get the supply demand".

The specific practice goes as the following: first, building the "Town and Park Industry Alliance" platform to lower the cost for information exchange. Hanyin County has compiled into a book the development needs of the enterprises in the agricultural parks, the contact information of the Township and village leaders and the first secretary and distributed it to the villages and enterprises, establishing the information exchange platform for poverty alleviation via industrial development in the county. The compiling and editing members include enterprise leaders, Township and village leaders, assistance staff in the villages and the first secretary. By the model of "Town and park alliance, village and community bearing, and participation of poor households", it has opened up communication channels for new types of business entities such as poor Towns and villages, parks, leading enterprises, and cooperatives in the county to achieve multi-party information interconnection and sharing and reduce information acquisition costs. Take Shuanghe Village as an example. The village is about 40 kilometers away from the seat of Hanyin County. It is characterized by remote geographical location, blocked information, and fear of market risks. In the past, farmers would only grow corns and rice, while young and middle-aged laborers kept on going out to work. Planting grain has relatively low benefits and there is no knowledge of what industry has a market and sales. Therefore, there was an increase in land abandonment. The launch of the "Town and Park Industry Alliance" has solved the confusion of villagers and made industry and market dynamic information convenient and available, thus greatly shortening the information distance between Towns and villages, farmers, enterprises and markets. Second, improving the working mechanism for industry connection to reduce the cost of cooperative organizations. Guided by the "Town and Park Industry Alliance" project connection, Hanyin County, on the one hand, organizes Township and village cadres to investigate and study in the agricultural parks, so that they can expand development ideas and increase their understanding of the development status of various parks, and then integrate local resources endowments and industrial foundations so as to form the initial judgment of the feasibility of related industry connection; on the other hand, it will promote the connection of the parks with the first secretary and Party branch secretary of each village, and each village will form a professional cooperative to organize farmers to engage in agricultural production. Through industrial technology training, the majority of farmers will have a clearer understanding of the development model of the enterprises in the parks and the enterprises will also have timely grasp of the development wishes of the villagers. Through the organized two-way investigation and observation, the mutual selection costs of the enterprises in the parks and Towns and villages are reduced, thus facilitating effective cooperation. In the two successive County-wide industry inspections, there were 26 heads of the relevant assistance units, 10 Township heads and heads of agricultural comprehensive service stations, first secretaries of 77 poverty-stricken villages and more than 260 representatives of some agricultural enterprises in the parks participated. Take the Wuyi Modern Agricultural Park as an example. The person in charge of the park said that in the past he wanted to expand production, but did not know the village information. He mainly contacted the farmers directly through publicity and acquaintance introduction, but this kind of communication is relatively fragmented and does not necessarily win the trust of the people. Through the "Town and Park Industry Alliance" platform, the park quickly signed a 33. 33 ha. toadstool planting contract with Hanyang Township after promotion, and reached initial cooperation intentions with nearly 20 villages in 7 other Townships. Third, improving the interest connection mechanism to reduce the cost for negotiation and gaming. In the process of guiding the industrial connection between the park and poor households, each Township cooperates with the enterprises in the parks by establishing village-level stock cooperatives and professional cooperatives. When signing the industrial cooperation contract with the enterprises in the parks, the opinions of the farmers are fully sought, and the two village committees, the first secretary, and the representatives of the farmers consult and vote, and report to the Township Party committee for approval. The "Town and Park Industry Alliance" balances the interests of all parties through a multi-party negotiation model, thus greatly reducing the cost of negotiation and gaming. Take Jingkang Modern Agricultural Park as an example. In October 2017, the park was just introduced from Foshan, Guangdong Province. Due to poor language communication and unfamiliarity with the local environment, and farmers had low trust in the park, it was difficult for the park to persuade farmers to plant traditional Chinese medicinal materials. Later, after coordination by the CPC county committee, the service center of the agricultural park and other department, it was possible to build more than 13. 33 ha. of lily and ginseng planting bases in two Townships. Driven by the "Town and Park Industry Alliance", many Townships and villages actively contacted the park in 2018 and quickly established 16 professional cooperatives. At present, more than 300 ha. of Chinese herbal medicine planting contracts have been signed, with the plan of planting 1, 000 ha. and driving more than 3, 000 households to increase income and become better off. Fourth, introducing support policies on industrial development to improve the efficiency in the use of funds. Through integrating financial funds and social assistance funds, Hanyin County has issued targeted incentive support policies to give full play to the guiding role of the poverty alleviation funds via industrial development and improve the efficiency of the use of poverty alleviation funds. Based on the county's resource endowment conditions, industrial basic environment and market demand prospects, Hanyin County has formulated the *Guiding Opinions on Poverty Alleviation via Industrial Development in Hanyin County* to clarify the idea of poverty alleviation via industrial development of "guided by the government and led by market players and capable people". The foundation of poverty alleviation via industrial development has been consolidated through the interest connection method of "poverty alleviation funds following the poverty-stricken households, the poor households following the business entities, and the business entities following the market". The county has formulated the *Reward Measures Hanyin County for Supporting Poverty Alleviation via Industrial Development* and the *Reward and Subsidy Measures of Hanyin County for Star Demonstration Family Farms (2018)*, through which the enterprises in the parks are guided to become big and powerful, and drive enterprises with strong capability to increase support. The County has formulated the *Reward and Subsidy Measures of Hanyin County for Industrial Development of Poor Households in Poor Villages*, through which to stimulate the poor households in the endogenous impetus and increase their enthusiasm for poverty alleviation.

2. 6. 1. 2　Poverty alleviation funds and mutual aid as development momentum

In order to improve farmers' ability of self-development, promote industrial development, and achieve sustainable poverty alleviation, mutual aid poverty alleviation funds have become an important move for Shaanxi Province to achieve poverty alleviation. It was as early as in 2009 that the exploration of mutual aid poverty alleviation funds began in Hanyin County. After nearly 10 years of long-term exploration and rapid development since 2017, Hanyin County has, centering on issues like "who provides funds", "who operates", "who guarantees and supervises", and "who serves and conducts management", formed an operating mechanism in which financial funds dominate the supply, the village cooperatives organize the implementation and operation, the farmers' joint guarantee and mutual aid for supervision, and the external professional services provide assistance, giving play to the advantages of different organizations' resources and ensuring the healthy operation of mutual aid funds. As of July 2018, there had been 87 associations for mutual aid poverty alleviation funds, which had fully covered 77 poor villages. A total of 11, 561 households had joined the associations, of which nearly 80% (9, 228 households) are poor households; the total amount of funds had reached 46. 3592 million Yuan, of which 91. 0% (42. 1772 million Yuan) were special financial poverty alleviation funds. The funds paid by the farmers as baseline funds accounted for 6. 4% (2. 982 million Yuan), and the funds for other projects for poverty alleviation cooperation accounted for 2. 6% (1. 2 million Yuan). The specific practice: first, financial poverty alleviation funds dominate and break through the predicament of credit fund supply. Mutual aid poverty alleviation funds are dominated by fiscal poverty alleviation funds, which account for more than 90% of the total mutual aid funds. With a small amount, low interest rates, and high convenience, it has realized targeted financial supply to rural areas, equivalent to moving the cost of capital supply to the county government, thus breaking through the plight of the serious shortage of rural financial supply. Second, The resources of village cooperative organizations are shifted, and the association is operated at a lower cost. The mutual aid poverty alleviation funds are managed by the village mutual aid funds association composed of 3 – 5 people who are responsible, have business ability, and managerial ability and who are elected from each project village. This is a management organization and has one chairman, one accountant, one teller and one supervisor. It is specifically responsible for the daily work such as auditing the project loan households in the village, fund issuance and recovery. In principle, the members of the village association team are concurrently served by members of the two village committees and are elected by the general assembly through democratic election. In order to mobilize the enthusiasm of the management staff of the association, Hanyin County has formulated and issued the *Management Measures of Hanyin County for Subsidies and Administrative Expenses for the Village-level Association of Mutual Aid Poverty Alleviation Funds*, to achieve "work by institutions, by people, and with money". Third, internal mutual credit supervision helps solve the problem of traditional decentralized supervision. The mutual aid poverty alleviation funds of Hanyin County are jointly guaranteed by five households for supervision, thus realizing internal mutual credit assistance and supervision, which solves the problem with traditional decentralized credit and supervision. Each project village association has set up a number of joint guarantee groups composed of five members. After applying for loan requirements and obtaining the guarantee signatures of all members of the guarantee team, members can enter the final evaluation link of the board of directors and the board of supervisors. In terms of supervision, multiple accountability mechanisms have played a check and balance role in breach of contract. The lender's loan information is networked with the credit union, and according to the signed loan contract, withholding can be performed according to law in the event of breach of contract; at the same time, those who fail to pay the debt will be announced in the village's black list, and the public opinion in the village provides an auxiliary punishment mechanism as an informal constraint. In the event that the lender is unable to repay, the guarantors have joint and several repayment responsibilities, forming an incentive for the guarantee team to carefully check the guarantee, so that the convenience and high efficiency of loans and the loan risk prevention are effectively balanced by the mechanism. Fourth, introducing market professional services to prevent various risks in capital management. By purchasing social services, Hanyin County has entrusted professional accounting firms to guide and sort out the accounts of the project village associations, so as to achieve the unification of general ledger, detailed account, cash journal, bank deposit journal, and accounting vouchers. The county strengthened the supervision of the associations, through the standardized management of "signature, account, cash and deposit", as well as the signing of safety agreements, strict loan procedures, open and transparent management, etc., to ensure the standard operation of the projects, and the Town's financial audit office is responsible for supervising the village-level mutual aid fund associations within its jurisdiction and include standardized management and performance in the annual audit. The county implements a special fund account escrow system to create a safe fund pool, that is, the county-level association opens a public account, the village-level association account is a zero balance account, and the bank deposits are managed by the county-level association for centralized management. After the village-level association issues each loan which is subject to approval, the county-level association will examine and verify it and apply for funding from the county-level association. According to statistics, the Hanyin County Mutual Aid Funds Association has collected more than 22 million Yuan of funds to be managed by a dedicated account, creating a safe fund pool for the county's poverty alleviation funds. This has effectively prevented problems such as "funding large accounts", "adding new debts without repaying the old ones", "overdue payments", and "minor proportion of households occupying mutual aid funds for a long time".

2. 6. 2　Basic results achieved

2. 6. 2. 1　Industrial guidance for factors integration and agricultural industry structure optimization in the county

By building the "Town and Park Industry Alliance", modern agricultural parks with better operating benefits and poor towns and villages cooperated to further expand production scale, gradually form a market-oriented leading industry, and optimize the county's industrial structure. The disadvantages of higher production costs of agricultural products in Qinling-Bashan mountainous regions and the advantages of producing selenium-enriched green agricultural products have forced enterprise subjects to adopt advanced production technology and ecological planting models and win market competition by improving the quality of agricultural products. Driven by the "Town and Park Industry Alliance", the agricultural industrial park has been expanded, providing sufficient raw materials for the deep processing industry of local agricultural products, as well as providing a development basis for the integration of agricultural tourism, thus realizing the improvement in quality and performance of agricultural products, and promoting the integration of the primary, secondary and tertiary industries. For example, Hanyin has a tradition of planting corns on dry slopes, but the poor taste and low yield of corn lead to low efficiency of the industrial development. Xiaocang Agriculture and Forestry Co. , Ltd. introduced new varieties of sweet corn, which have the characteristics of high yield, good quality and excellent taste, supplemented by advanced planting technology, the average income of sweet corn per hectare reaches more than 28, 358 Yuan. The company signed an agreement on poverty alleviation via industrial development with 548 impoverished households in 6 villages of 4 Towns including Donghe Village and Shuanghe Village in Xuanwo Town through the "Town and Park Industry Alliance" platform to develop a sweet corn planting base of more than 133. 33 ha. At present, mature sweet corns from more than 53. 33 ha. have been purchased, and after processing, they will be directly stored in the company's frozen storage, driving poor households to increase their income by more than 1. 6 million Yuan, which has truly improved the quality of agricultural products supply and the benefits of agricultural development. By improving the development environment of the agricultural industry, the "Town and Park Industry Alliance" has released the vitality of various parties such as modern agricultural enterprises, rural resource endowments, and farmer household production capacity, and has promoted industrial development, subject cultivation, and income increase for farmer households. As of the end of September 2018, the county had built 60 modern agricultural parks, 18 leading enterprises, 378 development cooperatives, and 701 family farms. Now, 110 villages have signed industrial alliance agreements with more than 70 enterprises in the park, and basically, reached full coverage of medium-and long-term industries in impoverished villages. A total of 5, 413. 33 ha. of industrial bases had been developed, driving 9, 327 rural households (including 2, 359 poor households) to increase income.

2. 6. 2. 2   Credit inclusiveness integrated into industry to activate the endogenous power of farmers for development

First, the industrial development environment driven by the "Town and Park Industry Alliance" expands the income-increasing channels for farmers. First of all, the poor households increase their income by means of rental from land transfer, salary from employment in the park, deposit from order production, and share dividends, and share the benefits of modern agricultural development. Next, through receiving training on production techniques related to work in the park and order production, farmers have mastered production skills, which has further improved the development capabilities of poor households. Finally, through the employment opportunities provided by the development of the park and the profit space above the market price in order production, the poor households are effectively encouraged to directly participate in the agricultural production link, and supplemented by the reward and subsidy policy for household planting and breeding, which fully enhances the endogenous dynamics in poor households for development. Shaanxi Fruit Industry Group Ankang Specialties Co. , Ltd. transferred 66. 67 ha. of land to build a kiwifruit industrial base. At present, kiwifruit grows in more than 33. 33 ha. of land, which can provide employment for more than 200 households in the Zhongba relocation community every year. Second, the mutual aid poverty alleviation funds have effectively solved the problem of shortage of production funds for farmers and enhanced their development capabilities. In the past, farmers in poverty-stricken areas would have difficulty in providing effective guarantee required by formal financial institutions for lending. At the same time, they would face many obstacles such as numerous loan procedures. Not only were they unable to increase their re-production input, but they were also stuck in debt due to temporary capital needs. The mutual aid poverty alleviation funds have easy access and low interest rates (generally lower than those of the local rural credit cooperatives), and poor households enjoy financial discounts, which solves the problems with getting loans and "expensive loan" for farmers. A man surnamed Wu from a poor household in Cigou Village of Puxi Town has three children who are attending school, therefore, he has large living expenses, and has difficulty in save money to invest in production. In August 2017, Mr. Wu received a loan of 5,000 Yuan from the mutual aid funds, enjoying a one-year financial interest-free subsidy. With this money, he purchased 10 piglets to raise, and purchased 500kg of corns to brew corn wine with local methods. These two projects earned him an income of more than 7,000 Yuan a year, which has not only helped him get rid of the dilemma of lending, but also greatly strengthened his confidence in getting rid of poverty. As of June 2019, Hanyin County had issued a total of 29.575 million Yuan of mutual aid poverty alleviation funds to support 3,437 farmers-times, of which 1,335 are poor households, accounting for 38.8% of the households with loans. With the support of mutual aid funds, households with loans raised more than 15,100 heads of pigs and more than 1,000 cattle, planted more than 366.67 ha. of flue-cured tobacco, more than 23.33 ha. of chrysanthemums, and over 233.33 ha. of konjac. Each household has received an additional income of more than 5,000 Yuan. The mutual aid poverty alleviation funds include individual farmers into the regional industrial development, which has effectively improved farmers' profitability and endogenous development momentum.

2.6.3 Experiences and enlightenment

2.6.3.1 Market orientation as the basic principle of poverty alleviation via industrial development

Market demand is the basic guide for poverty alleviation via industrial development. First, the "Town and Park Industry Alliance" model has fully exerted the role of the new type of agricultural management entities, especially the leading agricultural enterprises as the subject of the construction of modern agricultural parks generally have advantages over traditional small farmers in grasping market information and dealing with market risks, and they are able to form an industrial scale effect by using modern agricultural production technology, thereby reducing agricultural production costs and improving the efficiency of agricultural production. Second, the project connection of the "Town and Park Industry Alliance" is based on the equal and voluntary participation of enterprises and poor Towns and villages, and the two sides have formed a cooperation intention based on market rules, which has fully played the role of the market in the allocation of resources of both parties and reduced the market efficiency loss that may be caused by excessive government intervention. The government of Hanyin County mainly performs service functions in the process of poverty alleviation via industrial development, provides peripheral environment and support services for enterprises and towns and villages to connect and achieve industrial development. At the same time, it provides inclusive credit support through mutual aid poverty alleviation funds, and provides system guarantee for standardized operation through introducing a series of management measures, and strengthen business training and publicity guidance for village-level associations, promote policy implementation, guide poor households to embed in the industry chain for common development, and integrate farmers' independent production decisions into industrial development.

2. 6. 3. 2   Overall planning mechanism as the inner foundation for integrated development

If the poverty alleviation via industrial development wants to break through the double predicament of industry and capital, it must involve both industry driving and the participation of farmers. Hanyin County's practice in poverty alleviation via industrial development closely integrates industrial development with mutual aid funds. Based on the resource endowment conditions, industrial characteristics and market prospects of each project village, and in light of the industrial layout of "tea in the south, fruits in the north and rice and oil plants along the rivers", the country determines the industry support focus, and actively guides the associations to give priority to the registered impoverished households among the members in getting mutual aid funds, guides poor households to develop industries, and promotes poor households in increasing their income. Guanyinhe Village in Guanyinhe Town has cracked down on the problem of poor households with industrial development and of cooperatives with financing by following the idea of "poverty alleviation funds following the poverty-stricken households, the poor households following the business entities, and the business entities following the market", closely connecting the mutual aid funds with poor households, cooperatives and local industries to achieve a win-win result.

2. 6. 3. 3　Interest connection as a necessary condition for mutual benefit

Strengthening the interest connection mechanism is a necessary condition for agricultural enterprises, towns and villages, and farmers to achieve mutual benefit and win-win results in the industry chain. The "Town and Park Industry Alliance" and the mutual aid poverty alleviation funds embed farmers into the agricultural industry chain through various forms of interest connection, which not only keeps a stable enterprise expectation, but also benefits farmers in the long term. First, for parks that have strong development capabilities and use transfer land for "heavy asset" operations, farmers can earn income through land transfer and earn wages by working in the parks; for parks that adopt such "light assets" as order production for operation, the parks will provide seedlings and technology in a unified way to improve the quality of agricultural products and purchase at prices higher than the market price, so that farmers can obtain higher returns. Second, the mutual aid funds association and the industrial cooperatives with a certain foundation are combined. The industrial cooperatives and the farmers sign a land transfer agreement, an agreement on industrial management and protection or an agreement on cooperative and joint operation, the mutual aid association will determine the loan amount for support the cooperatives according to the number of members driven by the cooperative agreement signed with industrial cooperatives, and the cooperatives will obtain dual support of loans and discounts, and members of the poor households obtain stable income through land transfer, priority work, and income from dividends.

Chapter 3
Relocation from Inhospitable Areas: Cracking Down on the Problem of Living and Employment

On November 27, 2015, in his speech at the Poverty Alleviation and Development Working Conference of Central Government, General Secretary Xi Jinping noted that "where living conditions are severe and natural disasters occur frequently, the cost of access to water, road, and electricity is very high, and the poor people have difficulty in getting rid of poverty locally, it is necessary to implement relocation of the poor populations from inhospitable areas. This is a compulsory measure and a complicated systematic project. It is policy-oriented and requires deep and detailed effort. " To implement the policy of relocating the poor, we must not only need to make scientific planning to ensure that the poor people who need to be relocated can "move out", but also provide precise management and supporting services to ensure that the relocated people can "settle down"; at the same time, we must also solve the problems with employment for the relocated people and help the poor to realize their desire to "become better off". The Qinling-Bashan mountainous regions have actively made exploration and achieved remarkable results in terms of precise relocation, precise measures and fine management.

3.1 Shangluo Model of "Precise Relocation, Accurate Measures and Refined Management" for Addressing the Roots of Poverty

Relocation from inhospitable areas is part of the poverty alleviation by the Central Government. The poor people who live in areas with rough living conditions, frequent natural disasters, high cost of constructing facilities for water, road, electricity and heating, and difficulty in getting rid of poverty locally are relocated incounty seats, towns, and central villages with higher environmental carrying capacity and larger development space, as well as supporting industries and employment assistance, so that they are able to be lifted out of poverty, thus eradicating the problem of "Mountains and Streams Leave No Signs on Their People". The poor mountainous people who are relocated elsewhere express their infinite gratitude to the Party for its policy on relocation by writing couplets, some of which go to the effect that "The people are so moved by the relocation that they write couplets to express their gratitude to the Party", "Moving out of the mountainous area and marching on the road to a moderately prosperous society, living in new homes with gratitude to the Party". Shangluo City has been focusing on three key links before, in and after relocation and formulated a work system for relocation, that is, "precise relocation, accurate measures and fine management" so as to steadily advance the relocation of the poor people. In 2016, a total of 28,760 households with 110,859 people were relocated, including 18,027 households with 73,010 people relocated from inhospitable areas, and 10,733 households with 37,849 people synchronously relocated[①]. A total of 108 centralized resettlement projects were built with a total investment of 3.982 billion Yuan. In 2017, a total of 38,552 households with 141,546 people were relocated, including 35,852 households with 131,585 people being relocated from inhospitable areas, and 2,700 households with 9,961 people synchronously relocated. A total of 140 centralized resettlement projects were built with a total investment of 1.244 billion Yuan. Wang Yang, the then vice premier of the State Council, fully commented Shangluo City for its work on relocation during his investigation in Shangluo City. The experience in the model of "precise relocation, accurate

----

① Synchronous relocation: People living in poor ecological areas and areas with frequent natural disasters also include non-poor people who do not meet the poverty identification standards but also face survival risks and production difficulties. Synchronously relocating this group with the poor group to places suitable for living and implementing corresponding subsidies and assistance policies can make this group work better and live a better life.

measures and fine management" was introduced at the provincial on-site observation meeting and promoted throughout Shaanxi Province.

3. 1. 1   Constructing a ledger without loopholes for precise relocation

Relocation of poor populations from inhospitable areas is one of the ways to help people shake off poverty at the source. Only when the objects to be relocated are clarified can the original intention of relocation for poverty alleviation be realized. Regarding the question of "who to be relocated", Shangluo simultaneously carried out a series of actions including check of the relocation data, review of the relocation in South Shaanxi during the "Twelfth Five-Year Plan" period, and follow-up survey of the relocation of poor populations from inhospitable areas from four aspects of relocated objects, objects to be relocated, policy implementation, and policy connection, so as to achieve more scientific screening of the objects to be relocated, more accurate data, and more real relocation intention. Subsequently, four working teams, that is, the cadres of the immigration office of eachcounty, district and city, the working teams of Township and office cadres contracting or contacting villages, working teams of cadres from county departments who are working in villages, and village cadres, altogether 1, 200 people, were integrated. They were sent to 15 Townships and offices across the whole county to make a survey from door to door so that everything was done according to policies and based on the facts and all the people who should be relocated were resettled down in new places. A ledger of files was established in accordance with the standard of "one file for one household, one book for one resettlement, one book for one Township, one book for one county and one database for one city" so that the poverty alleviation information and relocation information systems are simultaneous integrated, laying a solid foundation for the relocation during the "Thirteenth Five-Year Plan" period. Today, in the market Towns or in a rural tourist area in Shuangluo City, everywhere you look, you will see buildings going up, populous and prosperous, with green mountains and clear rivers everywhere, presenting a thriving scene. Here you will feel the new atmosphere brought by the relocation of immigrants. Through the policy propaganda of the poverty alleviation cadres and the repeated data check and the use of the Internet for establishing a file ledger, the work on relocation in Shangluo was effectively implemented at last.

3. 1. 2   Accurate measures to ensure resettlement in an orderly manner

Shangluo City made precise planning and selection of resettlement sites so that the policies designed to benefit the people are more down-to-earth. Regarding where people want to move and where to move appropriately, Shangluo City made precise planning of resettlement sites, avoiding geological hazard-prone areas, flood disaster threatening areas, ecological protection areas and permanent basic farmland and being close totowns, central villages and parks or scenic spots. Jia Jiangang, governor of Zhen' an County, said: "In the selection and planning of centralized resettlement sites, Zhen' an pursues the basic principles of being close to parks, close to scenic spots, and close to communities, combines the construction of large and small sites, entry into cities and towns and resettlement in central villages, as well as resettlement in watershed and in market Towns, so that the site selection is scientific and reasonable, and the people can be relocated in places with development prospects. " Through scientific site selection, a total of 59 resettlement sites have been built in Zhen' an County during the "Thirteenth Five-Year Plan" period. Danfeng County focuses on relocation by households with the working idea of "determining housing by people, determining housing construction by households, and determining relocation by industry" and "relocated people will be engaged in their familiar fields". In light of the situation of different objects to be relocated, population structure, and poverty alleviation measures, work on classification, screening and sorting out was carried out to determine the resettlement location, types of resettlement housing, and resettlement year. Then, the agreement on relocation, the agreement on poverty alleviation and becoming better off, and the agreement on emptying and returning of homestead, were signed, thus achieving the goal of connection of people and housing and precise resettlement. Shangzhou District organized the development and reform, housing construction, land and natural resources, environmental protection and other departments for centralized office, established a "green channel" for the first-stage procedures of the project, and handled, together with the Township and office staff, the pre-procedures for the centralized resettlement project in demarcation, surveying and mapping, site selection opinions, land pre-review, project set-up and approval, and environmental assessment opinions, and at the same time, entrusted intermediary agencies to package the risk assessment of geological disasters and flood hazards for centralized resettlement projects, creating conditions for the rapid and orderly progress of the projects; in addition, it made full use of the stock housing in 8 completed resettlement projects including Yangxie Town and Songyun during the "Twelfth Five-Year Plan" period to accurately arrange the relocated objects from inhospitable areas. In accordance with local conditions, various counties, districts and cities shall strictly implement the policy on relocation to ensure that the relocation in Shangluo City was carried out in an orderly manner.

3. 1. 3   Fine management for promoting scheduled and steady poverty alleviation

Pursuing employment before relocation to ensure that relocation means getting rid of poverty. This is an important guarantee for the sustainability of the livelihood of the relocated people. In 2017, 39,100 households with 143,900 people were relocated from inhospitable areas and 138 centralized resettlement projects were performed, and industrial development plans were prepared for the centralized resettlement sites with more than 50 households in counties (districts), and supporting industries were also built for the resettlement sites. To help rural households achieve employment and entrepreneurship, Shangluo City has established a guarantee fund for poverty alleviation loans in cities and counties, and issued a total of 1.701 billion Yuan of "farmer loans" and 1.744 billion Yuan of "industrial loans", basically realizing full coverage of new agricultural business entities. Relocation is the means, and shaking off poverty is the end. After relocation, the people's overall standard of living has been improved, but at the same time the overall cost of living is also going up. The key to achieving sustainable poverty alleviation is to make the poor people have stable income. Considering the fact that some relocated people living in new communities are without land, the key is that how they can achieve employment and entrepreneurship as soon as possible. Before the commencement of the resettlement site, Chaiping Town, Zhen' an County transferred back all the land one km surrounding the Town and village and built four densely planted mulberry gardens with a total area of 33. 33 hectares. Close to the resettlement community, a silkworm rearing factory was built, adopting scale and intensive silkworm rearing technology, which offered jobs to the left-behind women of more than 100 households in the community, as a result, each household has increased their income by more than 5,000 Yuan. With such community factories and employment parks, the relocated people can find jobs locally and achieve seamless connection with the secondary and tertiary industries, helping the relocated people with accurate employment and accurate poverty alleviation.

The original intention of the state to implement the relocation of poor populations from inhospitable areas was to relocate the poor people living in areas lacking living conditions to other areas, and to help the relocated people shake off poverty and become better off by improving the production and living conditions of the resettlement areas, adjusting the economic structure and expanding income-increasing channels. It is not only a challenge for China to overcome absolute poverty, but also a test to deepen the improvement of China's capacity for governance. The ultimate revitalization of the countryside and prosperity of the nation will require the joint efforts of all the people. Just as General Secretary Xi Jinping pointed out, " after the problems of relocation are basically solved, the most crucial thing for subsequent support is employment. Only when one works in contentment can he lives in contentment. Securing employment is crucial for relocated people to settle down in their new homes, get rich and not fall back into poverty". [1]

---

[1]   During his inspection in Shaanxi, Xi Jinping emphasized to effectively keep employment, the financial sector, foreign trade, foreign and domestic investments, and expectations stable, ensure the employment of residents, the basic livelihood of the people, the market entities, food and energy security, stability of industry chain supply chain, and grass-roots operation, and strive to write a new chapter for Shaanxi to catch up and surpass in a new era, 2020-04-24(2) .

Achieving local employment near their new homes is the key to stabilizing the poverty alleviation results and the support of the people. Through the joint efforts of all the people, the rural revitalization and national prosperity will eventually be achieved. [1]

3.2 "Double Demonstration" Community in Zhen'an County

Relocation is essential for people in inhospitable areas to achieve strides in development. It is also an important approach to win the fight against poverty. The relocated people come from all directions, therefore, it is important to strengthen community building. [2] Zhen' an County, one of the 11 deeply impoverished counties in Shaanxi Province, has poor natural conditions, therefore, relocation is a heavy task. During the "Thirteenth Five-Year Plan" period, there were 8,139 households with 27,681 people who needed to shake off poverty by relocation in the County, accounting respectively for 40% and 45% of the registered poor households and poor people. In order to let the relocated people have more sense of gain, happiness, and security, Zhen' an County focused on creating " double demonstration" communities that are ideal for living and working, and in combination with the rural revitalization strategy, came out with the Zhen' an model of five measures, five types of households and five-small communities.

3.2.1 "Five Measures" to implement precise relocation

Zhen' an County makes an in-depth investigation of a series of issues such as who to be relocated, where to move, how to control the

---

① Lu Hang, "Make achievements in poverty alleviation stand the test of history", *Journal of Social Sciences in China*, 2020-04-24 (1).

② During his inspection in Shaanxi, Xi Jinping emphasized to effectively keep employment, the financial sector, foreign trade, foreign and domestic investments, and expectations stable, ensure the employment of residents, the basic livelihood of the people, the market entities, food and energy security, stability of industry chain supply chain, and grass-roots operation, and strive to write a new chapter for Shaanxi to catch up and surpass in a new era, 2020-04-24(2).

red line, how big a house should be, and how to build, etc. , to ensure precise relocation. In terms of object identification, the county strictly follows the policy definition of "Mountains and streams leave no signs on their people" and relocates all the poor people who should be relocated. Through data check, continuous investigation and verification, and dynamic adjustment for the relocated objects and other measures, it determines 8, 139 households with 27, 681 poor people to be relocated from inhospitable areas during the "Thirteenth Five-Year Plan" period, buttoning the first button in the relocation work. In terms of resettlement methods, the resettlement principle is that market Towns prevail, county seats and central villages supplement, and decentralized resettlement sites complement, thus scientifically and rationally arranging centralized resettlement sites. In terms of planning and site selection, the county pursues considering relocation, economic and social development, urban construction as a whole, and organically combines it with beautiful villages, tourist attractions, industrial development, and farmers ' income increase, and explores watershed resettlement models so that the relocated people living in the same watershed can not only move to communities which have easy access to medical care, education, and schooling, but also continue to generate income on their own woodland and land. In terms of the construction model, it took the lead in promoting the "EPC general contract" in the whole province. For the 30 centralized resettlement sites, a unified design, purchase, and construction were conducted, which accelerated the construction progress, ensured the project quality, and reflected the fairness and rationality in implementing the national policies that benefit the people. There were 320 resettlement houses in 3 resettlement sites were lived in the same year when the construction was commenced. In terms of policy control, the county adhered to the principle of determining the number of people to relocated first, then determining the construction of housing, and finally determining the relocation by households, put the "two red lines" at the forefront, and prevent in advance the problem of "exceeding the specified area and self-financing". In the process of constructing the resettlement housing, the resettlement housing shall be constructed based on the personal wishes of the relocated objects and family structure, and planned according to 20 square meters or so per capita. The decentralized resettlement housing adopted a small centralized model under the responsibility of Townships and villages and per capita construction area shall be guaranteed not to exceed 25 square meters; the per capita investment of the relocated people does not exceed 2500 Yuan, and a household can not exceed 10,000 Yuan. The attainment rate of the room area not exceeding the standard and the self-raised amount not exceeding the standard reached 100% respectively.

3.2.2   Five types of households division for targeted implementation

According to the actual situation of the relocated people and the intention of employment and entrepreneurship, Zhen' an County scientifically classifies the relocated households, implements tailored policies, and takes targeted poverty alleviation measures. For accurate aid to poor households, Zhen' an County subdivides the poor into five types: traditional farmer type, community worker type, tertiary service type, out-of-work type, and basic livelihood guarantee type.

Traditional farmer type: For the 2,158 relocated people who have the will of the agricultural industry and cannot leave the land, through the "Three Transfers" reform measures, priority was given to the relocated people in transfer of land and forest land, so that the relocated people can increase their turnover and rent while continuing to work on the land to increase income, thus forming a multi-channel for income increase. At the same time, the full coverage of "three belts and four joint's" was achieved, that is, the big households belt, enterprise belt, three cooperatives (cooperatives, credit cooperatives, supply and marketing cooperatives) belt and joint production, joint industry, joint stocks and joint ventures. Each household was allocated shares worth 50, 000 Yuan, getting an annual income increase of only 4,000 Yuan from dividends.

Community worker type: For those with skills who have the willingness to find employment at the doorstep and need to take care of the family, in combination with the resource endowments of each resettlement site, and relying on tea, silkworm, edible fungi, Chinese medicinal materials and other special industries and electronic processing industries, thecounty equips each centralized resettlement site with at least one community factory (poverty alleviation workshop), as a result, more than 2, 100 relocated people in the county realized employment and entrepreneurship at their doorstep.

Tertiary service type: For the relocated people who have certain service skills, strong service awareness, and understanding of operation and management, through incentives, financial support and other methods, thecounty encourages the establishment of agritainments, farmhouse inns and tourism specialty shops to allow 918 relocated people to engage in tertiary service business, thus increasing family income.

Out-of-work type: For the relocated people with a certain level of education, good physical fitness, and willingness to go out to work, through skill training and export of organized labor services, more than 2, 300 relocated people have achieved a stable increase in income.

Basic livelihood guarantee type: For the 663 "five guarantees" households with 705 people, thecounty adopted the immigration and relocation policy in building houses, and the civil affairs department provides basic livelihood guarantees with them. For the extremely poor "three no's" households (no work ability, no source of living, and no statutory supporters or dependents), the county adopted the "one yard, two systems" to implement turnkey projects. [1] For the disabled relocated households with multiple causes of poverty, the county help them get rid of poverty as soon as possible through the superposition of poverty alleviation policies, effectively stopping poverty from being passed on to the next generation.

3. 2. 3　Five-small communities to strengthen fine management

Many people who are willing to be relocated would ask a series of questions such as where to get vegetables after being relocated in new

---

[1]　By "one yard, two systems", it means that public pension institutions locate the supported elderly and the surrogated elderly in different areas. The area where surrogated elderly live can be leased. The personnel and charge within the lease area are operated in an enterprise-oriented and market-oriented manner. The "one yard, two systems" crack down on the institutional obstacles existing in public pension institutions in terms of responsibilities, rights, staffing, funding, and income distribution. For details, please refer to " Analysis of the ' One Yard, Two Systems' Reform of Public Pension Institutions", http: //www. yanglaocn. com/shtml/20151020/144534330059523. html.

resettlement sites, where to store our food and farming tools, if there is any place for weddings or funerals, where to buried after death, and what to do when shopping is inconvenient. In light of these questions, Zhen' an County explores the construction of "five-small communities" after repeated discussion, that is, supporting vegetable gardens, small living space, small council for weddings and funerals, small love-caring supermarket, and small public-interest cemetery, extending service to every corner of the people's life. Each community also establishes old age association and community theatrical troupe, which regularly conduct cultural and recreational activities, helping the relocated people integrate with each other and continuously improve their sense of belonging and happiness.

In creating "double demonstration" communities that are idea for living and working, Zhen' an County adheres to the construction standards, guarantees the progress, focuses on employment through industries, takes community management as the key, emphasizes coordination and cooperation, and makes efforts to solve problems such as "what industries to develop, how to raise funds, and where customers come from. Zhen' an County continues to improve the creation program, clarify the time limits, detail the division of labor, strengthen the responsibilities at all levels, so as to make up-and-down connection, overall coordination, and orderly promotion. In terms of fine management, the county establishes a high standard establishes "one file for one household, one book for one resettlement, one book for one Township, and one book for one county" to ensure the management of the relocation and resettlement of the county, Towns, sites, and households by means of ledger and the people, households, money, housing, and industry information are accurate and unified. The county continues to build civilized and safe communities and make entry of spiritual civilization and law into communities. As of December 2019, two communities in Zhen' an County had become provincial civilized communities, 6 communities had been awarded municipal civilized communities, and 30 resettlement communities in the whole county carried out activities on "double demonstration" for idea living and working. Six communities including Yunzhen Garden, Gaofeng Town, Pingjia Garden, and and the immigrant community in Fengshou Village,

Qinggongguan Town have accumulated rich experiences in deepening the work of "precise relocation, precise measures and fine management" and creating "double demonstration" communities.

3.3 "Community Factories" for Relocated People in Ankang City

Since 2014, in order to make the relocated people and poor people work locally, Ankang City, Shaanxi Province has, taking advantage of the opportunity of labor-intensive industries moving from the southeast coastal area to the central and western regions, vigorously developed community factories so that the relocated people can work near their homes. In addition, the county has also made active exploration and bold innovation to continually extend the industry chain, build an industrial system, create a service platform, provide all-round guarantees, and promote the steady improvement and upgrading and sustainable development of community factories.

3.3.1 Rented houses to a standardized factory

At the beginning, most community factories were in the immigrant communities, renting a few houses downstairs, and the working people were basically from the relocated and poor households from the communities and from nearby villages, so that they could both take care of the elderly and children and earn money to increase income steadily on their doorstep, which is indeed a good thing. However, as community factories grow, the existing plants, supporting facilities and extensive management, especially the congenital shortcomings of "community factories disturbing the people", etc., seriously restrict the further development of community factories. Standardized production and standardized management have become an inevitable choice for community factories to improve quality and performance and achieve sustainable development. In 2018, Ankang City issued the *Local Standards for New Community Factories in Ankang*, which makes it clear that the relocation community should be equipped with a community factory. The *Local Standards* require that the communities with a size of more than 300 households should build standardized factories, and those with a size of more than 100 households should build processing workshops. Moreover, they require that the production area and the residential area should be effectively separated, and put forward specific requirements for the conditions of the factory building, the operation entities, the production environment, the operating procedures, the management system, and the identification and withdrawal. As of the end of 2019, Ankang City had built 587 new community factories, creating 21, 000 jobs, including more than 7, 000 poor laborers; "New Community Factory Loan" had accumulatively invested 76. 94 million Yuan in 86 households, covering 154 resettlement communities and 156 new community factories, achieving full coverage of "new community factories" in the resettlement communities with over 100 households and the "new community factory loan" for those that have loan demand and meet the requirements for loans.

3.3.2   Plush Toys to Multiple Industries

Community factories of Ankang started in Baihe and took shape in Pingli. Now they have expanded to all counties and districts in the city. At first, they mainly produced plush toys, which belongs to a labor-intensive industry. In previous years, they were mainly concentrated in the eastern developed regions, most famous in Yangzhou, and their products were mainly exported to Europe and the United States. However, with the reduction of labor force and the increase in production costs, some enterprises began planning to transfer their industries to the western regions. The greatest advantage of Ankang, a city in deep poverty, is its abundant labor resources, especially the relocation communities have a large number of surplus female labor force. At the same time, there is almost no pollution in the production of plush toys, which is also very in line with the positioning and needs of Ankang's industrial development. In 2014, the first plush toy factory settled down in Baihe. In the next one or two years, plush toys flourished in counties and districts of Ankang. By the end of 2018, 165 plush toy community factories had been built and put into production in the city.

Ankang, as a key ecological function area and a water source conservation area of the South-to-North Water Diversion Middle Line Project, is restricted by the state from being developed. As a result, developing an eco-friendly industry represented by plush toys is the best choice for building its own industrial system. Therefore, starting in 2018, Ankang City has set its sights on undertaking industrial transfer to a wider field. In addition to plush toys, they have successively introduced electronic components, clothing processing, special agricultural products processing, folk handicraft production and cultural and creative industries of pollution free, low energy consumption, and low noise. It has included these five industries as the focus of the development of new community factories. At present, the community factories in Ankang City have shown a diversified layout and growth in multiple points, laying a good foundation for building an industrial system with Ankang characteristics.

3.3.3 Processing workshops to whole industry chain

Originally, most of the community factories were only production and processing workshops because they lacked creative design of products and raw material sources as well as sales and logistics. As a result, they had very limited value-added space for labor output, and the working people were unable to get higher wages, with an average monthly income of about 2700 Yuan. As community factories grow, the industry faces an increasingly prominent problem with improving quality and performance. For this reason, Ankang City makes a timely adjustment to the investment promotion ideas, transforming "inviting enterprises" into "inviting industries". With the introduction of plush toys as a breakthrough, it focuses on industry chain configuration and implements whole-industry-chain investment promotion to achieve updating and upgrading. At present, the plush toys factories have moved from simple production and processing workshops to the whole industry chain, and gradually realized the "one-stop" of creative design, raw material processing, production and sales. "Aiduobao" plush toy is the first community factory introduced by Ziyang County. During the investigation, we saw that a relatively complete industry chain has been established there, with product creative design, production of raw and auxiliary materials, product processing, packaging and finishing, warehousing and multi-channel sales. This year, Aiduobao headquarters has also settled down in Ziyang. During the investigation in Hengkou Town, we learned that they set up "five centers" including creative design of plush toys, wholesale of raw materials and auxiliary materials, product exhibition, logistics distribution, and e-commerce operation with the demonstration area as the core. At the same time, they speed up the construction of bases for important raw materials including PP cotton and fabric, and invited SF, JD. com, Shanghai Port, Ninggnag Port and other logistics and port companies to Ankang to open a special line for plush toy logistics. They also reach an *"Agreement on Ankang Dry Port"* with Shanghai Port Group. After completion, the containers for finished products will be directly declared and exported from the Hengkou dry port, leading to greatly reduced logistics cost. Not only stuffed toys but also other products such as electronic products, Chinese herbal medicines, and specialty agricultural products are also developing towards the whole industry chain.

3.3.4　Community residents to industrial professionals

The establishment of community factories provides a stable and reliable source of income for the poor and relocated people, and ensures that the relocated people can settle down and get rich after relocation. However, with the large-scale expansion of community factories and the significant increase in labor, some counties and districts have begun to find it difficult to recruit workers. At the same time, because the majority of community factory employees are relocated people and poor labor forces with little education, weakness in accepting new knowledge, bad labor habits and unstable attendance, which has also brought great difficulties to the management of community factories. In order to ensure the continuous and stable development of community factories and effectively solve the problem of "being difficult to hire qualified workers" and "labor cost being on the rise" for enterprises, all counties and districts have made every effort and adopted their own methods of publicity and subsidies for work to attract more community residents to work in the community factories; setting up technical posts and raising wages to attract more young and middle-aged migrant workers who have certain technical skills to return home for employment; in combination with the "Entrepreneurship plus Industry" training model, supporting Ankang University, Ankang Vocational and Technical College and relevant employment training institutions to carry out targeted, post-based and order-based training so as to train more localized, professional talents and operational experts for community factories; in combination with the construction of "sincerity, filial piety, thriftiness, diligence and harmony", integrating professional ethics, labor discipline and other contents into it, and striving to train ordinary farmers used to "work at sunrise, and rest at sunset" into skilled and disciplined industrial workers, providing solid human resources and talent support for Ankang's industrial development.

3.3.5   Employment and income security to all-round guarantee

Community factories also expose some problems during operation. Most of the employees working in community factories are married women, most of whom are in their 30s and 40s. They have to work to earn money and take care of their children, as a result, they can not guarantee working hours, coupled with frequent employee turnover, the product quality and the normal operation of the factories are affected accordingly. For example, the off-duty time is generally 6 pm, which is 2 hours later than the school hours of their children. The children are left unattended after school, especially in winter and summer vacations, therefore, most employees choose to take leave or resign to take care of their children at home; for many female workers, their husbands work out all year round, therefore, there are few opportunities for the couples to communicate. In addition to busy housework, they have to go to work, and take care of the elderly and children, which is very stressful and brings a series of family conflicts. For this reason, child care centers are established. During our investigation in Hanyin, we learned that among the 44 community factories in the county, 24 of them have built a "warm home" for women and children. The county has provided 2 public welfare posts at each factory to help employees take care of children, and tutor them in homework, which has solved the problem of the trusteeship of employees' children from school, weekends and holidays, and ensured that employees can work with peace of mind. "Factory plus home workshop". At the rattan community factory in Renhe Village, Jianchi Town, we found that this is a factory small in size and in scale, but its annual sales can reach more than 5 million Yuan, which has driven more than 200 villagers in Renhe Village and 8 surrounding villages to develop rattan industry. The community factory conducts special skills training for the people in the village and surrounding areas according to production needs. The government will pay for the training-related costs. Those who have completed the training will receive the raw materials from the factory and weave by themselves at home. The finished products will be purchased back by the factory. The advantage of this model is that the factory can expand production without expanding the plant, and the people can earn money in their own homes without delaying their housework. The Communist Youth League and the Women's Federation all participate. During the investigation, we saw that many community factories have Communist Youth Leagues, trade unions, and women's federation organizations, and they have set up special venues for female workers' training and rights protection to provide them with psychological consultation, rights protection, and skills training services. Enriching corporate culture. Organizing activities such as the selection of "Excellent Employee" and "Most Beautiful Female Worker" to allow employees to have a sense of belonging and honor in community factories, further enhance cohesion, and ensure that they work with peace of mind and stable employment.

In order to ensure continuous and stable development of community factories, Ankang City has played a "combination punch" with preferential policies since 2018. It has coordinated with the China Construction Bank Ankang Branch to innovatively launch "loans for new community factories" with zero guarantee, zero mortgage, and pure credit, to provide new community factories with a pure credit loan of up to 2 million Yuan per factory; providing free construction of standardized workshops and free decoration for new community factories, 3 years of rent-free, water and electricity fees free; for the new community factories that hire poor people, providing a one-time post subsidy of 1,000 Yuan per person; raising funds, establishing a fund pool, and providing timely financial support for enterprises, which greatly eases the enterprises' financial pressure caused by the long tax refund cycle.

3. 3. 6   Reflection over community factories

Taking the community factory as a breakthrough, Ankang City strives to build an industrial system with Ankang characteristics and is playing a "big game" of industrial transformation and upgrading. What is the basis for winning this game? Their approach is worthy of in-depth consideration.

3. 3. 6. 1   Seizing opportunities and taking the initiative

Ankang belongs to the contiguous poor areas in Qinling-Bashan mountainous regions. It is the core area of the main battlefield for poverty alleviation in China and the national key area for relocation. It can be said that it faces a heavy task of getting rid of poverty and great pressure of development. In order to shake off poverty, they have made every effort to innovate development ideas, focus on the development of characteristic industries, actively undertake the transfer of industries between the east and west, actively integrate into the Han River Ecological Economic Belt, hold fast to policy opportunities such as the cooperation between Jiangsu and Shaanxi for poverty alleviation, strengthen policy support, cracks down on development problems, and finally achieve the "multi-win" effect of helping the poor increase income, enterprise development, and industrial growth, providing examples for Shaanxi Province to seize development opportunities and adjust the structure, promote transformation and stabilize growth.

3. 3. 6. 2   Adjusting work style and delivering tangible outcomes

Success looks kindly on those with resolve, with drive and ambition, and with plenty of guts. The decision and entrepreneurship is not just about talking, writing, planning, but more importantly, relying on hard work. In a few days of investigation, we can really feel the strength of the Ankang people. In order to develop the industry, they have rushed to attract investment from all over the country, came up with "real money", and encouraged enterprises to invest in Ankang; in order to ensure the sustainable and stable development of the industry, they put up practical measures and make practical moves to solve the problems and difficulties encountered in the development of the enterprise on a one-on-one and point-to-point basis; in order to seize the opportunity and speed up development, they work and help with diligence. Under the circumstance that the downward pressure on the economy of theprovince continues to increase, the Ankang economy has risen against the trend and the growth rate of its GDP is ranked first in the Province for four consecutive years.

3. 3. 6. 3   Targeted green development

Ankang is located in the core area of water source protection of the South-to-North Water Diversion Project. In promoting development, they have neither "reinvented old industries" nor "waited for gains without pains". Instead, they firmly grasp the favorable opportunity for the economic transformation and upgrading of the southeast coastal areas and the transfer of a large number of labor-intensive processing enterprises to the central and western regions, and base themselves on the local resource endowments and industrial foundation. In accordance with the green cycle development ideas, they introduce high-standard, whole-chain industries that are pollution free and of low-energy consumption, realizing the intensive development and clean production of the industries, and effectively solving the problems of energy saving and emission reduction, ecological protection, and pollution control in the transfer industry, preventing the transfer of pollution "from east to west" and achieving "both ushering in invaluable assets and maintaining lucid waters and lush mountains".

3. 3. 6. 4   Optimizing the environment and improving services

A good business environment is productivity and competitiveness. Ankang people understand that the entrepreneurs have the most say about whether the business environment is good or not. In recent years, they have been thinking for the enterprises, responding to their needs, and following up in a timely manner. They would provide the services as what enterprises wish; providing related services to help enterprises extend the industry chain and enhance their competitiveness;

simplifying the examination and approval procedures, providing "one-stop" services, promoting online office, and opening up the "last mile" for serving enterprises. Their approach tells us that in order to improve the business environment, we must completely reverse the concept, truly realize the transformation from " management " to " service plus supervision", and strive to become a "golden waiter" that can both "add icing on the cake" and "provide yeoman's service".

3. 4   Traditional Industries Revitalization and Flexible Employment of Poor Population in Nanzheng County

Since 2016, Nanzheng District, Hanzhong City, Shaanxi Province, has given full play to the unique advantages of traditional industries in driving poor people to work nearby and from home, highlighting protection and development, digging deep into resource endowments, vigorously revitalizing traditional industries, and allowing more people to work steadily from home and realize income increase. They have explored a new way of "making people earn money by craftsmanship and using traditional industries to promote targeted poverty alleviation", helping to push poverty alleviation to the "fast lane".

3. 4. 1   Innovating inheritance to stimulate the vitality of traditional industries

Nanzheng is an important birthplace of Han culture, and the place name has been in existence for more than 2,400 years. Nanzheng District pursues giving the "old state new life" in the active inheritance, so that the traditional industry shows a new style in a new era. First, promoting development with protection. Nanzheng insists that the better protection and development is to focus on the ecological origin and declare geographical indication products. With the goal of "full census, forming a   comprehensive   database,   sound   institutions,   standardized management,   and   overall   protection ",   upon   the   principle   of "comprehensiveness, representativeness, and authenticity", Nanzheng pays close attention to the census and collection, summary and sorting out of resources. As a result, over 10 categories and more than 30 intangible cultural heritages with strong local characteristics including hand-made tea, folk embroidery, Handiao Guangguang, Xieshui shehuo, Chunguan Shuochun, wood engraving, etc. stand out, especially the traditional industries represented by palm weaves and rattan weaves, have been included in the third and fifth batches of intangible cultural heritage protection lists in Shaanxi Province, and "six-weave" skills such as bamboo weaving, fan weaving, straw weaving, and handicrafts are derived. Second, endowing modern elements. Nanzheng pursues the concept of innovation, always focuses on the traditional industry, and tightly follows the development law of "generation out of use, revitalization out of market, and changing out of the situation". It not only fully respects the regional culture and inherits the exquisite craft, but also combines with the contemporary life element with a new perspective, and promotes the innovation and creativity of the traditional industry. At present, there are 33,500 people engaged in the "six-weave" industry and the mianpi food industry. These two alone directly increase the annual income per capita by more than 65,000 Yuan. Third, innovating business model. It highlights the leading role and market operation and introduces combined measures of "demonstration base promoting employment, local employment in community factories and entrepreneurship by returned capable people" so as to continue to expand the traditional industry practitioners and improve the level of craftsmanship, thus, the traditional industries have achieved promotion in benefits and scale. In innovating marketing model, Nanzheng relies on the e-commerce platform at the district, Town and village level, actively promoting the "Internet plus traditional industries plus cooperatives plus base plus poverty alleviation" model, and realizing online direct sales of the district's hand-made tea, earthenware crafts, folk embroidery, and woven products. Palm weave and rattan weave are exported to other countries and regions, with an annual revenue of more than 6 million Yuan; the business scope of the mianpi food industry covers 29 Provinces (autonomous regions) and cities nationwide, with annual sales of more than 1.2 billion Yuan.

3. 4. 2   Fostering strengths and circumventing weaknesses to promote deep processing of traditional industries

Nanzheng District pursues to combine the revitalization of traditional industries with targeted poverty alleviation, focusing on resource elements, "carrying forward" the long-term employment of traditional industries from home, and "making up for" the shortcomings of fragmentation and weakness, and truly making traditional industries a "golden key" to stable poverty alleviation. First, building community factories. Nanzheng District pursues to integrate resources and building a platform to closely connect the inheritance of traditional crafts such as " government fund awards, inheritors teaching apprentices, and productive concentrated training" with targeted poverty alleviation, and encourages village cadres or skilled craftsmen and large households to set up professional cooperatives and form five production bases for rattan weaving and palm weaving in traditional craft resource concentration areas, communities and resettlement sites. It integrates financial development poverty alleviation funds industries, encourages craftsmen to return to their hometowns for starting businesses, and supports the poor to invest in industrial cooperatives and collective organizations to continuously improve the scale and organization of traditional craft industries. The whole district has established 47 various traditional industry poverty alleviation factories (bases), 5 associations including the Mianpi food association, the bee association, the tea industry association, the agritainment association, and the palm weaving association, and 10 cooperatives for poverty alleviation via industrial development. The whole district has already had 241 new type of business entities, driving 16, 261 households with 42, 219 people benefit from the industry chain, with an annual per capita income increase by more than 2, 000 Yuan. Second, developing leading enterprises. Nanzheng District pursues to take system and mechanism innovation and improvement of business environment as a breakthrough, strengthens the brand concept, makes good use of idle and existing resources, encourages the transformation and upgrading of "family workshops" through mergers and restructuring, technology grafting, and accelerates rise towards labor-intensive micro and small enterprises and leading enterprises; expanding "incremental", relying on the advantageous traditional industrial resources, actively attracting investment and wisdom, and developing leading enterprises in traditional industrial processing. A great number of traditional processing enterprises including Nanzheng Liangshun Rattan Company, Jinxiu rattan handicrafts, Feng Xu l fan weaving, etc. have developed rapidly, which effectively promotes the upgrading of traditional craft products from primary processing to deep processing, and transformation from traditional processing technology to the use of advanced and applicable technologies and high and new technologies. With the leading role, and by taking the order-based production model of production from home and enterprises purchasing back, an integrated production and marketing management model of "enterprise plus base plus farmers" is established, forming an interest connection mechanism for "small farmers" connecting "big market". At present, the district has developed 32 various types of traditional industrial processing enterprises, with an annual output value of more than 50 million Yuan, providing jobs to nearly 15, 000 people nearby, including more than 2, 600 poor people, and an annual per capita income increase by more than 3, 200 Yuan. Third, strengthening technological support. Nanzheng District focuses on strengthening the backbone of traditional industry talents and provides special financial funds for 90 representative inheritors of intangible cultural heritage and traditional skilled people and craftsmen, each of whom receives 2, 000 Yuan as fees for apprenticing. Masters are encouraged to have disciples and carry out "one-to-one" inheritance, so as to firmly grasp the traditional core craftsmanship. Nanzheng District strengthens the process alliance and technological research, makes full use of the Internet plus initiative, absorbs intermediaries, strengthens the integration of design, processing and marketing, and relies on intellectual resources and technical forces such as universities and creative teams to build 18 platforms (bases) for "firms, universities, and research institutes" of various traditional craft, which continuously inject traditional crafts with modern process and modern arts, thus effectively increasing the added value of entrepreneurship and employment from home. Nanzheng District continues to attach equal importance to "giving fish" and "teaching to fish", "supporting wisdom" and "supporting ambition", closely combines market demand and the will of the people, succeeds and establishes creative bases and entrepreneurial bases through teaching, delivers technology and services at home, and at the same time, relying on the advantages of the educational resources of vocational and technical schools in the district, gives play to the role of the social training institutions, increases the training of traditional craft, builds a bridge for flexible entrepreneurship and employment from home, and strives to make the poor people become better off. In 2018, a total of 6 traditional craft trainings were held, 282 people received training, and 139 new poor people increased income steadily through the traditional handicraft industry.

3. 4. 3   Following the trend and strengthening the traditional craft industry system

Industrialization is the only way to realize the resonance between traditional craft and the times and sustainable and healthy development. Nanzheng District has always taken targeted measures and spared no efforts to promote the work on demonstration sites, recommendation of industries, and integration, striving to build a traditional craft industry system with good quality, strong vitality and excellent structure. First, building a batch of demonstration Towns and villages. Upon the principle of "protecting solid state, inheriting active state, and improving format", Nanzheng District highlights the model of "one industry for one Town, and one product for one village", makes overall coordination, planning, and scientific layout, and elaborately prepares the development plans for demonstration Towns and villages with characteristic traditional crafts, focusing on the difference of the cultural connotations, technical methods and distribution of craftsmen of traditional craft, developing differentiated craft products, and creating more regional characteristics of craft brands. Huangguan rattan weave, Lianshui straw weave, Fucheng bamboo weave, Hanshan palm weave, and Lianghe fan weave, etc. have their own beauty and charm, with which more than 100 kinds of crafts are developed, for example, Erlong Xizhu (two dragons playing with a pearl), Longfeng Chengxiang (the dragon and the phoenix bringing prosperity), colorful unicorn, fairy flowering, etc. , which have improved the market competitiveness and economic added value of the traditional craft industry in the district. Second, running a good special event. Nanzheng District adheres to multi-angle and all-round publicity and promotion, actively communicates with foreign countries, and continuously improves and expands the popularity and reputation of Nanzheng's traditional crafts. Since 2019, it has held the "Five-Weave" (rattan, coir, fan, bamboo, handicrafts) competition, the first "Princess Cup · Hanzhong (China) Mianpi Food Contest", "The Mianpi Food Township Essay Competition", and the search for "Mianpi Food Xishi" and other activities. In November 2018, the Nanzheng Mianpi Foor Association was invited to participate in the first Liangpi Food Festival in Xi' an, with a revenue of more than 60, 000 Yuan in 3 days. The 2019 "Hanzhong (China) Mianpi Food Competition" will be upgraded to be hosted by the People's Government of Hanzhong City, and Nanzheng District will also determine the first week of April each year as "Nanzheng (China) Hanzhong Mianpi Food Snack Culture Festival". Third, developing a batch of integrated industries. Nanzheng District insists on doing a great article on traditional industry plus, focuses on the development of tourism within its jurisdiction, pays more attention to discovering the cultural connotation of traditional craft, and uses offline attractions such as tourist attractions and agritainment to build a "Nanzhen traditional craft experience center" based on social forces. It has opened various experience halls in clay pottery manufacturers, traditional oil-pressing workshops, rattan weaving and palm weaving production workshops, and organically combined traditional activities and cultural experiences, creating a group of excellent traditional cultural and folk tourism. It pursues to promote "production" with "tourism", makes an organic integration of material culture and intangible culture, and in the development of folk culture, folk craft experience tourism, further promotes traditional crafts to improve quality and form a brand. It supports cross-industry innovation and entrepreneurship such as traditional craft workshops, enterprise workshops, handicraft workshops, etc. , and actively explores traditional industries plus e-commerce, traditional industries plus exhibitions, traditional industries plus scenic spots, traditional industries plus consumption season and other models to cultivate new formats. Traditional industries have initially formed a three-dimensional and diversified new development pattern, which strongly promotes the positive interactions and steady advancement among protection and development of traditional crafts, flexible entrepreneurship and employment from home, as well as stable income increase and poverty alleviation.

Chapter 4
Endogenous Impetus for Poverty Alleviation through Ambition & Intellectual Enrichment

On November 27, 2015, General Secretary Xi Jinping instructed in his speech at the Conference on Poverty Alleviation and Development, " To win the fight against poverty, we need not only help the impoverished economically affluent, but spiritually and intellectually enriched. Our efforts for poverty alleviation and development aim at promoting people's all-round development. We need to increase cultural activities, improve people's well-being, maintain people's health, strengthen people's education and comprehensive qualities, and enrich people's intellectual lives. " Only through hard work can impoverished people be lifted out of poverty and achieve prosperity. To win the battle against poverty, Qinling-Bashan mountainous regions seek to enrich people's intellectual lives, adopt a people-centered approach to hamper the inter-generational transmission of poverty, and cultivate the endogenous impetus in getting rid of poverty and becoming better off.

4.1 Activation of Endogenous Impetus for Poverty Alleviation in Shiquan County

Shiquan County in Ankang City of Shaanxi Province is one of the key contiguous poverty-stricken counties in poverty alleviation and development of Qinling-Bashan mountainous regions. With 74 registered poor villages and 10, 027 poor households (24, 290 people) in the County, it is thus identified as a seriously impoverished County during the 13th Five-Year Plan. The inaccessible transportation, ill-informed communication, poor infrastructure, specially the lack of initiative to get rid of poverty and mere relying on assistance reveal key factors leading to the status of severe poverty. To address these problem and build a positive climate favoring the anti-poverty campaign, five people-centered measures have been adopted to stimulate the endogenous impetus of the local to fight poverty:

· Establishing a working system for poverty alleviation
· Strengthening the leading role of paragons
· Boosting employment and providing training for the poor people
· Enriching poor people's intellectual lives
· Establishing a comprehensive system for ambition advancement

4.1.1   "Shiquan Approaches" in Poverty Alleviation, Ambition Enhancement and New Folk Custom Construction

General Secretary Xi Jinping emphasized, "Publicity, education, training, and organizational work among the officials and general public should be strengthened to foster the idea of "better working hard for change than sweating out in endurance", arouse their activism and action to get rid of poverty through self-made diligent effort. "[1]

4.1.1.1   Establishing a working system for poverty alleviation

In August 2017, to promote the spiritual civilization and ambition for poverty alleviation, Shiquan County Party Committee released *Work Plan on Improving the Conduct of General Public* (hereafter *The Proposal*), after drawing experience from four projects and six village-level (community-level) projects for rural spiritual civilization construction. Following the principle of systematic planning, problem-solving orientation, targeted measures, long-term development and practical results, the four-phase system shortened as " education, governance, guidance and instruction" in which " Education " and " governance " serve as the key, " guidance " as the principle and

---

① *Anthology of Important Documents since the 18th National Congress (Volume II)*, Beijing: Central Party Literature Press, 2018, p. 49.

"instruction" as the goal, is implemented in ambition enhancement and the triple-6 project for value construction, problem resolution and goal setting is promoted in new folk customs building. To be more specific, *The Plan* aims to promote socialist core values into 6 places, namely communities, organizations, schools, enterprises, villages and households, resolve 6 noticeable problems in environmental management, and achieve 6 major goals in new folk custom construction. With a clear direction, it has established a working system for poverty alleviation, encouraged people's initiative to get rid of poverty through hard work, and contributed to an overall enhancement of productive labor and intellectual lives in poverty-stricken regions.

4.1.1.2 Strengthening the leading role of paragons

Shiquan County has exerted leading roles of paragons and publicized their exemplary deeds to encourage people's initiative in getting rid of poverty by diligence, and create a favorable environment for poverty alleviation. Through research, instruction and publicity, the leading function of paragons selected from party members, capable individuals and role models in poverty alleviation are fully and effectively promoted.

(1) Encouraging party members to play a leading role

Shiquan County has strengthened group learning among party members, imposed stringent learning requirements, and guided them to resist the waste and extravagance on birthday, weddings or funerals by signature.

(2) Nurturing capable persons to invigorate the village

Since 2017, Shiquan County launched the strategy of "Invigorating Villages by Capable Minds" to find and nurture capable individuals to help enrich people's intellectual lives. By tapping their advantages in knowledge, technology, and capital, the poor people is led to improve their custom and capabilities and activate the endogenous power for development among villages and poor households. The strategy planned to find and nurture 100 party and government elites, 100 outstanding village officials, 1000 technical personnel and 1000 locally respectful individuals. Since then, a large number of rural elites such as Yang Weidong, You Ziyong and Li Jindou, returned home to run business, and a host of local residents began to engage in scale agriculture operation or rural governance. 153 capable elites were elected in the working committees of the villages, of whom 22 have served as village directors and village secretaries. These capable individuals have played an effective leading role in poverty alleviation, intellectual enhancement, new folk customs construction and rural development.

(3) Awarding outstanding persons and setting up role models

To lead the public by fine examples, Shiquan County elects the "ten most advanced individuals" from the moral models and the anti-poverty paragons on a regular basis. 110 role models from different sectors including Paralympic champion Xia Jiangbo and Chengjiao were honored, and 12 of them have been approved and awarded as moral models by national, provincial and municipal governments. Besides, 300 honest villagers, 75 advanced units, 99 advanced individuals and 32 representative households were honored for their becoming better off through diligent work. The team led by outstanding officials and role models visit poor villages and conduct face-to-face and multi-dimensional teach-ins, motivating people across the county to learn from them and keep in alignment.

4. 1. 1. 3   Boosting employment and training for poor people

General Secretary Xi Jinping ever stated, "We should launch a training initiative to offer vocational skills for the poverty-stricken people, teaching them how to fish instead of giving fish, and train their capacity of employment. " For this target to deliver, Shiquan County has adopted four approaches in skill training, and provided four channels of employment, generating the morale of the poor to fight against poverty through hard work.

(1) Four approaches for skill training to add to their confidence to behave.

First, carry out collective management and separate training. Department of Human Resource and Social Security makes overall arrangement; vocational education centers at the county level train junior and high school graduates who fail to continue a higher education; various training institutions conduct short-term employment skill training; Agricultural and Forestry Bureau at the county level takes over practical rural skill training; Supply and Marketing Cooperative is in charge of e-commerce training; organizers at the township and village level are responsible for divide tasks on an equal basis.

Second, customize training to need. Trainers can teach at people's homes based on their needs, and training offices are set up at Townships and counties so that people can receive on-the-spot training near home.

Third, synergize training schools with enterprises. The local government serves as an intermediary in school-enterprise cooperation and enterprise-enterprise cooperation. Once a trainee is qualified, he or she will directly get employed in an enterprise. This will ensure that 80% of the trainees can get employed and over 70% of those who receive entrepreneurship training can successfully start their own businesses.

Fourth, combine training with specific industries. Shiquan County has provided the pre-job training of specific skills required by agriculture, e-commerce, tourism and service industries. The integration of training with specific industries resulted the "multiplier effect" of skill training, contributing to benign interaction among industries, enterprises and employment and income of the poor households.

(2) Four channels of employment

First, establish bases to boost employment. Shiquan County has established 3 incubation bases for business startups, 11 bases for poverty alleviation and 4 community factories. More than 600 business entities have settled here, providing over 3,000 jobs. The County has advocated paradigm like "base + business household + employment", "community factory + employment" and "labor migrant base + employment" and has been recognized as the national pilot County in supporting migrant workers returning home to start businesses. Second, develop industries to boost employment. Shiquan County has supported industrial parks and fostered modern agricultural to create over 2, 000 jobs in the neighborhood for rural households in agricultural companies or cooperatives. Third, develop tourism to boost employment. Shiquan County has promoted the development of new cultural tourism, eco-tourism, leisure tourism and the tertiary industry. It sought to build scenic spots, like Guiguzi Cultural Town, Chihe Sericulture Town and Zhongba Workshop Town, in communities and create a market by enlarging shops to boost employment. Fourth, offer public welfare jobs to boost employment. To address the problem of unemployment and low income faced by over-aged people, Shiquan County has offered 1000 posts in public service within the County and 1,500 within the villages for them to work near home.

4.1.1.4　Establishing a comprehensive system for ambition advancement

Shiquan County highlights the joint development of all villages in an all-round way. It has taken five measures to establish a comprehensive system for ambition advancement at village level, enriching people's intellectual lives across the county. The five measures are:

· Formulating village regulations and non-governmental agreements
· Fostering family culture by publicizing good family rules
· Establishing four village-level committees
· Building cultural places and teams for arts and sports activities

(1) Guidance: formulating village regulations and non-governmental agreements

The County has guided 161 villages (communities) to amend and improve the village regulation and non-governmental agreement (community convention) highlighting the value of "honesty, filial piety, frugality, diligence and harmony ". More detailed clauses and corresponding punishment were systematically enshrined into it, including the standards for hosting weddings and funerals, and requirements of active labor, respect for the elderly, filial piety for parents, honesty and obedience of law. A total of 485 obligatory clauses were added and 599 unqualified clauses were deleted to make the regulation simple and clear, practical and effective, standard and highly operational. As a result, a code of conduct has been commonly recognized and observed by all villagers.

(2) Instruction: fostering family culture by publicizing good family rules

The County has carried out selection activities such as " the happiest family", "fine family traits and family rules" and "the most outstanding family in implementing new customs" among people in all villages (communities). 120 family rules from the Hu's Family, Feng's Family, Chen's Family and Gan's Family were selected, properly amended, and then publicized on bulletin boards of the villages and communities. In this process, excellent family rules have been popularized, including "loyalty, filial piety, property and righteousness; frugality in household management; respect for seniority; self-cultivation for self-perfection". On this basis, Shiquan County has carried out activities of "setting up family rules, passing down family disciplines, straightening out family tradition and enhancing family morality". People were guided to strengthen family education, cultivate family culture and establish good family rules.

(3) Main body: establishing four village-level committees

Shiquan County has made solid efforts in setting up the four committees, namely Village Moral Appraisal and Discussion Committee, Wedding and Funeral Affairs Committee, Villager Committee and Anti-Drug and Anti-Gambling Committee. In shifting the term of office for the party branch committee and the village committee, the County government further improve 158 village-level (community-level) organizations of the four village committees by enrolling 2,000 locally respectful individuals into the organizations as major forces in poverty alleviation and ambition advancement. Among the four, the Moral Appraisal and Discussion Committee plays an outstanding role to poverty alleviation and ambition enhancement. The committees were founded in 161 villages (communities) around the county and run by locally respectful persons, retired officials and party officials elected by the people. Besides, rules and regulations have been formulated for regular morality appraisal and discussion. Since 2018, a total of 430 publicity and education activities and 684 morality appraisal and discussion meetings have been carried out. 161 bulletin boards have been set up in the villages, on which over 400 cases have been publicized. The committee has appraised 610 role models and figured out 265 negative ones. Over 600 applications for poor household subsidies have been proactively recalled due to the fair work delivered by the committee.

(4) Platform: building cultural places and teams for arts and sports activities

To address the problems faced with rural people such as spiritual emptiness, gambling, excessive drinking and demoralization, Shiquan County enlightens the poor people by cultural enrichment and focuses on improving their moral integrity and civilization quality. With places, teams, system, equipment and funds provided, cultural activity squares and farmers' libraries have been established in all administrative villages and communities, and moral lectures were held on a regular basis. Besides, 45 art associations have been organized to hold regular cultural activities to enrich people's cultural life. A platform for publicizing village culture, consisting of moral lectures, farmer's libraries, teams for arts and sports activities and cultural activity squares, has basically taken shape.

(5) Stimulus: the "love shops"

To further incentivize villagers who perform extraordinarily in poverty alleviation, Shiquan County has built 75 "love shops" in all registered poor villages and some non-poverty villages. The 11 aspects of performance of poor households including poverty alleviation work, spiritual outlook and sanitation are assessed on a monthly basis. The results will be transferred to corresponding credits which can be exchanged for goods in the "love shops". So far over 2000 poor people have made such exchanges and such a move contributes greatly to the sound development of rural folk customs.

4.1.2   Major achievements of poverty alleviation and ambition enhancement in Shiquan County

4.1.2.1   Solid progress in poverty alleviation and ambition advancement

For the all-around, comprehensive, in-depth and long term poverty alleviation and ambition enhancement, Shiquan County effectively implemented the seven concrete approaches, namely carrying out moral evaluation and discussion, enforcing village regulations and non-governmental agreements, building the four committees, publicizing positive family rules, improving public etiquette and ethical standards, promoting cultural and ethical progress among the public, removing outdated customs and habits, carrying out cultural activities, and performing governance according to law.

4. 1. 2. 2　Improvement of public morals

Shiquan County has greatly improved its social morality by taking vigorous measures to counter bad trends and performances such as extravagance and waste, vulgarity, gambling and "keeping up with the Joneses". Compared with 2017, the number of feasts held by the local people has dropped by 60% and the expenses for cash gifts and social engagement decreased by 80% and 90% respectively. The poor people proactively devoted more money to starting up businesses and more energy to building up family fortunes. Fewer people appeal to the higher authorities for unreasonable demand. Diligence and frugality gradually prevail across the county, creating a strong spiritual power.

4. 1. 2. 3　Enhancement of moral qualities and civilized manner

Nearly 1,000 role models emerged from the long-term and in-depth improvement of public etiquette and ethical standards. Inspired by them, the pursuit of goodness and beauty has become people's conscious action. Shiquan County has witnessed a significant improvement in people's moral concepts, ethical awareness, social civilization and moral qualities. Fewer disputes but more harmony emerge among the villagers; more people dedicated themselves to get rid of poverty and become better off; less people idle about relying on assistance. The county has seen an overall enhancement of civilized manner, order and ethical standard

4. 1. 2. 4　Upgrading of social governance and development environment

Shiquan County has witnessed a comprehensive improvement in social governance, the officials' work efficiency and service quality, and the administrative and business environment. The rule of law, the rule of virtue and self-governance across the county have improved the overall environment for development. In recent years, no major criminal cases, nor vicious public security cases occurred and Shiquan ranked first in Ankang City in terms of public satisfaction for social security and political legal organs. At the same time, it has been graded "Excellent" for six consecutive years in the comprehensive assessment of target achievement and responsibility fulfillment by the municipal government.

4. 1. 2. 5   Stimulation of endogenous impetus for poverty alleviation

The solid development of poverty alleviation and ambition advancement has created a good atmosphere throughout the County, and has fully inspired people's endogenous impetus in poverty alleviation. With confidence and impetus, people were proactive to get rid of poverty through their diligent work. From 2016 to 2018, 14 poor villages, 4, 114 poor households and 13, 360 poor people in the County have been lifted out of poverty. Shiquan was approved as "Excellent County in Performing Poverty Alleviation" in Shaanxi Province for two consecutive years. In February 2020, it has been removed from the list of registered poverty-stricken regions.

4. 1. 3   Shiquan experience in ambition enhancement and custom construction

In enhancing the ambition and combating poverty, Shiquan County has inspired the endogenous impetus among people and realized comprehensive economic and social development based on systematic arrangement, far-reaching planning, and public contribution.

4. 1. 3. 1   Systematic arrangement to seek joint efforts of all parties

Shiquan County has carried out far-reaching planning on the clear orientation and the distinctive work objectives and framework. It has given full play to the leading role of party organizations at all levels and effectively united people to provide strong political guarantee for poverty alleviation. At the same time, it has effectively mobilized various organizations, and has worked out a pattern with joint coordination of multiple forces in which publicity departments take the lead, involved units perform their duties and social organizations take an active part.

4. 1. 3. 2   Working system to consolidate achievements

Shiquan County has built a comprehensive work system at the village level, creating an overall good environment across the county in poverty alleviation, ambition enhancement and new folk customs construction. Only by establishing a mature working system can the achievements of poverty alleviation be effectively consolidated to sustain good rural customs.

4. 1. 3. 3   Key groups to award role models

Key groups are critical to inspire endogenous impetus among people. Therefore, it is important to give full play to key groups, cultivate advanced models, and build platform to publicize and practice their exemplary deeds so as to guide people to shake off poverty with strong motivation and diligent work.

4. 1. 3. 4   Public power to motivate endogenous impetus

Public participation and support are crucial to secure a success in poverty alleviation. Shiquan County has inspired people's power and wisdom by involving them in formulating rural regulations and building the four committees. By encouraging people to supervise, learn from and help each other, it has achieved practical results in poverty alleviation and can work towards people's self-management, self-education, self-service and self-constraint.

4. 2   "Love Shops" to Generate Village Cohesiveness in Danfeng County

To combat poverty, first enhance the ambition of poor people. General Secretary Xi Jinping stressed, "Getting rid of poverty and becoming better off requires us to be determined in spirit and action. As long as we have the ambition and confidence, we can step over any hurdles in the way ahead. "[1] Some poor households have become accustomed to waiting for, relying on and asking for public or private assistance. Policy contrasts between between the poor and non-poor households have brought with some conflicts among villagers and impeded the efforts for poverty alleviation. Since the fight against poverty, a large number of impoverished villages have set up the "love

---

[1]   Research Institute of CPC History and Documentation, *Anthology of Xi Jinping's Speech on PA*, Beijing: Central Party Literature Press, 2018, p. 132.

shops" in supply of daily necessities donated by people from all sectors of the society, enterprises and the government. Poor people who take an active part in production, public services and elderly respect and care will be rewarded credits to be exchanged for goods in the "love shops". These measures will promote poor people to work harder, be independent, and contribute to the rural customs construction. By raising funds from various parties, Danfeng County has built ' love shops" in every village and set up a redeeming credits system. It has promoted poverty alleviation through a two-way track of material rewards and spiritual incentives: people can get " love points " by actively participating in village affairs or moral evaluation, and then exchange their points for daily necessities in the "love shops". This approach has greatly encouraged people to get rid of poverty through diligent work, eased the conflict between the poor and non-poor households, and created a harmonious atmosphere for shaking off poverty and becoming better off.

4. 2. 1　Main practice

Since 2017, in order to encourage the poverty-stricken households to fight against poverty, Danfeng County has raised funds from various channels to build the "love shops", implemented the redeeming credits system, and formulated detailed and strict rules and regulations to promote poverty alleviation.

4. 2. 1. 1　Joint participation of multiple parties to build the "love shops"

In addition to government funds, Danfeng County has raised money from designated units, warm-hearted people, enterprises and social organizations to jointly build the "love shops". The government and party officials have appealed to various support units, warm-hearted people and enterprises from different sectors for material donations. As of February 2018, a total of 155 "love shops" have been built across Danfeng County, [1] which stand out at the center of the villages

---

[1]　"Danfeng County strives for lifting 25,000 people out of poverty", February 14, 2018, http://www. shangluo. gov. cn/info/1057/74048. htm.

(communities) for the convenience of people. After completion, the village committees implement standard management in the "love shops", and Danfeng County Party Committee conducts supervision on a regular basis to ensure standard operation. The government of Danfeng County has also actively raised donations from multiple parties, including warmhearted people, enterprises, social organizations, public welfare organizations, chambers of commerce (associations), individual industrial and commercial households across the County, to ensure the "love shops" with sufficient supplies to and normal operation can deliver real benefits to more people, and further strengthen its role in stimulating and boosting the poor people to get rid of poverty.

4. 2. 1. 2　Redeeming the credits rewarded for village service

Danfeng County has implemented the credit redeeming system in the "love shops" to standardize goods purchase and distribution. On the basis of a fixed amount of "love points" distributed every month, each person in the villages (communities) can earn additional ones by complying with laws and regulations, contributing to poverty alleviation, environmental improvement and rural customs building. The " love points" can be exchanged for life necessities in the "love shops". The redeeming points system can ensure a timely distribution of "love points" compared with the previous temporary assistance. It also guarantees efficient and sufficient supplies, and provide people with what they really need. In the "love shops", people can openly choose articles of daily use, and pay with "love points", saving the troubles arisen in the previous multi-layered distribution. The Danfeng County Party Committee can distribute rewarding "love credits" to those who contributes to village governance, such as infrastructure construction and environmental protection, thus raising people's sense of participation in village affairs.

4. 2. 1. 3　Detailed rules and regulations for awarding and punishing

To ensure the long-term stable incentives of the "love shops" to poverty alleviation, Danfeng County attached equal importance to construction and operation management after completion, formulated detailed rules and carried out regular supervisions on the management of the "love shops". First, internal donations should be put into charity donation boxes before registration while external donations only need to be registered. Second, managers of the "love shops" should record and store donations in strict compliance with the financial management system, to ensure the statement of account are clear and accurate. Third, goods prices should be clearly marked. Managers of the "love shops" should make timely registration of each transaction made by "love credits", and avoid any wrong deductions. Fourth, the "love shops" should regularly publish the statement of account for public supervision. Finally, villages are entitled to add or deduct "love points" based on their daily behavior and performance in poverty alleviation. Those who perform good deeds and act proactively in poverty alleviation will be awarded additional "love points", while those who conduct bad behaviors, such as littering, fighting, impiety, dishonesty and slackness in poverty alleviation, will be punished by deducting "love points". Points are rewarded to exemplary models selected by morality committees and removed to those idling for assistance so that a favorable custom of kindness and generosity is bred in the village.

4.2.2   Major achievements

The redeeming credits system in the "love shops" have not only contributed to civilized rural customs and harmonious village environment, but eased the contradiction between poor households and non-poor households, and stimulated people's impetus in poverty alleviation. Danfeng County has regenerated people's will to fight against poverty through concerted efforts, enhanced solidarity and coordination in the villages, and collected a joint driving force for poverty alleviation.

4.2.2.1   Cultivating endogenous impetus for poverty alleviation
People are motivated to participate in village affairs and rural governance by the redeeming points system. More people take it a shame to merely rely on and wait for assistance, but act proactively and honorably toward poverty reduction through their diligent work. The "love shops" ensure abundant living products so that people will go burden-free when starting up businesses. Besides, people become more proactive to learn from those who were awarded "love points" for good, and those

who behaved well are willing to help others. All people have become more active in village affairs and worked harder for poverty alleviation, thus creating a good atmosphere of becoming better off with mutual help. The non-poor households drive forward the poor by collaborating in industrial development. An unprecedented good atmosphere where everyone aspires and strives to get rid of poverty is thus created.

4. 2. 2. 2　Creating a harmonious, united, civilized and friendly environment for poverty alleviation

Thanks to the redeeming credits system in the "love shops", the enthusiasm and initiative of all villagers to jointly participate in village construction and service affairs have been motivated, and the collective cohesiveness have been enhanced. The rules and regulations secure an effective management of the " love shops ", promote collective consciousness and rural governance, and guarantee safety and stability of the villages. Strict implementation of these rules and regulations not only stimulates people's impetus to get rid of poverty, but also properly punished those who behave badly. People are motivated to obtain self-improvement and offer mutual assistance, easing the conflicts between poor and non-poor households, and strengthening the solidarity and harmony. Besides, people act proactively to make joint efforts in environmental sanitation, including rural garbage treatment, sewage treatment, and toilet renovation, to better the environment. They take the initiative to perform good deeds, lead a healthy lifestyle, and develop good living habits. A harmonious neighbourhood relationship and united and friendly environment for poverty alleviation has been created across the county, greatly enhancing village cohesiveness and improving rural customs.

4. 2. 2. 3　Concentrating collective efforts for poverty alleviation

Concerted efforts have been delivered by all walks of social life in building and managing the "love shops", demonstrating the traditional Chinese values of moral generosity and willingness to helping the needy, as well as the new customs of our times – benevolence and readiness to help. The *Proposal on Making Donations to "love shops" for Poverty Alleviation* jointly issued by United Front Work Department of the Party

Committee, Federation of Industry and Commerce, Supervision Department, and Department of Civil Affairs in Danfeng County calls for warm-hearted people, enterprises and organizations from different sectors to offer donations for the "love shops", creating strong joint force for poverty alleviation. In attracting donations, the provincial and County government cooperate closely while assume different responsibilities, and make concerted efforts to raise work efficiency, contribute to the management of "love shops" effectively, and promote the poverty alleviation greatly.

4. 2. 2. 4 Laying solid foundation for rural revitalization

Rural areasas the natural, social, and economic territorial complex, bears multiple functions of production, living, ecology, and culture. It coexists and interacts with the urban areas to jointly constitute the main space for human activities. Rural prosperity leads to national success, while its decline causes national decay. General Secretary Xi Jinping put forward the strategy of Rural Revitalization in the report of the 19th CPC National Congress with a general target of advocating and pursuing prosperous industry, ecological livability, rural civilization, effective governance, and affluent lives in the rural areas. By setting up the "love shops" and the redeeming credits system at village level, Danfeng County not only stirs up the endogenous impetus of the public in poverty alleviation, but also greatly arouses their enthusiasm to participate in village building and service affairs. As a result, together with better infrastructure and living environment, the living standards, habits, health concepts, and intellectual outlook in the villages have been constantly improved, and the rural customs have embodied more solidarity and friendship. "Love shops" project has prepared a solid foundation for pursuing rural revitalization.

4. 2. 3 Experience and enlightenment

Danfeng County has joined multiple forces in building and managing the "love shops", demonstrating a spirit of solidarity, friendliness, and readiness to help in modern times. The redeeming credits system have motivated the villagers to participate in public campaign and affairs, raised their basic living standards and enhanced the cohesiveness of the village as well. The formulated scientific village rules and regulations both award positive incentives to fine actions and put relevant constraints to poor behaviors.

4. 2. 3. 1   Base: material incentives

The "love shops" is an important resource to help people get rid of poverty and improve their living standards. Daily necessities and life supplies have filled most shelves in the "love shops", which can be exchanged by redeeming points. Through the participation in village affairs, people can obtain articles of daily use, which is a reasonable approach to meet their basic needs and serves as a positive guide meanwhile. Enterprises, social organizations and warm-hearted people from all walks of life have actively responded to the initiatives of the party committee and government by making donations to the "love shops", which has created a virtuous circle of "all for one and one for all".

4. 2. 3. 2   "Red lines": rules and regulations

Rules and regulations serve as an important means to ensure the effective management of the "love shops" and a security to the utmost effectiveness of such a move. They guarantee the redeeming points system running smoothly, serving as "red lines" to ensure the "love shops" producing the best possible results. As is advocated that "You can't get a proper square without a ruler or a circle without a compass, or literally, ruler and compass, rules and regulations define the successful drawing of square and circle". Detailed and strict rules and regulations, which ensure fair rewards and penalties through "double-pronged" or "multi-pronged" approach, are necessary for running the "love shops". Besides, the strict implementation of the rules and regulations has inspired villagers' confidence to fight against poverty, enhanced their solidarity and cohesiveness, and guaranteed the "love shops" to exert its expected mission in full swing.

4. 2. 3. 3   Means: positive competition

Positive competition is of great importance to encourage people's initiative to get rid of poverty and become better off. Danfeng County has established a redeeming points system for the "love shops", guiding villagers to serve villages business in exchange for points, and then redeem points for goods. It is not merely to serve the impoverished people but all villagers, including the non-impoverished, who are encouraged to participate in, thus dissolving the conflict between the poor households and the non-poor households. Therefore, a positive competitive atmosphere is created, which further motivates people to get rid of poverty through concerted efforts, and contributes to village construction and rural governance.

4. 2. 3. 4　Key: ambition and intellectual enhancement

"Teaching one to fish is better than merely giving him the fish. " As an important part of poverty alleviation, boosting people's ambition and intellectual life is the key to inspire their endogenous impetus to fight the poverty and unite as a whole. This is also the motive why the "love shops" were originally built. People from all walks of life actively make donations, guaranteeing the goods supplies in the "love shops". The redeeming points system fosters a good environment for positive competition. The detailed rules and regulations encourage villagers to be active in village construction and services. These measures seem to be independent of each other, but actually are interconnected, jointly creating a virtuous circle and bring remarkable results. On one hand, the "love shops" have enriched people's intellectual lives by changing the outdated living habits, fostering a harmonious environment that encourages people to help each other, respect the elderly and love the young. On the other hand, they have stimulated people's endogenous impetus to get rid of poverty and become better off, strengthened their collective consciousness, risen their sense of responsibility and enhanced the cohesiveness.

4. 3　Tailoring Poverty Alleviation to Three Categories of Households in Zhen' an County

"Ninety percent of mountains, half water and half land ";

"mountains stretch hundreds of miles One after another without a half mile of flat land in sight"... These are the true portrayal of geographical condition of Zhen' an County located in the southern foot of the Qinling Mountains. Restricted by natural endowment, Zhen' an County has lagged behind in economic development with a large poverty-stricken population. It is one of the 11 severely impoverished counties in Shaanxi Province. By the end of 2017, 90 villages had been registered as poverty-stricken villages, totaling a sum of 16, 000 households and 47, 000 people and the poverty headcount ratio reached 19. 1%. Its battle against poverty is the most difficult one: most of the poor households living in mountainous areas are deeply impoverished, bringing great difficulties to poverty alleviation and a high risk of returning to poverty after being lifted out. To achieve the goal of eradicating poverty by 2020, Zhen' an County formulates the policy of "three categories and well-targeted assistance". Based on their family situation, causes of poverty, future development, and changes in development, poor households are divided into three categories: labor-capable households, less labor-capable households, and labor-incapable households. The county government tailors targeted assistance to different kind of households. This policy has hit the nail on the head, effectively and precisely helping each poverty-stricken household. On May 7, 2019, the Shaanxi Provincial People's Government approved Zhen' an County to withdraw from the list of poverty-stricken counties as the first impoverished country being lifted out of poverty.

4. 3. 1　Door-to-door and person-to-person investigation

General Secretary Xi Jinping stressed that poverty alleviation requires targeted measures. The targeted measures should be implemented based on people's cause of poverty and their impoverishment types. On the basis of the current information of poor households, Zhen' an County has conducted door-to-door, person-to-person investigation to further clarify people's family situation, causes of poverty, health conditions, development potential and policy implementation situation. County officials guide village officials to conduct a thorough and detailed investigation on poverty-stricken households with a village as a unit, to ensure correct and complete information with no omission or error. The main information they surveyed includes family size, health condition, labor capability, employment situation, cause of poverty, family income, policy implementation, standards fulfillment, and people's wishes. In line with the updated information, corresponding actions have been carried out. First, any ineligible household shall be strictly removed from poverty-stricken household list in accordance with the rules. Second, any eligible poverty-stricken household yet to be registered, or any household that has returned or fallen into poverty due to accidents, shall be registered as poverty-stricken household timely, and policy assistance shall be provided accordingly.

Based on the basic information of poor families, Zhen' an County has made an assessment of their labor capacity. Together with other factors taken into account, all poverty-stricken households are classified into three categories. First category, labor-capable households, refers to the impoverished households with basically healthy members, relatively sufficient labor force and stable source of income. Bench-marking the five standards set for out-of-poverty households, families that have reached all 5 standards are identified as the relieved households, while those who have not reached one or more of the standards are identified as the inadequately-relieved households. There are 7, 914 labor-capable poverty-stricken households in the County, 48.2% of total impoverished households, including 5,406 relieved households and 2,508 inadequate households.

Second category, less labor-capable households, refers to the impoverished households with weak, sick and disabled family members, relatively inadequate labor force and unstable source of income. Among them, families that can reach the out-of-poverty standards in the same year are identified as the PA-capable households (households capable of poverty alleviation), while those who cannot get rid of poverty are identified as the tanking households. There are 3,826 less labor-capable households in the county, accounting for 23.3% of its total, including 3,215 PA-capable households and 611 tanking households.

Third category, labor-incapable households, refers to the impoverished households with all family members incapable of working, or losing capacity of work due to illness, disability and age. Among them, those who are entitled to receive assistance as households in dire poverty are identified as the extremely poor households, while those who are not entitled to are identified as the allowance-subsisted households. There are 4,691 labor-incapable households, accounting for 28.5% of its total, including 3,490 extremely poor households and 1,201 allowance-subsisted households.

However, some households tend to change their household registration to escape the duty of supporting and caring senior parents. In response to this immoral phenomenon, Zhen' an County has put forward a new practice of recording the households with poor elderly people. First, the households with poor elderly people, whose children have a stable income and good living conditions but fail to perform their obligation of supporting parents, will not be registered as poverty-stricken households, or will be removed if registered. Zhen' an County then sends "four teams", First Secretary of the anti-poverty leading group, the working team stationed in villages, the leaders of anti-poverty assistance, and Village Party Branch and Village Committee, to have a door-to-door guidance and education to their sons and daughters. If it doesn't work, the Judicial Department will force them to perform their duties in accordance with the law. They are guided to sign agreements, promising to provide money for the basic life of the elderly.

Second, the households with poor elderly people living alone, whose children are not poor households but have great difficulties in living, will be identified as the "filed households with poor elderly people" to be registered by county-level poverty alleviation bureau after the officials of anti-poverty assistance collect testimonies from 5 households, based on the discussion and deliberation by Village Party Branch and Village Committee, and after the approval of villager representatives. If there is no objection after publicity, they will be entitled to enjoy the benefits of all poverty alleviation policies. As of July 2018, the county has identified 1,128 people of 728 households in total. Besides, the elderly people, who are actually helpless because their sons and daughters have been out of contact for more than two years due to marriage, migrant employment and other reasons, will be directly included into the allowance-subsisted households if meeting the requirements, and being removed if not.

4. 3. 2　Targeted policy and assistance to individuals and households

The " three categories and tailored assistance " policy aims to provide targeted assistance based on the specific analysis of different causes of poverty and different labor conditions for each household. The government has truly dovetailed the policy with its targeted households, and specifically planned the targeted policies in line with the criteria of poverty alleviation. For labor-capable households, industrial development and employment assistance are the key. Integrating long-term industries that require long-term investment and development with short-term industries that yield quick returns, Zhen' an County has proposed employment assistance for each labor-capable household in more than two short-and long-term industries, and have issued industrial support policies on providing rewards and subsidies meanwhile. Zhen' an County has set up special funds for industry awards and subsidies, established industrial bases, and supported the establishment of community poverty alleviation factories. A total of 163 million Yuan of industry awards and subsidies were distributed throughout the year, about 4, 733 hectares of land was transferred to build industrial bases, and 208 poverty alleviation factories (workshops) were set up. Concerning the relieved households, great importance should be attached to consolidating the achievements and improving the quality of poverty alleviation; for households with missing information, it is necessary to record the missing items and fill in the information item by item; poor households with unqualified dilapidated houses will be relocated or renovated. For less labor-capable households, employment assistance is the priority. Zhen' an County has implemented the poverty alleviation policies on the targeted population, including organizing labor skill training for the poor people who long for employment and entrepreneurship, creating public service jobs nearby, arranging stables jobs at poverty alleviation factories (workshops), mobilizing local leading enterprises, professional cooperatives and other major business owners to create jobs and ensure stable employment for the impoverished. For some poverty-stricken households "just relying on assistance", measures to inspire their ambition and motivation to get out of poverty are implemented. For the tanking households, an annual assistance plan is formulated based on the family situation. With clear timelines and emphasis on continuous assistance, people will be lifted out of poverty year by year. For the labor-incapable households, targeted policy assistance is the key. In addition to implementing the basic policy without compromise, the major task is to provide individual support for people living in extreme difficulty, and to guarantee food, clothing, education, medical care, and housing of the households receiving basic living allowances, so as to ensure the poverty alleviation is achieved on schedule. For extremely poor households with the elderly, the disabled, or people under the age of 16, who have no labor capacity, no source of living, no legal provider, supporter, or fosterers, or whose legal obligors fail to perform their duties, implementation of aid and support policy targeted at people in extreme poverty, and providing concentrated and individual support are essential to achieve poverty alleviation. For the households receiving basic living allowances, the major task is to guarantee them the A-type basic living allowance[①] and to overcome weaknesses.

After implementing the " three categories and well-targeted assistance" policy, government leaders, officials and the people in Zhen' an County have been working hard on their duties, establishing a harmonious and stable relationship between the government and the people. Zhen' an County has witnessed the stable development of industries, the rise of people's motivation to poverty alleviation, the improvement of rural outlook, and the steady increase in people's income. On May 7, 2019, the Shaanxi Provincial People's Government approved Zhen' an County to withdraw from the list of poverty-stricken counties. Zhen' an County's poverty alleviation path undoubtedly scores high in poverty alleviation exam.

---

① The basic living allowance is divided into three types of ABC according to poverty measurement. A-type is the long-term targets who have no working ability, no source of income, no legal provider and supporter, and enjoy full subsidization in accordance with the standard.

4. 4   Mutual Aid and Cooperation to Boost Poverty Alleviation in Liuba County

Liuba County in Hanzhong City is one of the key contiguous poverty-stricken counties. In 2014, the poverty headcount ratio was as high as 30. 81% . Since the battle against poverty, Liuba County has focused on the goal of "two no worries (food and clothing) and three guarantee (education, medical care, and housing) ", insisted on institutional innovation, and established a " Poverty Alleviation Cooperative" (hereafter referred to as the "PAC") at village level, which integrates production and operation, village management and public services. 82. 6% of farmer households and 100% of poverty-stricken households in the County are all embedded in the industrial chain, which has greatly promoted agricultural development and farmers' income. In 2018, the whole County was lifted out of poverty.

4. 4. 1   Problems in industry-sustained poverty alleviation

"We have walked almost all the detours", speaking of the development process of the village, Yu Haibing, secretary of the party branch of Shaba Village, Madao Town, Liuba County, smiled bitterly. In the past, there was no industry. Ordinary people couldn't get out of poverty and become better off at their hometown. Most young and middle-aged people went out to work, and left the elderly and children at home. Generally, people had very low income and no stable economic guarantee of life. In order to change this situation, the village party branch mobilized the people to develop industry, but successively encountered setbacks. Around 2010, the people were organized to participate in giant salamander breeding. Soon, the market shrank and the entrepreneurship failed. In 2013, the party branch took the lead in breeding bamboo rat. Due to the lack of technical support, the bamboo rats died of the disease and people lost almost all their money; in 2014, poor families were organized to produce bagged edible fungus. Due to the lack of management experience, people was hired with "a guaranteed salary" and therefore some of them worked without effort, resulting in a poor product quality and a loss of tens of thousands of RMB; later, the village party branch mobilized the people to plant herbs, or to engage in breeding, which all ended up with nothing for various reasons. The poverty situation did not change. Even worse, the village owed more than 200,000 Yuan to the involved people and they complained: we should not follow the leaders because they will lose all our money for whatever they initiate. The village party members and officials were troubled and bewildered because their effort didn't work, nor being appreciated.

This situation is not unique to Shaba Village. In the battle against poverty, Liuba County found that although many villages have funded the project which seemed developing, but before long, most of them would fall into half-dead dilemma. After a review and analysis, it was found that the enthusiasm of local village leaders and poverty alleviation officials doesn't work alone. Loose organization, lack of management and market knowledge will inevitably lead to great loss. How to solve this problem? It is obviously unrealistic to equip each village with a host of energetic and capable leaders. Great efforts must be delivered on the innovation of management and organization so as to organize every single farmer, extend the industrial chain, turn small businesses into great industries, sell products into bigger markets, and achieve poverty alleviation and pursue prosperity. In 2016, based on an in-depth study of the facts across the county, and advanced experience learned from other regions, Liuba County explored the establishment of Poverty Alleviation Cooperatives at village level, and conducted trials in some Towns and villages.

4.4.2   "Overall Framework" of poverty alleviation cooperatives

In the poverty alleviation cooperatives newly established, the village secretary serves as the chairman of board, the village director as deputy chairman, and the first secretary of officials living and working in the village as the chief supervisor. The specific fabric mainly includes three aspects as followed.

4. 4. 2. 1　Economic Shareholding Cooperatives centered on production and mutual assistance

Village Economic Shareholding Cooperatives have undertaken the economic management functions of the poverty alleviation cooperatives through pooling project funds, connecting leading enterprises and ordinary farmers and serving as a main platform for industrial development. From the perspective of equity, the total share includes 15% collective stocks, 15% government stocks, and 70% individual stocks, respectively. The government stocks are held by the County's enterprises of industrial investment & development on poverty alleviation. In terms of the profit allocation, 10% of the annual net profit is used as a provident fund for expanding production, and 5% is used as a public welfare fund, and the remaining 85% is distributed according to the share allocation. In terms of organization structure, each cooperative has a construction project team, an e-commerce service team, a tourism service team, and agricultural production service teams in correspondence to industries of each village, such as edible fungus, seedlings and flowers, and bee breeding production service team. In line with County policies, the construction project team undertakes rural construction projects with investment of less than 300, 000 Yuan and simple engineering technology to boost the cooperative's income at a quick speed. The other teams are mainly responsible for organizing the workforce to work for the development of relevant industries. Each team leader is capable and familiar with the industry. Public villagers, with the poor household holding priority, voluntarily join in and earn their salary by labor-hour. The average daily income per person is about 100 or 200 Yuan. From the perspective of production and operation, the County builds an industrial base in the management architecture of "leading enterprise + cooperative + farmer household", adopts the model of "3 unified and 1 separated" in production and management, namely unified procurement and acceptance, unified audit and settlement, unified transfer payment, and separated management. Taking the edible fungus industry as an example, the "3 unified and 1 separated" refers to the unified production, technical guidance, sales, and separated management. Unified production could solve the problem of low yield of the previous individual production; unified technical standards and complete technical services could solve the technical problems of farmers; unified storage of the mushrooms in the industrial park and on-the-spot purchase arranged by the poverty alleviation cooperatives, could solve the problem of sales at low prices. In addition to paying a certain production cost, farmers only need to do daily management and mushroom picking with relatively low technical requirements and large labor input, so that enterprises, cooperatives and farmers can do its bit for the good of all, forming a joint force to achieve a win-win result. This method was first piloted in Shaba Village. An edible fungus industrial base was launched in Shaba that year which put an end to the loss and generated a profit of 15, 000 Yuan. This year, it is expected to make a profit of at least 200, 000 Yuan.

4. 4. 2. 2   Public service teams centered on public service and mutual assistance

Due to the shortage of fund, platform and /or personnel, various policies and measures for rural governance have not been implemented in most rural areas for a long time. The infrastructure is often "built, used, but uncared". To address these issues, Liuba County has set up "Three teams", "Two sessions", "One rule" and "One house" Mechanism for managing public affairs in the village and truly implementing rural governance. The "Three Teams" are service teams for the sanitation management, water management, and road management. They are mainly responsible for the daily maintenance of the infrastructure and environmental sanitation in the village, also carry out the specific work of rural residential environment improvement, and undertake most of the projects such as "toilet revolution", garbage classification and village appearance promotion. The "Two Sessions" stands for the "Open Meeting" and Village Ethics Review Committee. The "One rule" refers to villager's rules and regulations and the "One House" is the house of virtue. The "Open Meeting" allows all villagers to participate in discussing and deciding on all major issues of the village and the poverty alleviation cooperatives. The Village Ethics Review Committee is a democratic review and evaluation body, regularly reviewing and grading villagers' implementation of rules and regulations, and performance of poverty-stricken households in independent poverty alleviation. Villagers can exchange daily necessities with their grade points at the house of virtue, and the collective dividend at the end of the year is also associated with their grade points.

4. 4. 2. 3   Poverty Alleviation and Mutual Assistance Fund Association centered on mutual financial aid

In supporting rural industries, the lack of funds is a prominent problem encountered by many regions. For this reason, many poor households couldn't participate in the in-depth development of the village industry, let alone start up their own business. To tackle this problem, Liuba County establishes the Poverty Alleviation and Mutual Assistance Fund Association supported by provincial and municipal policies. The County allocated 300, 000 Yuan for each association as the principal base funds. Based on extensive publicity and the principle of voluntariness, Liuba County has mobilized poor households, well-off households, and new business entities to take a stake by share-holding, 1, 000 Yuan per share, at least one per holder. Poor households enjoy the subsidy from supportive organizations, can hold shares free of charge and enjoy full financial discounts. Members can apply for a mutual aid loan of up to 10, 000 Yuan for one year for industrial development. Interest on loans is distributed to stakeholders in proportion to their holdings each year. At the same time, policies are also improved in keeping with the industrial development. For example, in 2018, Shaba Village approved to adjust the loan amount of the Association after a group discussion on the "Open Meeting" to change the loan limit per household from 10,000 Yuan in one year to 3,000 Yuan for three years, which provides greater support and effectiveness for farmer households to expand production.

4. 4. 3   Effect analysis of mutual cooperation in poverty alleviation

Based on the good results achieved in the pilot project, Liuba County has promoted the anti-poverty cooperatives for production and mutual assistance throughout the County. At present, a total of 75 anti-poverty cooperatives have been established in all 75 administrative villages, greatly enhancing the vitality of rural development.

4. 4. 3. 1　Continuous development of agricultural industry

The County has built 128 industrial bases of various types and developed 221 large production households. In 2018, the total sales of agricultural products reached 100 million Yuan. In the first half of 2019, the pig, chicken and edible fungus industries increased by 73%, 66. 7% and 77. 6% year-on-year respectively.

4. 4. 3. 2　Sustained growth of the collective economy

In 2016, there were 36 "shell villages" with weak economy and fiscal deficit in Liuba County, accounting for almost half of the administrative villages; by the end of 2018, collective economic accumulation at village level reached 16. 06 million Yuan, with the richest village exceeding 1 million and the least reaching 50, 000 or 60, 000 Yuan. The "shell village" was completely eliminated.

4. 4. 3. 3　Progressive increase of farmers' income

In 2018, by industrial development, poverty alleviation cooperatives, industrial trusteeship, land transfer, and dividends in the county, the total income of poverty-stricken households exceeded 20 million Yuan, and the average household income was nearly 20, 000 Yuan. The poverty headcount ratio reduced from 10. 34% in 2016 to 1. 08% in 2018.

4. 4. 3. 4　Constant improvement of the rural outlook

Today, in Liuba, the rural roads are paved, the garbage on the roadside is picked up, and the broken water pipes in any household will be repaired just through a phone call. Over 200 advanced role models who are self-independent in poverty alleviation have emerged, and more than 300 exemplary deeds have been publicized on theHonor List. The rural outlook continues to improve with people's happiness and sense of gains increasingly enhanced.

4. 4. 4　Reflections

4. 4. 4. 1　Cementing the party's leadership in rural areas

The rural grass-roots Party organizations are the basis of all work.

No matter how the new institutions and forms are innovated, the party's leadership will never waver. Liuba County clearly stipulates relevant articles that the poverty alleviation cooperative is a collective cooperative led by the village party branch, and the secretary of the village party branch shall serve as the chairman. By integrating the work for economic development, rural governance, and public service into the anti-poverty cooperative under the leadership of the party branch, a closer and practical connection between the party governance and the normal production and life of the general public has been established. In addition, the party's cohesive force, appeal, and influence have been significantly promoted and its core leadership given full play.

4. 4. 4. 2   Fully respect the pioneering spirit of the grassroots

The grassroots are the base of practice, and people are the most creative. In poverty alleviation and rural revitalization, we must further stimulate the vitality of the grassroots, encourage local leaders to explore, innovate and dare to take the tests, and allow more "indigenous methods" and good experience to be full played to guide local practice. For deviations and mistakes that emerge in the exploration, we should be tolerant to avoid frustrating local officials and people while actively correct timely; for some systems and institutions that lag behind the development, we must modify and innovate them timely, making more innovative measures a powerful driving force of development.

4. 4. 4. 3   Establishing a working system with integrated functions and clarified responsibilities

At present, the diversification of investment subjects and investment forces is common in rural development. To advance poverty alleviation and realize rural revitalization, it is necessary to coordinate all forces for them to do its bit for the good of all, but also to be integrated and mutually cooperated for solidified outcome. Through the poverty alleviation cooperatives, Liuba County has integrated the functions of village party branches, village committees, poverty alleviation teams and other forces, simplified some old links in rural governance, improved rural self-development capabilities, and meanwhile, rationally clarified the power and responsibility among various subjects. Necessary process must be completed and some accounts must be separated to avoid problems such as buck-passing and entanglement.

4. 4. 4. 4   Forming an effective supervision system

To make leaders and officials play their parts, political empowerment is necessary; to guarantee a fair and transparent governance, an effective supervision is required. Liuba County has empowered the village leaders via the poverty alleviation cooperative, and enforced constraints at the same time: the first secretary serves as the chief supervisor of the poverty alleviation cooperative and the commissioner for public integrity; the financial management of the poverty alleviation cooperative at Town level is outsourced to accounting firms, and the project audit of the poverty alleviation cooperative is conducted by external audit firms hired by the County Audit Bureau; leading officials of the party branch, the village committee, and the poverty alleviation cooperative are not allowed to run business in poverty alleviation cooperative projects, nor to get paid in project implementation by leasing large machinery. Such approaches give full play to the supervising systems and guide the masses and officials to devote themselves to poverty alleviation and social development.

Chapter 5

Sustainable Development of Poverty-stricken Mountainous Regions through Ecological Construction

On August 24, 2005, Xi Jinping, then Secretary of the Zhejiang Provincial CPC Committee, put forward that "the harmony between man and nature or between economy and society we strive for can be expounded as our desire for both the lush mountains ecologically and gold mountains (invaluable assets) economically. "[1] The sustainable development of poverty-stricken mountainous regions like Qinling-Bashan mountainous as both the poverty-stricken region and the key eco-functional region relies heavily on attending and preserving the ecological environment. In the poverty elimination, localities here made utmost use of their ecological resources and exert respective ecological advantages in line with the local conditions, promoted the sustainable development of regional economy through ecological protection and management, and embarked their unique ways in "ecology-sustained poverty alleviation".

5.1　Ecology Construction and Development Driven by Poverty Alleviation in Mountainous Regions of Shangluo City

Poverty alleviation via eco-compensation is a component of the five special poverty alleviation strategies package issued by the Central Government. Most of the contiguous poverty-stricken areas are located in

---

[1]　Xi Jinping, *Essay Collection along Zhijiang*, Hangzhou: Zhejiang People's Publishing House, 2007, p. 153.

mountainous regions where there display relatively fragile ecological environment and bear important ecological functions. It is therefore of vital importance to coordinate ecological construction and poverty alleviation and to rationally utilize the ecological resources for lifting the population out of poverty in contiguous and concentrated poverty-stricken areas. [1] Since the 18th National Congress of the Communist Party of China, all people and governments in Shangluo have been learning and following Xi Jinping thought on ecological civilization, practicing the green development concept of "lucid water and lush mountains as gold and silver mountains, or literally, sound ecology as the invaluable assets", oriented ecological construction at poverty alleviation and took ecological building as the main measures for poverty alleviation. The projects including grain for green, featured forestry industries, ecological compensation, and ecological management posts setting, etc., were comprehensively implemented and the road for poverty alleviation sustained by ecology construction and green development was blazed out.

5.1.1　Prompt provision of subsidies following ecological poverty alleviation policies

As is stated by General Secretary Xi Jinping, poverty alleviation can be attained through the ecological environment preservation and management in regions with fragile living conditions to be protected and restored for the significant ecosystem. Accordingly, Shangluo launched a series of policies on ecological construction to assist the poverty alleviation guided by principles of scientific planning, in-site guidance, preferable support and anti-poverty orientation.

5.1.1.1　Grain for Green Project

Fulfilling the principle of "most-probable satisfaction over the

---

① Poverty alleviation by ecological compensation means that ecologically-benefited areas provide compensation in forms of funds, projects, and talents to motivate areas providing ecological value in pollution and damage reduction. The compensation can help get rid of poverty by expanding income sources for farmers and herdsmen.

applied quota", Shangluo prioritized poor counties, poor Township or sub-districts, poor villages (communities) and poor households in project quantity distribution, i. e. , the county government will give priority and directly assign in full the plan and quantity to the villages and households when the rural poor population applied for the grain for green project. After implementing the project of returning farmland to forest, the subsidy funds are promptly provided in accordance with the relevant cashing policy after the project being assessed and approved by the municipal and county forestry administrative departments and other agencies. In 2017, the project farmers received a de-farming cash subsidies of 301. 2 million Yuan and afforestation and seedling subsidies of 753 million Yuan. The new round of Grain for Green (returning farmland to forest or grassland) Project organized and implemented greatly increased the forest area and the vegetation coverage and effectively improved the ecological environment. As of September 2018, Luonan County of Shangluo actively implemented the Grain for Green Project and put the policy of returning farmland to forests into actual effects: 1, 2407. 8 Mu (about 828 ha) of farmland of poor villages has been returned to woodland; 2. 09 million Yuan of subsidy been offered, 13, 400 people from 3, 368 households benefited, average annual income per household increased by 620. 5 Yuan, and the per capita annual income increased by 156 Yuan. [①] At the same time, the afforestation construction teams organized in project implementation received the practical training on forestry technology, expanded the source of household income and improved their labor capacity as well. Li Chunwen, a poor villager of group 2 of Zhongcun Village, Qingtongguan Town in Zhen'an County, has a family of 6 and 22 Mu (about 1. 5 ha) of hillside farmland. Before the project, his family used to live on the grains cultivation on large area however with little yield, and the family annual income was only a bit up 2, 000 Yuan deducting the cost on seeds and fertilizers. The ecology-sustained poverty alleviation project brought humongous changes to his family. In 2017, Li was enrolled into the de-farming and afforestation construction team set up by Zhen'an County

---

① "Five Measures of Luonan to Promote Ecology-sustained Poverty Alleviation", 2018-09-04, http://www. shangluo. gov. cn/info/1057/77945. htm.

and trained on practical techniques such as pruning, planting, formula fertilization, pest control, etc. by forestry experts and technical backbones. Currently, Li Chunwen increased his income by 6,000 Yuan through planting and seedlings nursing in the spring and autumn seasons. Besides, he also changed the cultivation of grains to tobacco on nearly 20 Mu (about 1.4 ha) of farmland, increasing an estimated net income of 30,000 Yuan.[1] In September 2016, Shangluo Municipal Office of Grain for Green Project was jointly approved as National Model Agency for Greening Work by the National Forestation Commission, the Ministry of Human Resources and Social Security and the State Forestry Administration.

5.1.1.2　Ecological compensation provision

To carry out ecological protection and restoration in rural areas and improve the function and stability of rural natural ecosystems, Shangluo constantly refines the ecological compensation mechanism, levels up the scientific use of natural resources and lifts up the comprehensive benefits of ecology preservation and restoration. Programs such as natural forest resource protection and key protective forests in Shangluo actively upgrade forest quality and accelerates the construction of the ecological security barrier for the whole city. The lands unsuitable for farming or unused were fully reserved for afforestation to increase forest vegetation. From 2009 to 2015, the area for public welfare forests subsided by central and provincial governments steadily increased from 2.644 million Mu (about 176, 267 ha) to 7.9021 million Mu (about 526,807 ha) with 6.4801 million Mu (about 432,007 ha) subsided by central government and 1.422 million Mu (about 948 thousand ha) by provincial government, totaling a compensation fund of 420,908,700 Yuan cashed to the rural households. Beneficiaries are 713,000 people of 171,000 households, 4315 villager groups, 781 villages, 81town or sub-districts, 6 counties and 1 district in Shangluo City, among them are 64,000 poor households and 272,000 poor people who received a per capita

---

①　"Poverty Alleviation by Forestry Ecological Projects Benefited Households in Zhen'an County, Shangluo City", *Shangluo Daily*, 2018-11-15.

compensation of 150 Yuan in 2015. [1] Jin Chuanan, a poor villager in Duanwan Village, Wuguanzhen Town of Danfeng County, received a subsidy of 1, 587 Yuan for returning farmland to forest in 2017 and earned more than 10,000 Yuan for mowing lacquer the same year, easily alleviating from poverty by utilizing forestry and ecological resources. The implementation of ecological compensation increased the income of the poor to a certain extent, secured their fixed income, protected the ecological environment and forged ahead an ecological compensation system oriented by government subsidy and supplemented by a variety of market-based compensation mechanisms to assist poverty alleviation.

5. 1. 1. 3　Job positions set for ecology management

In Luonan County, the selection and employment plan of ecological forest rangers was formulated and implemented in line with the actual situation of the county and the working scheme of "management by the county, construction in the towns, contract with the stations, and work in villages". From 2017 to the end of July 2018, 396 eco-forest rangers from the registered impoverished population were selected, hired and subsided 600 Yuan monthly. The total pay to 1, 495 ecological forest rangers of 396 households reached 4. 5144 million Yuan, increasing the annual household income by 7, 200 Yuan and annual per capita income by 1, 907. 2 Yuan. [2] To promote scientific management of ecological forest protection posts, each Town or sub-district set up an afforestation and fire brigade of 30 members from poor population able to work to bear duties like forest fire fighting and key afforestation projects in Township jurisdictions through government procurement of services. The per capita annual salary is 5, 000 Yuan and the measure directly lifted 3, 000 people out of poverty. [3] Zhashui County from 2018 on has been formulating a mind-map of "training each forest ranger to master the management technology for one kind of forest and fruit, to successfully

---

① "Research Report on Ecology-sustained Poverty Alleviation by Shangluo Forestry Bureau", 2016-07-27, http: //www. slzxw. gov. cn/html/2016/hyzt_0727/1118. html.

② Yao Bochao, Lu Genliang, "Five Measures of Luonan to Promote Ecology-sustained Poverty Alleviation", 2018-09-04, Http://www. shangluo. gov. cn/info/1057/77945. htm.

③ "Investigation Report on Ecolog-sustained Poverty Alleviation by Shangluo Forestry Bureau", 2016-07-27, http: //www. slzxw. gov. cn/html/2016/hyzt_0727/1118. html.

manage one Mu (about 667 m^2) of economic forest and to earn an annual income of 10, 000 Yuan". The technical staff of Zhashui Forestry and Featured Products Industrial Development Center and Zhashui Forestry Station offered technical training to forest rangers in various Towns and villages, illustrated theories in class and practiced in the woodland, assessed the on-site operations of each ranger to ensure their command of management technology on at least one branch of forest and fruit. After training, 798 rangers mastered management techniques for both chestnut and walnut, and 165 rangers grew into the forestry technology leader of their village groups owing to their techniques for beekeeping, seedling nursery, herbs farming, fungus and mushroom pocketed cultivation and mixed fruits tree pruning and management. [1] Zhang Hongxue, a poor farmer with a disabled wife from Xiwan Village, Jinsixia Town of Shangnan County, had low income and severe poverty status. After being selected and trained to be a forest ranger by ecological poverty alleviation project, he was paid a monthly subsidy of 300 Yuan (400 Yuan per month since 2018) and his living conditions have improved significantly. According to him, "the government policy really did me good by offering me the post of a ranger, which paid me every month and made it possible for me to take care of my family members while working nearby. " The setting of ecological management posts, as an important measure in poverty alleviation assisted by green development, lifted some poor population out of poverty quickly, guaranteed their sustainable livelihoods, and accelerated the pace of reducing poverty and becoming rich.

5. 1. 2　Development of green industry to increase the farmers' income

Since 2012, Shangluo has highlighted the green development course, adhered to the development of green industries, scenery cities and landscape countryside, and embarked a green road to poverty alleviation based on the ecological advantages.

---

[1]　"860 ranger families in Zhashui Lifted out of Poverty within the Year", 2019-10-09, http: // www. shangluo. gov. cn/info/1057/84816. htm.

5. 1. 2. 1   Characteristic economic forestry industry

Shangluo vigorously push forward characteristic economic forest industries in implementing the Grain for Green Project. Based on scientific planning suitable plants in line with local land conditions while fully respecting the willingness of farmers, cash forests of walnut, chestnut, peony, pepper, Huashan pine and others were planted to increase the farmers' income in constructing the Grain for Green Project and to sustain the poverty alleviation and enriching of impoverished population. The "Three Leading Entities and One System Innovation" Development Model (leading entities: leading enterprises, leading cooperatives and leading household; one system: Poverty alleviation through financial inclusion) and "Three Transfer" Reform (Three transfers: transfer resources into assets, transfer capital into shares, transfer farmers into shareholders) were further explored and implemented to effectively promote forestry industrialization, fund capitalization, targeted poverty alleviation and continuously increase the income of poor households. [1] Shangluo also developed its traditional forest and fruit industries as long-term poverty-alleviation scheme. The Wulongshan Walnut Processing Plant with an annual processing capacity of 150 tons of dried walnuts was established in Rencun village, Jinlingsi Town of Shangzhou district to mainly produce jujube-walnuts snacks, fine walnuts and fried salty walnuts. The walnut products are sold in supermarkets and specialty stores and the profits were increased by about 30% than mere selling of raw walnuts. By joining walnut cooperatives for farmers who have transferred walnut woodlands or poor households with labor capacity and organizing professional teams for technology, farming and processing, 95% of poor households in the village got rid of poverty relying on the walnut industry. Based on the natural resource advantages of Mangling Mountains, Yuling Township government of Danfeng County led the local people in setting up a Tzxus Chinensis industrial base of 12, 000 Mu (about 800 ha) in Liangchahe village for poverty alleviation where 49 yew seedling greenhouses were built, 1. 5 million yew trees

---

① Dang Liang, "New Achievements of Ecology-sustained Poverty Alleviation in Zhashui", 2020-01-06, http: //www. shangluo. gov. cn/info/1057/86465. htm.

planted, and a professional cooperative with 150 members including 70 poor households established to lead the poor to increase their income.

5. 1. 2. 2   Characteristic agricultural industrial system

In recent years, supported by local characteristic agriculture, Shangluo focused on industry-sustained poverty alleviation mainstream and followed the development strategy of "large industries to greatly drive forward massive poverty alleviation" in building the eco-agriculture demonstration city in Qinling regions and developing characteristic modern agriculture. The "4 + X" agricultural anti-poverty industrial system in fungus, medicines, fruits, and livestock have been formed, and 147 leading companies such as Senfo, Junwei, and Huamao have been nurtured. Through contract farming agreement, the fungus and walnuts produced by poor households are inspected and purchased by the poverty alleviation corporations and sold to large enterprises such as Eastern Airlines and China Railway Group, ensuring the stable sales of agricultural products of poor households and the quality of goods procured by enterprises. 186 million bags of edible fungus were cultivated in Shangluo in 2018 and the practitioners of this industry involved more than 100,000 people and 50,000 households. The average income of mushroom farmers in the main production areas exceeded 20,000 Yuan and the per capita income reached 5, 000 Yuan. 20 professional cooperatives for edible fungi farmers were organized, 4 edible fungus development and processing enterprises established, 11 fungus production plants built, 23 edible fungus materials and machinery stores opened, and more than 1, 500 large edible fungus purchase and sales households formed. In the same period, Shangluo has farmed 3. 36 million Mu (about 224 thousand ha) of walnuts, 2. 689 million Mu (about 179, 266 ha) of chestnuts, 2. 0854 million Mu (about 139, 027 ha) of Chinese medicinal herbs, 2. 883 million live pigs and 39. 934 million poultry. The output of fungi, fruits and herb industries rank first in Shaanxi Province and a number of county-specific anti-poverty industries in chestnut, tea, konjac, sericulture, and kiwi emerged intensively in Shangluo.

5. 1. 2. 3   Photovoltaic power generation project for environmental-friendly income

As one of the Ten Targeted Poverty Alleviation Projects approved by the State Council Poverty Alleviation Office in 2015, Photovoltaic power generation project constructs household and village-level power stations or larger-scale centralized power stations in areas with plentiful sunshine, [1] farmers and the impoverished population can use the electricity themselves and sell the surplus to the national power grid to add a stable income to their revenue. Since 2016, the photovoltaic power generation industry vigorously developed in Shangluo and the provincial-level PV subsidy in 2017 reached 6. 6 million Yuan and the cumulative power capacity of photovoltaic generation projects installed and under construction exceeded 385 Megawatt. All poor villages and poor households in 5 counties (districts) have been fully covered by the photovoltaic industry now and the development of the photovoltaic generation industry not only provides policy support for leading all people to practice green development and protect green ecology, but also contributes to the energy structure upgrading and beautiful countryside construction. Wuzhuang village of Yangyuhe Town, Shangzhou District actively launched the distributed photovoltaic roofs and increased the income of poor household through "photovoltaic + Chinese herbs" and "photovoltaic + edible fungi" and other integrated development approaches.

5. 1. 3   Eco-tourism industry by building "Lucid Water and Lush Mountains" scenery

Development modes for scenery cities, green industries and landscape countryside proceed thoroughly in Shangluo City. Led by green development philosophy, Shangluo is propelling the featured All-for-toursim Industry, breaking the natural resources restrictions of "80% mountains + 10% water + 10% farmland", building beautiful countryside where people and villages resident in scenic nature

---

[1] "Opinions on the Implementation of Poverty Alleviation by Photovoltaic Power Generation", *NDRC Energy*, No. 621, 2016.

environments, and developing itself the picturesque backyard garden of Xi'an and top holidaying and tourists destination in Qinling Mountains.

5.1.3.1   Characteristic towns construction

Taking tourism as an important engine to promote economic and social development, Shangluo strives to build the "Leisure Capital in Qinling and Industry and New City along Silk Road". With "all-for-tourism" as a strategic pillar industry, Shangluo successfully brought forth innovated high-quality scenic spots of Jinsixia Canyon, Tianzhu Mountain, Niubeiliang Forest Park and Muwangshan Park, created a number of the national beautiful leisure villages in mountains and waters and characteristic thematic Towns like Beikuanping Sports Town in Shangzhou District, Music Town in Luonan County, Tea Town in Shangnan County and other characteristic cultural and tourism towns, and built assembles of scenic, cozy and sentimental boutique home-stays, all which constituted colorful and comprehensive tourism product and evolved into top destinations for the original eco-tourism in Qinling. Meanwhile, through integrating the tourist attractions construction with the resettlement of rural residents, relocated farmers were employed as their dreamed staff by the tourism spots and enjoyed the economic benefits of the natural ecology.

5.1.3.2   Health-care and tourism industries environment building

In active response to the call for Healthy China Initiative and fully optimizing "Health for All" development opportunity, Shangluo profoundly merged the "Tourism and Healthcare" industries, developed healthcare-tourism industries like the elderly nursing and leisure health preservation in scenic spots of Jinsixia Canyon in Shangnan, Tianzhu mountain in Shanyang, Muwangshan park in Zhen'an and Niubeiliang forest park in Zhashui, and initially forged a standardized healthcare-tourism demonstration zone with distinctive regional characteristics. At the same time, Shangluo actively carried out special tourism, leisure and fitness programs, created a number of outdoor sports and tourism routes, and formed a fitness and leisure service system matched with tourism, rehabilitation, catering and other supporting facilities, among which are popular tourists destinations like Chinese herbs specimen garden and

Chinese herbal medicine ornamental gardens in Shangnan County, Shima Peony Sightseeing Garden in Shanyang County and Manchuanguan Modern Agriculture Demonstration Garden in Shanyang County. In all, Shangluo embarked an anti-poverty road through green development of its ecological advantages.

5.2   Win-win Interaction Between Eco-environment Protection and Poverty Alleviation in Yinghu Town of Hanbin District

Since 2016, Yinghu Town of Hanbin District, Ankang City, Shaanxi Province has worked to implement the development philosophy of "lucid water and lush mountains are invaluable assets like mountains of gold", blended economy with ecology and promoted industrial transformation and upgrading with eco-environmental protection. Such an endeavor continuously improved the ecological environment and the income of the public steadily, and concluded a win-win situation between eco-environment protection and poverty alleviation.

5.2.1   Industrial transformation driven by green development

In the 1980s and 1990s, to develop hydropower industry, Huoshiyan Hydropower Station was launched 18 kilometers west of the Ankang city. The dam was finished in 1990 as an artificial water body with an area of 77 square kilometers and capacity of 2.6 billion cubic meters, hence the current Yinghu Lake.

The dam sank a large amount of surrounding farmland and posed new challenge to the life of the residents who have lost the land around the reservoir area. Following the traditional Chinese concept of "making a living on the local natural blessings", since 2000, residents around were advocated to engage in aquaculture industry in the reservoir water. The fishing technology developed from the ecological culture to the cage farming and 34,000 fish cages were cultivated in all the lake and 23,000 in Yinghu Town alone by 2016, making fisheries the main source of income for localities.

However, with the continuous expansion of scale, new problems emerged: too much bait feeding increased the nitrogen and phosphorus concentration in Yinghu Lake excessively, the water body was more and more severely entrophicated and heavily polluted, being listed in the key cases for supervision and rectification by both the central and provincial government. How could the desire for development and meaning of environment protection be appropriately balanced? The CPC committees and government at municipal and district levels finally are determined to adjust the industrial development ideas and launched the "Industry-ashore" project in accordance with the concept of green development and environmental protection, transforming main industries from fisheries to others ashore. By the end of April 2018, 30, 000 aquaculture cages and management houses of more than 500 households and nearly 2, 000 people of Yinghu Town were completely demolished and 900 thousand kg of fish sold in just 5 months, reversing water quality in the reservoir to the national standard.

What industry to develop to secure the household income after quitting fish farming? What measure to take for poverty alleviation? With the instruction and assistance from the municipal and district governments, the "Three Transfers" (Three transfers: transfer resources into assets, capital into shares, farmers into shareholders) development model was proposed and launched in Qiaoxing village of the core region of Yinghu to spawn and breed new industrial forms, and effectively solved the problems in "demolishing the unsuitable industry, securing the present order and income, and striving for prosperity".

5. 2. 2   Transformation to green circular quality development

The consequent major problem encountered by Yinghu Town is to select the right alternative industry and solve the production and living difficulties of the people in the reservoir area as quickly as possible. Based on in-depth investigation and deliberation, both the traditional industries with solid foundations like planting, breeding, tourism, etc. and the emerging industries with quick benefits like new community factories and e-commerce were taken as options for industry transformation under the guidance of the new concept in pursuit of green, circular and high-quality development.

5. 2. 2. 1　Transfer from waters to mountains

After the cages were demolished and fish farming were banned in the lake, farmers were encouraged to leave the water for the forests for new forms of industries. One transformation is to develop new leading industries. Qiaoxing villagers originally had the tradition of tea planting in their back mountains. To expand the scale of planting and set up the leading industry, the villagers transformed the original tea garden into standardized tea plantation of 850 Mu (about 57 ha) and built new tea plantation of more than 2, 000 Mu (about 134 ha). 4 tea cooperatives were reorganized based on the former seven fish farming cooperatives and 29 poor households joined in. Tang Hanbang, a leading farmer who previously operated a fisheries cooperative with 8 shareholders, invested all the 5 million Yuan of dismantlement compensation to develop 500 Mu (about 34 ha) of tea plantation in the back mountains which can be harvested for benefits next year after their " fishery parks " were dismantled and all 1, 360 cages removed in May 2018. The second transformation is to develop characteristic agricultural industries. In consideration of the loquat cultivation tradition in Yinghu and the position of Qinquang Loquat as national geographical product, Yinghu Town takes Qingquan village as the leading entity in championing farmers to plant grapefruit, loquat, bayberry, citrus and other fresh fruits on the hillside land. The "10-thousand-Mu (about 667 ha) fresh fruit base around the lake" was created and 13 surrounding villages were motivated to vigorously develop modern agriculture with characteristics. Ai Jiahong of Qiaoxing village originally planted only 5 Mu (about 0. 3 ha) of loquat. After the fish cages were dismantled, he expanded his loquat garden to 150 Mu (about 10 ha) through land transfer and earned an income of 500, 000 Yuan this year. The third transformation is to develop a green recycling industry. Characteristic farming industries like raising chicken and pigs in forests are vigorously promoted for a recycling development: chickens under the tea tree cleaned the insects and weeds and provided quality manure fertilizer to the tea tree; pigs fed by weeds in the forests satisfied the high-quality pork demand of the villagers and local household agritainment consumption and pig manure be returned directly to the forest field. Till now, 31,500 Mu (about 2100 ha) of tea garden, 10,000 Mu (about 667 ha) of fresh fruit orchard, 8,000 Mu (about 534 ha) of walnuts forest, and 1,000 Mu (about 66.7 ha) of vegetables base from the foot to the top of the mountain of various altitude in the Yinghu reservoir area are cultivated, forming an ecological and hierarchical layout of characteristics and efficient agricultural industry in the mountains.

5.2.2.2   Transfer from farming to producing industries

Based on the current situation and guided by the long-term vision, industries like agro-products processing and community factories were synchronically strengthened while consolidating farming industry to continuously optimize the income structure and expand income sources of the local people. First move is to enhance deep processing of special agricultural products. The three agricultural products processing enterprises in Qiaoxing village signed farming and sales contracts on potatoes and sweet potatoes with more than 120 villagers and 34 poor households around and processed the raw produce into starch and vermicell and added their value. The collective entity of Yingtian Walnut Processing Plant was established in Tianzhushan village to improve the output value and benefit of nearly 6,000 Mu (about 400 ha) of walnuts trees. The processed products like walnut oil, walnut-in-jujube snacks extended the industry chain and constantly increased the income of farmers. The second is to build new community factories. Championed by the overall community factories development scheme throughout Ankang city, Qiaoxing village built a plush toy factory facilitated with canteens, nurseries, and elderly homes and employed more than 120 women, elderly and other weak laborers in the community factory. Currently, 4 community factories in Yinghu Town employed a total of more than 400 people with an average salary of about 2,000 Yuan and an optimum of 6,000 Yuan monthly. The third is to set posts for public benefits. Some older fishermen in the Town were employed as forest and river rangers with a total of 600 posts altogether in the Town to patrol mountains and lakes on regular duties and transferred their job from "fish farming" to "mountains and water protection". The fourth is train farmers vocational skills. The free skill training on forest and fruit tree cultivation, tea management, catering and cooking, civilized etiquette, etc. were held to improve the capacity for employment and prosperity-pursuing of villagers in the reservoir area. Sun Yang, a paralyzed and disabled villager in Qingquan village, also an internet celebrity and spokesperson for the e-commerce platform of Hanbin district, operated an online loquat store after learning e-commerce himself actively. He manipulated chopstick by his teeth to key in the computer board to sell the loquat of his own and the neighbourhood villagers. "Qingquan loquat" sales boomed because of his image and effort and he himself earned an annual income of more than 200,000 Yuan.

5. 2. 2. 3　Transfer from fishing to tourism industries

As the largest artificial freshwater lake in the northwest region, Yinghu lake has its unique strength not in "fishing" but in "touring" which can transfer the lucid lake into "mountains of gold". Therefore, Yinghu Town adjusted its industry orientation, optimized and integrated scenery resources, and promoted the upgrading of its tourism industry. One of the measures is to introduce leading enterprises. Ankang Cultural Tourism Company jointly set up by Ankang Municipal Government and Shaanxi Cultural Investment Group re-framed and re-built the integrated resources of Yinghu scenic spot, and distributed dividends to the poverty-stricken households and villages with a sum of separated funds. For example, Qiaoxing village in the core scenic area was rationed a collective share of 480,000 Yuan and 126 poor households a per capita share of 20,000 Yuan with a guaranteed dividend of 8% per year. The company also hired a third-party organization to evaluate the original shipping company and private vessels for unified purchase, management and operation. Cao Wenlong, a villager in Qiaoxing Village, received a compensation of 60,000 Yuan for his small boat and 240,000 Yuan for the big boat, as well as a monthly income of 4,000 Yuan for being employed to drive the houseboats. The second move is the establishment of industrial alliances. The individual vendors and self-employed households were joined in the Yinghu Scenic Spot Industry Alliances. Tang Ruibang, the Party Secretary of Qiaoxing village, initiated a catering company and joined 9 other agritainment households to set up an industrial alliance with the unified style, decoration, pricing, ingredients, reception and main serving of "Yinghu Fish Banquet", earning an average annual net profit of over 300, 000 Yuan per household. The third is to build distinctive brands. "Tangjialianzi" fishery cultural tourism in Qiaoxing village was jointly forged by Yinghu Lake Administrative Committee and Ankang Cultural Tourism Company, three major zones for rural experiencing, ecological farming and comprehensive services been initially created and rural tourism products such as countryside leisure, fisher customs, eco-agricultural sightseeing, flavored catering, and characteristic home-stays been developed. Completion of the project will reinforce the endogenous development of Qiaoxing village and expand the income-increasing channels of local people.

5. 2. 3   Enlightenment of Success in Eco-environment Protection and Poverty Alleviation

The "Three Transfers (transfer resources into assets, capital into shares, farmers into shareholders)" Reform in Yinghu Town checked by problems and targets have concluded initial results in industry transformation so far. The right transformation navigation, wise successive industry selection and disruptive breakthrough of the localities set a fine model for eco-environmental protection and industrial transformation in Shaanxi Province. The following are the enlightenment their success brings:

First, transformation predicts the trends of development. "Gold mountains are what we desire for, same is lucid water and lush mountains", "Protecting and improving the ecological environment is securing and increasing productivity" and other remarks by President Xi Jinping are not only the insightful judgement concluded in long-term practice, also the basic norms to be resolutely followed and implemented in the agricultural industry development. The outdated agricultural industry based on extensive consumption of natural resources input and huge investment in the long run has led to the over-exploitation of agricultural resources and the degradation and fragility of ecological environment. The "red lights" warning of resources and environment checked an inevitable agricultural development trend and orientation to adjust the industrial structure toward green and circular development and to manage the win-win interaction between ecological protection and industrial development for high-quality development.

Second, transformation deserves courage and resolution. Transformation promises opportunities while brings with pains. It is really difficult to give up anything that took much effort to achieve in the past. No exception to Yinghu Town, neither the local government nor the general public can accept for a while abandoning totally the fishery industry that has been working as the main source of income of the local leading industries and the local households for many years. However, most rebirth rise up in ashes and thorough changes are needed to address severe adversity. With this consensus, more than 30, 000 cages were dismantled, all people living in the reservoir area properly resettled within 5 months and no case of petition appealed. The firm determination and resolved implementation are accompanied by courageous commitment, solid transformation and meticulous work, driven by reforms and institutional innovation and secured by enterprising party branches and the leading party members.

Last, transformation shall navigate appropriate orientation in line with local conditions. Lucid water and lush mountains are natural and ecological reserves, as well the social and economic fortunes. Most people live on the natural environment while the key is on what manner to live. In detail, mountains where people reside can be applied for both traditional crop and livestock farming and modern characteristic agriculture with the latter adding the income by managing tea and fruits orchards, developing deep processing of the fresh produce to increase the additional value of products. Water body gives life to both fishing or boating industries with the latter enriching tourism resources, promoting rural traveling and blending the agricultural, production and tertiary industries. Besides, positions for public welfare and community factories are constructed to prosper the life of villagers in multiple channels. It is reflective enlightenment that Yinghu Town developed a "characteristic economy" based on its local conditions, amplified the "beautiful economy" supported by natural advantages, scientifically transferred the ecological value of lucid water and lush mountains into "gold mountains of invaluable assets", and harvested overwhelming success in ecological preservation, economic profit and social progress.

5. 3   Turning Ecological Strength into Invaluable Assets through Implementing " Ecological Plus " Anti-poverty Initiatives in Ningshan County

Ningshan of Ankang City in Shaanxi Province, is a poverty-stricken county with the characteristics forest zone, ecological function, reservoir area to supplement Weihe River from Hanjiang River, and water source area of the middle line of South-to-North water diversion project, etc. With a total area of 367, 800 hectares, Ningshan administrates 12 communities and 68 villages, 11 Towns, a total population of 74, 000 including about 60, 000 farmers. Since 2016, Ningshan County has been actively implementing "Two Mountains Theory" by General Secretary Xi Jinping to advance the green and renewable development model for pursuing other areas based on their ecological resources of 90. 2% forest coverage. Through the deep integration of ecological construction and poverty alleviation, Ningshan County explored the "Ecological Plus" strategy to get rid of poverty, turning the lucid waters and lush mountains into "gold mountains" of the poor households and secure the general public with "gold bowl" by activating and releasing ecological bonuses. By now, the new "Ecological Plus" model has been a powerful drive to promote the project of poverty alleviation and rural revitalization. Among the registered 7, 240 low-income families in 2018, 73. 4%, or about 5, 300 families were covered by the ecological poverty alleviation policy. In 2019, 81. 5%, about 5, 800 families, of the registered low-income families were lifted out of poverty by the ecological construction. At the same time, 46. 79% of the low-income families received the ecological financial allowances on poverty alleviation in 2019 and Ningshan County fully shake off poverty in February, 2020.

5. 3. 1   Optimization of Ecology plus Industry to enrich the farmers

Ningshan County achieved win-win situation between ecology and industry and shared prosperity between farming and farmers, and they vigorously promoted the development of ecological forestry, featured agriculture and leisure agriculture and took the implementation of industrial poverty alleviation as the fundamental solution to lead the whole population out of poverty and increase their income. According to the actual forestry situation and features, they actively constructed five forestry industry bases for nuts (Chinese chestnuts and walnuts), forest tours, forest medicine herbs (edible mushrooms), breeding and cultivation, flowers and seeding plants. They also introduced and constructed processing lines on walnut oil and Chinese chestnuts to extend the industry chain and build a solid foundation to increase the masses' income following the idea that the first, second and third industry should develop in an integrated way. Ningshan County had built high-standard walnut orchards of 122, 100 Mu (about 8, 140 hectares), Chinese chestnut orchards of 210, 000 Mu (about 14, 010 hectares). Besides, they cultivated 1, 800 musk deer and sika deer and forest medicine herbs like gastrodia elata and grifola of 146, 600 Mu (about 9, 780 hectares). In 2019, Ningshan County had constructed 44 poverty alleviation exemplary bases, developed characteristic economic forest of 72, 000 Mu (about 4, 800 hectares), cultivated forest mushrooms of 14, 800 Mu (about 990 hectares), planted about 5, 200, 000 bags of edible mushrooms with recyclable wastes, bred 542, 000 livestock animals, kept 15, 000 boxes of bees and added 200 musk deer and sika deer into the deer industry. As for flowers and trees planting, 5, 500 Mu (about 370 hectares) of golden chrysanthemums, oil sunflowers, lacquer trees, kiwi fruits, Sichuan peppers and tea trees were farmed. What's more, in synergetic development model of "the enterprises + the agricultural parks + the cooperatives + the farmers", new business entities including 6 leading enterprises at the city level, 28 modern agricultural areas and 219 cooperatives were bred up in Ningshan County. The three leading enterprises continue to grow stronger and one of them is acknowledged as the forestry economy demonstration base at the national level. Relying on the "Three-Transfer" reform, Ningshan County inset the low-income people into the industrial chain, guaranteeing their steady income increase by taking part in the cooperatives production, shareholding, land transfer, contract farming, getting employed, etc. All the walnut, Chinese medicine herbs and edible mushroom planting are improved by the leading enterprises. 37

leading processing plants were constructed in the Towns and villages, Ningshan gastrodia elata and pig poria cocos approved as national landmark product and "Top Ten Shaanxi Medicines", and the "Tianhua Mountain" certified as the provincial famous mushroom brand. In 2019, 90% farmers of 11 Towns in Ningshan County were included in ecological industry and all 40 poverty-stricken villages were covered by the forestry industry. 4,800 Mu (about 320 hectares) of economic forest were newly planted in the poverty-stricken villages and 7,610 Mu (about 510 hectares) of economic forests developed by the impoverished population brought a total income of 2,470 thousand Yuan from forestry industry to 4,717 poor people of 2,423 poor households.

5.3.2   Activation of Ecology plus Reform to improve the income in ecological dividend

As the first batch of collective forestry comprehensive reform experimental demonstration zone in China, Ningshan has blazed out a new path on the forestry industry reform with the idea that "Farmers become well off and natural environment get preserved". by exploring bravely in the four aspects of the socialized service system, the financial supporting system, the public welfare forests operational system, the transfer mechanism and institutional improvement of forest ownership.

5.3.2.1   Increase the income by transferring ecological resources into assets

Ningshan County took the lead in transferring the ownership of 3,062 thousand Mu (about 207,300 hectares) of forest from collective to private and issuing 17,300 forest property certificates with a certification rate of 99%. The County had cumulatively mortgaged the ownership of 50,200 Mu (about 3,350 hectares) of forest, issued the mortgage loans of 78,720,000 Yuan, transferred 731,100 Mu (about 48,800 hectares) of forest land in 1,734 cases and transacted a total revenue of more than 700 million Yuan up to June, 2019. The forest's ownership transfer rate in Ningshan County reached 35%, 15% higher than the average of the whole country. Ningshan County granted 1,800 thousand prepaid mortgage loan for the first batch of public welfare forest in Shaanxi

Province, increased the annual income of 1,626 people of 742 poverty-stricken families by a per capita average of 510 Yuan through being shareholders for their forestry assets or revenues of financing. In 2019, Ningshan County enhanced the construction, training and management of socialized organization of forestry, and established two more socialized service organizations. Besides, the supporting system for the forestry professional managers is explored, new forestry businesses are supported and the forestry professional managers are encouraged to invest and become a shareholder. Ningshan County established a "forest right mortgage loan through train" system to conduct a unified assessment and credit of the forest rights, public welfare forest pre-revenue rights, and forest land management and transfer rights of all farmers in the County so they can finish all procedures in the same financial window. The service functions and application channels of the "smart forestry" big data platform have been expanded. Three forestry expert workstations have been established and four forestry associations formed to convert all ecological forest protection personnel and natural protection forestry personnel into forest product supply and demand information personnel. The seamless integration of forest farmers and e-commerce information helps forest farmers increase their income through poverty alleviation through consumption

5.3.2.2　Increase the Income by Perfecting Forest Subsidy Mechanism

Ningshan was the first poverty-stricken County using its own fiscal revenue for ecological compensation in 2016.6.5 million Yuan was allocated to increase the compensation standard for 650,000 Mu (about 66,700 hectares) of provincial public welfare forests from 5 to 15 Yuan per Mu, equal to the national compensation level. In July 2017, Ningshan County Forestry Bureau was jointly approved by the Ministry of Human Resources and Social Security and the State Forestry Administration as the "Advanced Collective of the National Collective Forest Right Reform". In 2018, Ningshan County was appointed pilot demonstration area by the State Forestry and Grassland Bureau in the new round of national collective forestry comprehensive reform. In 2019, Ningshan timely and accurately cashed the ecological benefit compensation funds to 10,745 people from 3,463 households, totaling a compensation area of 337,900 Mu (about 22,540 hectares) and a compensation amount of 3.259 million Yuan.

5.3.3 Concretizing Ecology plus Employment to increase income in attending the ecology

In order to give full play of the farmers' initiative to protect the ecology, Ningshan County had explored a poverty alleviation approach in which the poor people could work as ecological forest rangers, constructing a ecological environment grid monitoring system for forestry, land, water and environmental protection. 812 registered poor people able to work as ecological foresters are selected from 40 poor villages in principles of "managed by the county, employed by the town, and work in the village" and through government purchase of public services. Fund was raised to continuously increase the employment of ecological forest rangers. The number of ecological forest rangers employed throughout the county has increased year by year from 812 to 844, increasing the income of a total poor population of 3,000. All the ecological forest rangers are trained before taking the job. Each manages a forest area of over 500 Mu (about 330 hectares) with the annual salary of 7,000 Yuan. All rangers are dynamically assessed and contracted once a year.

The employed ecological forest rangers are under a strict management shortened as "One Supervision, Two Publicity, Three Assessments and Four Ones". As to the details, "Two Publicity" includes two aspects. On the one hand, every village makes billboards about the ecological forest rangers' work performance, publicizes their position description and the hot-line for supervision at the County, Town and village levels. The masses are encouraged to supervise and report the ecological forest rangers' work performance and get an award of 200 Yuan a time if the report proves true. On the other hand, the management areas and duties of ecological forest rangers are published on their doors to remind them to perform their duties at all times. "Three Assessments" means to assess the work performance of the ecological forest rangers every day, every week and every month. Those who cannot fulfill their duties regularly or fail to have standard attendances will be fired immediately. " One Supervision " refers to the professional supervision team that Ningshan County set up to randomly investigate and supervise the ecological forest rangers' performances at least in two villages a Town and two Towns a month.

As to the phenomenon that some of the Towns and villages have poor daily management on the ecological forest rangers, the Forestry Bureau of Ningshan County put forward two measures to solve the problem. One is the Work Plan on Forest Ranger Performance Supervision and Verification Sharding formulated to mobilize the whole bureau in forest rangers work performance supervision. Through entrusting the bureau leaders with supervision responsibility for certain areas, subordinated offices for certain Towns and the individual cadres for certain villages, a complete monitoring system was set up to verify whether the 844 ecological forest rangers are normally performing their duties, whether the ecological forest staff employment process files are standardized and perfect, whether the employment contract has expired and not renewed, and whether the attendance registration form is inconsistent with logic; etc. Whether they can perform after being relocated, and the treatment and treatment procedures for abnormal conditions found by ecological forest rangers when they patrol the mountains. On the other hand, the Forest Bureau of Ningshan County organized activities like "turning forest rangers into messengers" or the "Five Stars Competition" to vote stars in enrichment through hard working, stars in science and technology, stars in public health, stars in family tradition, stars in dedication to work, etc. to precisely manage the ecological forest rangers and precisely shake off poverty. Since the implementation of the policy of ecological forest rangers, a total of more than 16. 96 million Yuan in wages, 4. 22 million Yuan in 2019, has been paid. By appointing eco-forest rangers, each family household earns an additional 7,000 Yuan and the per capita income increases by more than 2,000 Yuan, achieving expected results in "one member works as the ranger and the whole family get out of poverty".

5. 3. 4　Refining Ecology plus Projects to prosper the farmers in livable environment

Ningshan County increases the farmers' transferable income through the construction of ecological project. Priorities were given to the poor households in poor villages in hiring labors for the construction of various key forestry ecological engineering projects. Social capital is introduced to carry out forest tending, the public welfare forest management investment mechanism is innovated, *Plan on Supporting the Establishment and Implementation of Forest Management Professional Cooperatives in Ningshan County (Trial)* is promulgated, and 9 forest management cooperatives are newly established. Up to now, more than 50, 000 Mu (about 3, 333 hectares) of forest tending have been implemented. The people relocated to the bottom of the mountain were subsidized for their house site vacation and a new round of farmland-to-forests returning. The poor villages and poor households are strongly supported during the implementation of the project. 1. 5 Mu (0. 1 ha) of land per person is allocated to each poor household that meets the conditions for returning farmland to forest policy. In 2019, a new round of subsidies for returning farmland to forest was completed in time and beneficiaries were 1, 516 poverty-stricken households and 4, 924 people of 22 villages and 2 communities in 7 Towns in poverty. 4, 835. 7 Mu (322 ha) of land were returned to forest and the subsidy funds of the poor population reached 1, 957, 676 Yuan. At the same time, through renovating the dilapidated houses in rural areas, the comprehensive rural human settlement environment was improved and the ecological functions restored. The comprehensive improvement of the rural settlement environment and the renovation of poor households in 40 impoverished villages were undertaken, and 29, 000 Mu (1933 ha) of forests planted, 19, 500 Mu (1300 ha) of land afforested in the spring of 2019, and 206, 600 trees were voluntarily planted.

By releasing the ecological dividends and studying the poverty alleviation pattern on ecological protection, Ningshan County had explored the replicable and exemplary "Ningshan Mode" to alleviate poverty with the idea that "lucid waters and lush mountains are invaluable assets. " The poverty alleviation work of Ningshan County has been attended continuously by the central and provincial governments and its methods and experiences of "Ningshan Mode" have been summarized and promoted throughout the whole country. Wei Zengjun, vice-governor of Shaanxi Province, had given full recognition on the poverty alleviation work in Ningshan County. "Ningshan Mode" was presented in the national seminar of forestry ecological construction and targeted poverty alleviation and covered by many authoritative medias including the official website of the State Council, China Central Television, the Xinhua News Agency, etc. The practices of poverty alleviation via "Ecological Plus" programs successfully turned the lucid waters and lush mountains into invaluable assets for the impoverished population in the Qinling-Bashan mountainous regions.

5. 4   Consolidation of Anti-poverty Achievements by Ecological Economy in Xichuan County

Xichuan, a county in the administrative area of Nanyang City in Henan Province in the Qinling-Bashan mountains, got its name for the alluvial plain formed along the reaches of the Xi River. Xichuan is the most impoverished County in Henan Province with 670,000 people in 17 Towns on the land area of 282,000 hectares. In 2017, Xichuan County was included as one of the "National Important Ecological Function Area" according to Notice on Clarifying the Types of Newly-added National Key Ecological Function Zones by NDRC (National Development and Reform Commission). As the water source area of the middle line of South-to-North water diversion project and an extreme poverty-stricken County, Xichuan actively implemented the "Two Mountains" theory by General Secretary Xi Jinping, held fast to the bottom line of ecology, and took initiatives to innovate poverty alleviation modes on the basis of the eco-economy sustainable development.

5. 4. 1   Practicing the "Two Mountains Theory" to fulfill the responsibility of water protection

Since 2013, Xichuan County has been actively carrying out the

"Two Mountains Theory" (LUCID WATERS AND LUSH MOUNTAINS ARE INVALUABLE ASSETS, we desire both the ecological benefits and the economic gains), strictly fulfilled the duties to protect the water source for the country, and implemented the "Four Development Strategies" of surviving the County by ecological industry, strengthening the County by manufacturing industry, thriving the County by tour industry, and prospering the County by innovative industry. To ensure the water storage to 170 meters in the Danjiangkou Reservoir, 416,000 Mu (about 27750 hectares) of the best farming land in the river valley of Xichuan County was drowned, and about 400 thousand people were relocated. In order to ensure the water quality of the water source, more than 380 mining factories were closed, 50 thousand fishing net cages and 600 livestock farms were banned. Finally, the water quality of Danjiangkou Reservoir is maintained above the second class standard all the year round, and water quality in Taocha water-intake reached the first class standard. As the water source area and the start of the water canal of the middle line of South-to-North water diversion project, the national wetland nature reserve and the provincial tourist attraction of Henan, Danjiang Lake scenic spot is currently constructed by Henan Fusen Group in accordance with the national standard for 5A scenic spot, aiming at building a leisure resort and holy place in Henan for people to enjoy scenery, acquire knowledge, have fun, entertain and keep fit, vividly demonstrating the effectiveness of the "Two Mountains Theory" and its implementation against ecological degradation. To safeguard the "ecological bottom line, ecological red line, ecological high-pressure line" of the first-tier water sources, and change ecological pressure into a transformation impetus, Xichuan County took the ecological economy as the central task, acted according to the local conditions to cultivate specialties in clusters, built featured ecological brands like "water source" "forest sea" "fruit home" "medicine storehouse", and "leisure resort", and formulated a short-, middle-, long-term poverty alleviation mode via sustainable development of ecological economy. All these endeavors secured the national water source safety, also established reliable industries to combat poverty and concluded sound benefits in ecology, economy and social development.

5. 4. 2 "Short-, Middle- and Long-term" Development Mode to combat poverty via ecological economy

Xichuan County helped the masses to steadily increase their income by activating their dynamism in developing ecological industries following the philosophy that the short-, middle-and long-term plans motivate, drive and complement each other, to ensure real alleviation of targeted population will never fall into poverty again. In water source protection and poverty alleviation, Xichuan County explored the characteristic "Short-, Middle- and Long-term" modes to achieve sustainable poverty alleviation based on ecological economy. The "short-term plan" is to help farmers conclude remarkable effects and shake off poverty within the same year by developing the featured industrial clusters on edible fungi and traditional Chinese medicinal materials, etc.; The "middle-term plan" is to help farmers result great benefits and become rich in three years by developing the featured industrial clusters on soft-seed pomegranates and thinly shelled walnuts. The "long-term plan" is to ensure the sustainable proficiency in five years and a lasting prosperous life by developing the ecological tour industrial clusters. After persistent efforts, the featured industries in every Town, production bases in every village and income-increasing plans in every family were basically constructed. The "Short-, Middle-, and Long-term" industrial clusters achieved a comprehensive output value of over 13. 8 billion annually, with 31 leading companies above the city level set up, 1152 farmers corporations supported and 916 home farms established, lifting one third of the low-income families out of poverty steadily.

5. 4. 2. 1 Short-term plan of developing industries on edible fungi and traditional Chinese medicine materials to reduce poverty within the year

By playing the comparative advantages of the local ecology, resources, climate and featured industries, Xichuan County had striven to develop their advantageous industries with "solid industrial foundation, promising market potential and high current efficiency", focused on the industrial clusters of featured planting and breeding, photovoltaic project and labor-service economy for higher benefits with little investment in a short period. Each poor households will be covered by at least two "short-term" projects to realize an increase of 10, 000 Yuan per household a year and shake off poverty within the same year. Planting edible mushrooms and traditional Chinese medicinal materials is a traditional advantageous industry also the optimal choice of industry in Xichuan County located in Qinlin-Bashan mountainous regions. To build the edible mushroom industry base, leading companies like Lvdi, Yirui and Danjiangqing were integrated in the mode of "company + cooperatives + base + poor farmers" to build the poverty-alleviation demonstration area via shiitake mushroom industry to include all the local low-income families in two years. Till now, 40 million bags of edible mushrooms have been produced and 6500 families participated in the industry with an income increase of about 5000 Yuan per household. In the construction of traditional Chinese medicinal materials industry base, Xichuan County had formed a development mode of "production-processing-sales" relying on biotech companies like Fusen, Jiuzhoutong and Aierkang in Henan Province. The "company + cooperatives + base + low-income farmers" mode has been adopted to continuously plant 50, 000 Mu (about 3340 hectares) of medicinal herbs like honeysuckle, wormwood, forsythia, red-rooted salvia and rosemary. In average, every low-income family has one Mu (667 m^2) of medicinal herbs with an annual income increase of about 5000 Yuan. The Fusen Medicine Company of Henan Province, listed on the Main Board of Hongkong this year, is the largest enterprise on the production of cold medication with the coptis herbs. Planting of herbs like honeysuckle and forsythia employed more than 2000 people, 350 families in 23 villages and 4 towns, with the peak employment of above 6000 every day and increasing the household income by 18, 000 Yuan a year. The industries of edible mushrooms and traditional Chinese medicinal materials in Xichuan County formed a whole chain mode of "planting base + processing base + global marketing". As for breeding industry, Xichuan County successfully built the largest breeding and distributing base of crayfish and white-jade snails based on the abundant water resources and the mode of "village party branch + cooperatives + poor household". Till now, more than 20, 000 Mu (about 1, 333 hectares) of crayfish, an average of 1 Mu (about 667 m^2) of shrimp per household, have been farmed to increase the average annual household income by 4, 000 Yuan; and more than 50 million white jade snails are bred in 40 villages and 5 Townships, increasing an average annual household income by about 6, 000 Yuan. Besides, the Xichuan County strove to develop "photovoltaic + farming" projects, taking the photovoltaic projects as important ways to alleviate poverty following a mechanism "led by the government, managed by the market" for "seizing opportunities and activating the resources". The labor service economy covered all the low-income people who are able to work, attracting labor force at 40s or 50s by workshops and industry bases which are designed to alleviate poverty. More than ten thousand welfare working posts are developed to solve the problem of unemployment in the resettlement area, and the young labors are trained to work in cities, effectively consuming the surplus labor forces.

5. 4. 2. 2   The middle-term plan of developing the featured forestry and fruit-tree industrial clusters to enrich low-income families

In order to consolidate the achievements of short-term poverty alleviation and strive for a prosperity in a systematic overall plan, Xichuan County put great effort in building profitable and ecological forestry and fruit-tree industrial clusters, such as soft-seeds pomegranates, apricot and plums, thin-skinned walnuts, large cherries, according to the idea of "regional layout, large-scale development and industrialized operation" on the county's actual situation that 70% of the farming lands are infertile ones in hilly areas and 80% of the County land are strictly under the ecological conservation red-line. They employed the mechanisms like "Separation of Three Rights" (the system for separating the ownership rights, contract rights, and management rights for contracted rural land), "Subcontracting", and "Guaranteed Labor Division" to develop the industries in large scale by transferring the lands. Relying on the local leading companies, they gave priority to the industry of soft seeds pomegranates, building 100, 000 Mu (about 6670 hectares) of poverty alleviation demonstration areas on soft seeds pomegranates in the towns like Jiuchong, Xianghua and Houpo in the plain-hilly area, which entitled the county as "Hometown of Soft Seeds

Pomegranates" and achieved the profit of 15,000 Yuan per Mu. Relying on the leading company including "Fruit Excellence" of Nanyang City, they gave priority to the thin-skinned walnuts industry, consolidated the achievements on fishing and planting, and developed the large cherries industry in hilly Towns like Jing Ziguan, Siwan, Xihuang and Maotang, finally built poverty alleviation demonstration areas of thin-skin walnuts of 100,000 Mu (about 6670 hectares) and fishing and planting industry of 10,000 Mu (about 667 hectares). Led by "Apricot and Plum Forestry" company near the middle line water source area, the industries of apricot, plum and large cherry were developed, thin-skinned walnuts and soft seeds pomegranates industries consolidated, featured industrial and tourist belts of economic fruit trees built, and the featured forestry and fruit-tree industries promoted by the industrial cluster effect in Laocheng Town, Dashiqiao Town, Taohe Town, Shengwan Town, Jinhe Town and other reservoir areas. By now, more than 300,000 Mu (about 20,000 hectares) of economic fruit trees with 50% of inter-planting area under the trees, at least 1 Mu (about 667 m^2) of fruit trees per family, were cultivated by farmers including almost all the low-income household. About 160,000 Mu (about 10,672 hectares) of the fruit trees have begun to bear fruits and they will be in full productive period in two years, increasing their income annually by more than 6,000 Yuan per household and primarily realizing the greening of the lands, prospering of the farmers and thriving of the industries.

5.4.2.3   Long-term plan of developing eco-tourism industry to ensure sustainable alleviation of poverty

In order to achieve the goal of sustainable poverty alleviation, Xichuan County is striving to develop eco-tourism industry as the long term plan to alleviate poverty, aiming at exploring more room to help the masses prosper in the long run. All the tour industries in Xichuan County could be promoted to a higher level by the driving force from scenic areas, leading power from typical spots, and the unified strength from association, which will help the masses increase their wealth in the eco-tour industrial chain. In order to ensure the sustainable poverty alleviation by tourism, the Xichuan County has promoted and upgraded many scenic areas and spots like the Head of Water Diversion, Danjiang

Park, Zen Valley, Xiangyan Temple, the Eight Immortals Caves in constructing the "Five A" Danjiang national scenic area. Great effort was levied in the construction of Danjiang Lake tourism circle by building the reservoir-ring-road with high standards and quickening the working schedule of the Xian-Shiyan highway. What's more, the tourism poverty alleviation project focusing on the poor villages along the lake was formulated to better use the tourism resources, implementation plans for poverty alleviation via rural tourism was promulgated, tourism development funds and incentive support methods for farmhouse hotels were set up. Altogether 10 key tourism Townships, 36 key tourism villages, 40 rural tourism industrial parks, more than 500 farmhouses and special guesthouses developed precisely inlet the poverty chain into the tourism chain, and led 2,300 poor people of more than 500 poverty-stricken households on the road of rural tourism development. In order to deeply integrate tourism with agriculture, forestry and sports industry to expand all-for-one tourism, Xichuan County has built the anti-poverty project of "Hani Terraced Fields"of a thousand Mu (about 667 hectares) at high standards in managing mountains, waters, forests, fields, lakes, grasses and waste lands as a whole system. The tourist spots like botanical gardens, picking gardens and breeding gardens were expanded based on the 300,000 Mu (about 20,000 hectares) ecological fruit trees industry in the County; the afforestation project made the county rank the front in Henan Province in ten years as to the planting area; many important sporting events were successfully held in the mode of "tourism + sports + poverty alleviation". The featured tourism industry added a per capita income increase of 3,000 Yuan to at least 1,000 poor people.

5. 4. 3   Enlightenment of sustainable poverty alleviation in Xichuan County

5. 4. 3. 1   Party-building to push forward sustainable poverty alleviation

Tackling poverty is a matter of national prosperity, national rejuvenation and people's happiness. With high quality integration of poverty alleviation and Party Building, Xichuan County promoted the anti-poverty work through Party building, fully exerted the Party leadership in primary-level organizations, pooled the extensive strengths of the Party officials and provided the career of poverty alleviation with strong supports from the Party.

5. 4. 3. 2　Adhering to economic rules to increase income at multiple levels

Pursuing the "Featured plus Green" regional economy cluster guided by "Two Mountains" theory, Xichuan County continuously promoted the supply-side economic structural reform, integrated the short-period plan of poverty alleviation and the long-term prosperity of the poor households for both economic development and ecology protection. The short-, middle-and long-term development plans drive, complement and activate each other in solving issues related to water quality protection and water resources conservation and establishing the competitive and development advantages for the long run. Constant exploration and practice of the "Short-, Middle- and Long-term" development modes enriched income-increase measures at multiple levels and guaranteed that the impoverished population could get rid of poverty within a short time, become rich in three to five years, and maintain their prosperity in a long run.

5. 4. 3. 3　Innovating win-win systems to pool effort for poverty problems

Poverty alleviation is a systematic project which requires enthusiasm and concerted power of all parties. The local government's leadership, the leading companies' driving force, the associations' linking power and the low-income families' initiatives shall be activated by innovating the profit-linking systems like "Separation of Three Rights", "Guaranteed Bonuses" and "Subcontracting", with equal consideration of benefits of the companies, the banks, the village collectives, and the farmers.

5. 4. 3. 4　Securing risk prevention and control to protect all-around development

The economic development and risk prevention and control shall be concerned together to achieve sustainable and flourishing poverty alleviation. The risk prevention and control determines the successes of industries. Great effort shall be delivered to provide comprehensive protection in policy support, talent introduction, tracking services, etc. , to persistently enlarge and strengthen industrial clusters and leading enterprises, but also to promote the poverty alleviation on banking businesses to a new step by introducing flexible financing systems like agricultural guarantee and insurance in comprehensive and multiple ways.

Chapter 6
Designated-area Poverty Alleviation: A Campaign to Lift Designated Targets out of Poverty

On June 23, 2017, President Xi Jinping pointed out at the Symposium on Poverty Alleviation in Deeply Impoverished Areas that "China's poverty has regional characteristics. When the national large-scale poverty relief campaign was launched in 1986, there were 18 designated impoverished regions where poverty exists over extended areas. The northeastern Fujian area where I was working was one of them. At that time, even in eastern China, many people's lives were very difficult. After over 30 years of continuous efforts, most of the poverty-stricken areas have taken on new looks and people's lives have been significantly improved. "[①] Danfeng County of Shaanxi Province is a targeted poverty alleviation County of the Chinese Academy of Social Sciences (CASS). Based on local conditions, CASS has explored effective ways to achieve poverty reduction in such an area of extreme poverty, which has made Danfeng's contribution to the success of the poverty alleviation campaign as scheduled in China.

6.1　Development of Rural Collective Economy—the Road to Dramatic Change in Meizhuang Village, Wuguan Town, Danfeng County

Located in the deep mountains of Wuguan Town, Danfeng County,

---

① Xi Jinping, "Speech at the Symposium on Poverty Alleviation in Deeply Impoverished Areas", 2017-08-31, http://cpc. people. com. cn/n1/2017/0831/c64094-29507970. html.

Shaanxi Province, Meizhuang Village is at a disadvantaged position due to unfavorable geographical conditions. In the village with 7 villager groups, 255 households and 1062 people including 37 CPC members, 241 people in 68 registered poverty-stricken households amounted to a poverty rate of 23% in 2017. In the past, Meizhuang was referred to as a village of "two no's and two many's" (no leading industry, no collective economy, many poor households, many migrant workers). It was virtually an "empty village". To transform the current situation of abject poverty, Meizhuang has taken the expansion of the collective economy as the focus and breakthrough point, actively developing poverty alleviation industries and innovating the benefit linkage mechanism. The "four-in-one" collective economic development model of " party branch + cooperative of shareholding economy + enterprises + poor households (farmers) " has started the village's collective economy from scratch and developed it into a strong one.

6. 1. 1   Main Practices

Since 2016, Meizhuang has relied on reform, innovation and cohesive breakthroughs to promote the model of " party branch + ' threetransfers' reform + collective economy + poor households". All the efforts have finally lifted the village out of poverty and the village has now taken on a new look.

6. 1. 1. 1   Strengthening party building, an "engine" for grass-roots work

As the saying goes, it's better to have a good Party branch than to just receive relief money and materials. The capabilities of the village leadership committees directly dictate the overall development of the village. By carrying out activities themed as "Party Flag Leading the Way out of Poverty", the village party branch has served as a driving force for the development of the collective economy with the party carders and members as the core.

First, leadership by the party branch. In 2018, seven well-respected individuals with high overall qualities and sense of responsibility were elected into the village's two leadership committees, building a strong grass-roots battle fortress. The newly established party branch have taken the lead to shoulder their responsibility, earnestly implemented the rural collective property right system reform issued by the central and provincial governments, and carried out the asset and capital verification to confirm the total assets of the village. In April 2018, the Meizhuang Village Cooperative of Shareholding Economy was established, solving the problem of the legal person's identity that had long plagued the development of the rural collective economy and removing the obstacles to the development mechanism from the root.

Second, role model demonstration. In accordance with the constitution of the newly established cooperative, the general assembly of members (representatives) elected the village party branch secretary as its chairman, the director of the village supervision committee as the chairman of the board of supervisors, and the other five members of the village committees as managing staff, thus building a village collective economic organization structure of " party branch + cooperative of shareholding economy + company ". When the first village-owned enterprise Dangu Shiitake Mushroom Company was set up, its development was challenged by serious shortage of funds and low participation of the villagers. The party branch secretary took the lead in investing 100, 000 Yuan, and the remaining six village cadres each invested 30,000 Yuan in the construction of mushroom growing sites. 40 poor households who were not involved in any industry were mobilized to get a loan of 5000 Yuan each from the village mutual aid fund① to join the cooperative. The cooperative invested 600, 000 Yuan, and 548, 700 Yuan of village collective operating assets was converted into shares and did not receive dividends within three years. Through the demonstration of the role models, the villagers were encouraged to participate extensively in the village company which entered the fast lane of healthy development.

---

①　Poverty-stricken Village Development Mutual Aid Fund: a financial assistance fund which composes of special capital offered by the government and farmers' own investment in the form of capital shares. In the poor villages, the fund is owned, used, managed by farmers for the benefit of farmers. The fund is expanded through constant lending among villagers. The fund is focused on offering capital needed by poor farmers to develop production, thus promoting the sustainable development of poor villages and poor farmers.

Third, party members taking the lead. According to local conditions, we have tried to first help party members to become successful farmers or to cultivate successful farmers to become party members, and then to invite successful farmers who are party members to join the village leadership committees. Therefore, the party members can lead other villagers to increase income, reduce poverty, develop collective economy. Eight leading party members, both as "administrators" and "technicians", have been fully involved in supporting the development of the collective economy with capital, technology, or management as their investment; more than 30 party members have served in all aspects of industrial poverty alleviation, becoming the main force in promoting collective economic development.

6. 1. 1. 2 Developing a poverty alleviation industry as a "cash cow" for the village

To develop and strengthen the collective economy, industry is the foundation and the core. Meizhuang Village has been focused on the goals of industrial development and collective income increase, and made great efforts to explore new ways to diversify and develop the collective economy.

First, strengthening reform-driven mechanisms. Meizhuang has comprehensively promoted the rural collective property right system reform and established 8 village-level and group-level asset and capital verification teams. After the verification, the total assets of the village included 1. 52 million Yuan in operating assets, 4 million Yuan in non-operating assets, 99 hectares of arable land, and 1, 307 hectares of woodland. There were 1, 002 cooperative members of 258 households, setting up 1, 002 population shares, all of which became part of the shares in the collective economic organizations. At the same time, the village's collectively constructed CA freshness storage warehouse, water wells, industrial roads, and industrial base supporting facilities were converted into collective operating assets. After the integration of the government-invested Jiangsu-Shaanxi Cooperation Project Fund, Shaanxi Financial Special Fund, and the village collective economic support fund, all the funds were managed and allocated by the Meizhuang Village Cooperative of Shareholding Economy. All the village's operating assets, resources and funds were converted into shares of all shareholders, effectively activating resources and consolidating the foundation of collective economic development.

Second, strengthening the project-driven approach. Utilizing the advantages of abundant mountain resources, large mountain areas, and rich solar and thermal resources, the working team residing in the village helped to formulate the collective economic development plan which included the development direction, projects, pathways, and operation mode. The industrial layout was tea in spring, mushrooms in three seasons, and photovoltaic power generation in four seasons, forming a development model of long-term industry guaranteeing stability, short-term industry offering stable income growth, and integration of the primary, secondary and tertiary industries promoting the market's development. The long-term and short-term industries complemented each other so that industries can effectively increase the income of locals.

Third, strengthening policy's stimulus effect. By seizing the opportunities of three major policies, Meizhuang had striven to make great strides in its collective economy. With the rural property right system reform and the reform of the "rural three changes", namely "resources changed to equity, capital to shares, farmers to shareholders", the village had transferred idle land, revitalized resource assets, and actively explored the shareholding development model incorporating village collectives, enterprises, well-off households, and poor households, encouraging more impoverished households to become shareholders and share profits. To seize a series of preferential policies and opportunities introduced by the central and provincial governments, the village had implemented targeted poverty alleviation. Based on the local conditions, the village built industrial bases and promoted the continuous growth of the village collective economy, embarking on the road of sustainable development with the poverty alleviation transformed from a "blood transfusion" mode to a "blood-making" one. The Opinions on the Implementation of the Development and Strengthening of the Rural Collective Economy issued by the Shangluo Municipal Party Committee and Municipal Government helped the village to further enhance the development concept, innovate the development path, take full use of the supporting policies, and accelerate the development of the collective economy in an all-round way.

Fourth, strengthening multi-party cooperation. The village has actively explored diversified development paths and strongly enhanced the development of village collective economy. One, development by photovoltaic industry. By taking advantage of the national PV poverty alleviation policy and the Jiangsu-Shaanxi Cooperation Project, the village managed to get government financial investment to build a 140-kilowatt PV power plant, which was operated and managed by the village cooperative. The power plant's revenues have become an important income source of village collective economic funds and solved the problem of lack of capital money for the collective economic development. Two, development by economic entities. Economic entities such as village collective enterprises were established according to local conditions. In May 2018, the village economic cooperative founded Dangu Edible Mushrooms Development Company with a registered capital of 1.08 million Yuan, 4 hectares of transferred land, 60 Shiitake mushroom greenhouses, and a CA freshness storage warehouse of 400 cubic meters. At the same time, technicians from the County's Edible Mushrooms Research Institute were employed as consultants, invited farmers who know how to grow Shiitake mushroom but were migrant workers in other places to return to the village to form a technical guidance team. While focusing on professionalism, specialization and branding, the local mushroom brand Dangu became well-known. Led by Dangu, the Shiitake mushroom industry in the village has expanded to 109 households with 1 million bags of logs in 2019, which not only achieved local employment of the poor and surplus labor, but also effectively lifted farmers involved in the industry out of poverty. Three, development by land. Through land transfer, the concentration of land into the collective economic organizations has changed the situation of decentralized operation of individual household, and promoted the operation of land on a moderate scale. The village economic cooperative transferred 66.7 hectares of land from Ruanling Group and Meiziwa Group, which was built into a tea garden operated by the cooperative. With such a large tea plantation, it is possible to develop a tea industrial chain linking the pre-production, production and post-production processes. It has also addressed the mismatch between non-standard tea produced by individual households and the demand of the large commercial market, thus developing the local agricultural industrialization. Four, development by enterprises. According to the "village collective capital—enterprise—dividend" model, 1 million Yuan of collective idle capital is invested in Huamao Livestock Group with a fixed annual dividend of 6%, which increases the village's collective economic income. Five, development by mutual aid fund. The Meizhuang Village Mutual Aid Fund has attracted 206 households (including 122 poor households since 2013), issuing a total of 555,000 Yuan of loans, and withdrawing 15,000 Yuan of public welfare funds every year. The smooth operation of the mutual aid fund has not only increased the value of the fund in operation, but also enhanced the strength of village-level collective economy.

6.1.1.3　Implementing linkage shareholding and benefits, giving reassurance to farmers

The key to developing a collective economy and helping farmers increase their incomes and reduce poverty is to establish a mechanism of interest linkage and risk prevention and control, and effectively stimulate the enthusiasm and motivation of the people to participate in development. Meizhuang Village has explored and initially established "three mechanisms":

First, a share linkage mechanism. With the village leaders taking the initiative in holding shares, villagers' capital contribution as shares, and the collective's capital investment in the shares, the shares link together the interests of the collective, leaders, and the villagers to form a community of interests. In terms of benefit distribution, 20% of Dangu's annual net income is allocated as provident fund and the bonus for leading cadres, and the remaining 80% is distributed according to shares (of which 600,000 Yuan contributed by the village economic cooperative accounts for 55.6% of the shares, 280,000 Yuan by cadres, 25.9% of the shares, and 200,000 Yuan by poor households, 18.5%). Forty percent of the net income of the cooperative is withdrawn as welfare fund, provident fund, risk fund and management fees, and the remaining 60% is distributed to the villagers according to the equity owned by them to achieve shared benefits. Among the 60% of the cooperative's revenues, 70% is distributed to 241 poor farmers according to the headcount shares and 30% is averaged to all 1, 002 villagers according to the headcount shares during the poverty alleviation period. When poverty alleviation is achieved, the cooperative's dividends will be distributed evenly to all shareholders.

Second, a benefit incentive mechanism. Preferential policies and measures are drawn up to encourage village cadres to lead and assist in collective economic and industrial development. For cadres who are involved in the collective development, they are not require to participate in working shifts or daily affairs, but can still take bonuses. Ten percent of the annual net income of Dangu is used as the bonuses for leading cadres. The Dangu board of directors will evaluate the participation and contribution of each individual and bonus will be distributed accordingly with the consent of the village economic cooperative. For the poor farmers who work for the company, salaries are paid according to their workload. If some of them are not active in the job or do not take good care of the subcontracted mushrooms, they will be disqualified from having the cooperative shares, forcing the poor farmers to actively participate in the work. For the 60 mushroom greenhouses, the property rights being owned by the village economic cooperative are managed and operated by Dangu. Among the 60 greenhouses, 36 are directly operated by the company, and 24 greenhouses are offered to 15 mushroom farming households for free during the poverty alleviation campaign. Starting from 2021, the 24 greenhouses will be leased to the villagers, and the rent will be included in the revenues of Dangu).

Third, a risk prevention and control mechanism. When choosing a village-level collective economic project, local conditions should be given careful consideration while strengthening risk assessment, expanding the leading industry's insurance coverage, and establishing a multi-entity and multi-channel risk sharing mechanism. When important decisions are made about the collective economic project and related issues, they should be proposed at the party branch meeting, discussed at the two village leadership committees, deliberated at the party members' assembly, voted upon at the villagers' representatives assembly or villagers' assembly. Both the resolution and its implementation results should be made public to all the villagers. The members of the two village committees are cross-appointed. The secretary of the village party branch and the director of the village supervision committee also serve as the chairman of the village economic cooperative and Dangu's chairman of board of supervisors respectively, thus strengthening internal management. According to the Guidance for the Village Collective Economy Income Distribution, annually 10% of the net profits will be allocated into a risk prevention and control fund, which is mainly used for fast response expenses for natural disasters or unpredictable disasters to safeguard the interests of the village collective and farmers to the largest extent. The village-run enterprise Dangu Mushroom Company takes out part of its net income every year as the incentive bonus for leading cadres, raising the reasonable income of the two committees' members, and as rewards to the party members who contribute to the development of the village's collective economy. This practice has shown to other villagers that as long as you are committed to the collective economy, you will be awarded.

6. 1. 2 Major achievements

6. 1. 2. 1 Enhancing economic strength

Through the establishment of the village collective enterprise and mutual aid fund, Meizhuang has focused its efforts on building a diversified industrial development pattern and the collective economy has achieved steady and rapid development. By the end of 2019, the net income of Meizhuang's collective economy reached 370, 000 Yuan (including 95,000 Yuan from PV, 185,000 Yuan from Dangu Mushroom Company, 60, 000 Yuan of fixed dividend from Huamao Livestock Group, and 30,000 Yuan of welfare fund from mutual aid fund). When the newly planted tea trees of 66. 7 hectares start to make profits in 2021, Meizhuang will achieve a gorgeous transformation from an "empty village" with little collective economy to a "village with strong economic entities".

6. 1. 2. 2 Boosting motivation to poverty reduction

Supported by the diversified development of the village, 55

households including 40 poor ones were motivated to grow mushrooms and 68 poor households to develop the tea industry. Altogether 160 poor farmers were employed. In 2018, the per capita net income of the villagers was 9,737 Yuan, 13 percentage points higher than the County average, and the poverty rate fell to 1.4%. A total of 230 people from 59 households were lifted out of poverty, which meant Meizhuang would no longer be referred to as a poverty-stricken village. In 2019, the poor households increased their income by more than 8,000 Yuan on average, and seven farmers of six households were lifted out of poverty, which injected a strong impetus into poverty alleviation.

6.1.2.3   Stimulating development vitality

Through the linking of village collective economy and the interests of the villagers, the poor are encouraged to actively participate in the development of the village industry, rely on labor to increase their income and become well-off, eliminate the mentality of coming to terms with living in poverty, thus forming a good atmosphere of promoting progress and hard work. Meanwhile, by participating in the processing and production of edible mushrooms and tea, the farmers have mastered practical techniques and some even have become local farming experts, providing talent and intellectual support for poverty alleviation and rural revitalization.

6.1.2.4   Enhancing the organizational ability

The development of the village collective economy has enhanced the two leadership committees' ability to work for the people and the self-governance of the villagers, achieving the goal of reviving rural traditions, enriching cultural life, and beautifying the environment. Through a series of measures to develop the collective economy, the enthusiasm of village cadres has been fully mobilized and stimulated. The pioneering role of party members and cadres has been effectively demonstrated. The cohesion, fighting power and appeal of village-level organizations have been significantly strengthened. The people's sense of gain, happiness and security has been enhanced, and the party's ruling foundation in the rural areas consolidated.

6.1.3 Experiences and enlightenment

Meizhuang Village takes full advantage of the party branch's leadership, corporate operation and participation of all villagers to mobilize all the resources of the whole village to develop collective economy. The four-in-one development model of "party branch + cooperative of shareholding economy + enterprises + poor households (farmers)" has help the village to embark on a path of prosperity with distinctive characteristics and enlightening values.

6.1.3.1 Party building as the core

Rural grass-roots party organizations are the core of leadership in economic and social development. If the leaders do not take the lead, the other villagers do not dare to venture into any project. To do a good job in the countryside, we must rely on a good grass-roots party organization and a group of reliable leaders. The four-in-one village collective economic organization structure of "party branch + cooperative of shareholding economy + enterprises + poor households (farmers)" explored by Meizhuang has provided a strong organizational guarantee for the whole village to get rid of poverty, and has also laid a solid organizational foundation for rural revitalization.

6.1.3.2 Path selection as the key

The key to developing the village-level collective economy is to choose the right path. To develop village collective economy in poverty-stricken mountainous areas with relatively scarce resources, we must adapt to local conditions, dig deep into the potentials, and insist on taking multiple measures and multiple linkage development paths. Meizhuang has taken advantage of PV industry, economic entities, land, enterprises and mutual aid fund to minimize market risks and ensure the increase of the collective economy's revenues. In particular, in the process of industrial development, the poor farmers should always be incorporated into the industrial chain. By cultivating leading enterprises, extending the industrial chain, and improving industrial efficiency, the people's confidence in relying on industrial income to increase wealth can be boosted.

6. 1. 3. 3　Increased benefits for farmers as the purpose

Farmers' participation and benefits are the starting point and goal of the development and expansion of the village-level collective economy. It is not only just to make a big "cake", but also to reasonably share the "cake" so that the poor can truly benefit from the collective economic development. The collective land, barren hills, houses and the contracted management rights of the poor farmers' own cultivated land and forest land are converted into the shares of the village collective economic organization to achieve sharing by activating resources. The financial funds and poverty alleviation funds invested in the village by the government are quantified into shares held by the village collective or the poor people, helping the poor to increase their income through returns on equity.

6. 1. 3. 4　Mechanism innovation as the guarantee

Mechanism innovation is a booster for the development and growth of the collective economy. Only by exploring feasible mechanisms and insisting on scientific operation and standardized management can we ensure the healthy and orderly development of the village collective economy. It is necessary to realize the integration of the interests of village collectives, shareholding companies, village cadres, and farmers through the establishment of share linkage, incentives, brand sharing, and risk prevention and control.

6. 2　Supporting Leading Enterprises to Achieve Targeted Poverty Alleviation

President Xi Jinping pointed out that poverty alleviation is not just to help people in need, but to guide and support all those with working abilities to rely on their own hands to create a better future. For the poor people who have the ability to work, cultivated land or other resources, but do not have funds, industry or skills, they should be encouraged to take advantage of local resources, such as agriculture, forestry, animal husbandry, business, tourism. By supporting the development of featured industries that give full play to local people's abilities and resources, poverty alleviation can be achieved locally. Promoting industrial poverty alleviation, realizing the organic connection between the poor and the poverty-relief industries, and solving problems like market risks and technical challenges faced by the poor in developing industries rely on effective measures to deepen government-enterprise cooperation and play the leading role of major enterprises. The Danfeng County government has strengthened the policy support for the Danfeng Huamao Livestock Group, a private enterprise that focuses on broiler farming and processing. The policies have encouraged Huamao to give full play to the advantages of the entire industrial chain, help poor households to increase income through multiple channels, and explore a road of industrial poverty alleviation featured by the government-enterprise linkage, complementary advantages and win-win results for the enterprise, people and the society.

6. 2. 1   Strengthening policy support to cultivate leading enterprises

Danfeng has long attached importance to the cultivation of leading enterprises, laying a solid foundation for leading enterprises to play a role in poverty alleviation. In accordance with the idea of "building leading enterprises, achieving industrialized operation, and developing industrial parks", Danfeng strives to build industrial bases, to develop leading industrialized enterprises such as Huamao Livestock Group and Shangluo Minle Modern Agricultural Technology Development Company to accelerate the transformation and upgrading of modern agriculture, and promote the continuous increase of farmers' income. As of the end of 2014, Danfeng, with the aim of building standardized production bases of 50 million broilers, focusing on the promotion of modern livestock and poultry farming equipment technology, had built standardized production bases of broilers in villages like Wangyuan in Shangzhen Town, and Tumen in Tumen Town. In these bases, there are 6 automatic overlapping cage-raising chicken houses and 40 FRP standard chicken houses, helping Huamao continue to grow and develop in an enabling environment[1]. Since the start-off of the fight against poverty, governments at all levels have continued to increase assistance to Huamao, and have provided comprehensive support and guarantees in terms of policies, funds, talents, and mechanisms, which has greatly enhanced Huamao's role as a leading enterprise in alleviating poverty. In 2016, when developing agricultural industry, Huamao obtained a loan of 10 million Yuan with assistance of the Shaanxi provincial government to expand the industrial category, and also provide support to more than 1.8 million Yuan of dividends for workers in financial difficulties. In 2018, when Huamao suffered from insufficient capital flow, it obtained a low-interest loan of 15 million Yuan with the help of the provincial government again. With the company's own efforts and the strong support of the government, Huamao has been listed as one of the "National Staple Food Processing Demonstration Enterprise" by the Ministry of Agriculture, and "Shaanxi Modern Agriculture Park" and "Key Shaanxi Agricultural Industrialization Leading Enterprise" by Shaanxi Province. [2] Huamao has become the major enterprise for industrial poverty alleviation in Danfeng, and the key industry for farmers to get rid of poverty and become well-off, which plays an important role in the development of poverty alleviation industries.

6.2.2　Deepening government-enterprise cooperation and improving industrial assistance

In the poverty alleviation campaign, the Danfeng government strengthened cooperation with Huamao, the leading enterprise. Huamao also set up a targeted poverty alleviation leading group with full-time poverty alleviation staff, and determined the idea of "the unified leadership of the general party branch, the responsibilities of the local party branch, and piloting role of party members" for the PA

①　"Danfeng County Joining Forces to Build Ten Industrial Bases", 2014-12-26, http://www. shangluo. gov. cn/info/1057/45655. htm.

②　"Leading Enterprises' Power in Poverty Alleviation", 2019-12-30, http://www. shaanxi. gov. cn/info/iList. jsp?tm_id = 166&cat_id = 18014&info_id = 157582.

campaign. Through the "government + enterprise (cooperative) + poverty-stricken households" working model, poor households are involved in all links of the whole industry chain of breeding, processing and distribution, which directly helped an accumulative total of 7, 795 persons from 2, 346 registered poverty-stricken households in the PA campaign with a total net income of 11. 83 million Yuan.

6. 2. 2. 1　Strengthening the use of funds to help poor people to gain dividends

Building poultry farming bases and cultivating large-scale chicken farmers are effective means to help poor households to start businesses and increase income. The Danfeng government determined the idea of "3393" in thepoverty alleviation campaign[①], which meant to make good use of 30 million poverty alleviation funds in 3 years in supporting 900 poor households to drive 3,000 poor people out of poverty in the broiler chicken breeding industry chain, and carried out in-depth cooperation with Huamao to let the whole industry chain of the enterprise to play the leading role in the anti-poverty campaign. As poor households were unable to afford the cost of building broiler farms due to lack of funds, the local government and the company jointly adopted assistance measures to provide financial support to the poor. It takes more than 300, 000 Yuan to build a second-generation house, for which the government and the company will provide interest-free loans of 150, 000 Yuan and 50, 000 Yuan respectively. Farmers themselves only have to raise the rest 100, 000 Yuan and the loan is deducted by the company in installments from the purchase of broilers. In addition to building chicken houses, poverty-stricken people also benefit from gaining dividends by using capital or forest land to invest in shares. In Zhaogou Village under the Longju Sub-district Office, where there are a large number of poverty-stricken people to carry out under-forest chicken farming, Huamao invested 8 million Yuan to transfer 21. 53 hectares of woodland, and established three professional farming cooperatives of free-range chickens, providing opportunities for 691 people from 211 poverty-stricken households. The farmers joined the cooperatives at 2, 000 Yuan

---

① "Danfeng Leading Enterprises Increasing Farmers' Income", *Shangluo Daily*, 2016-08-12.

per share with an average annual minimum dividend of 1, 000 Yuan. This, together with the transfer of land and labor income, made the average annual household income increased by 5, 300 Yuan, and 156 households were lifted out of poverty within one year. At present, a total of 5, 055 people from 1, 497 poor households have become shareholders of Huamao, and they have received dividends every year.

6. 2. 2. 2   Strengthening technical training and enhancing production skills of the poverty-stricken people

Aiming at the fact that poor households are lack of technology and funds, Huamao provided them with tailored services called "eight unification and four exemptions", which means unification in design of chicken coops, supply of chicks, supply of feed, immunization program, technical standards, purchasing price of chickens, processing and sales, and cooperation methods, to ensure that poor households without large-scale farming experience can also smoothly carry out breeding, and that the product quality is stable; "four exemptions" means that farmers are exempted from the costs of chicks, insurance, epidemic prevention and technical training to reduce the investment of poor households as much as possible. In 2019, while the market price of a chick is 2. 6 Yuan, the company provides chicks at 1 Yuan each for farmers, and the cost of chicks and feed offered to farmers will only be deducted when broilers are purchased from farmers. Danfeng also held a provincial professional farmer training course—Farmer Training Course of Haofeng Vocational School in cooperation with Huamao, provincial agricultural training bases, and private schools. This course focuses on the production skills for large-scale chicken breeding, attaches importance to various aspects of chicken farming and standardized techniques and forms a professional farmer training model of "agriculture bureau + private school + leading enterprise", which has been actively promoted throughout the Province. Many poverty-stricken people who have been trained are offered employment at Huamao[1]. Since 2016, a total of 452 persons from 141 poor households have been employed in

---

[1]   "Danfeng County Vigorously Developing Professional Farmer Training", 2012-06-12, http://www. csxfc. com/2010/html/news/express/2012/0612/22044. html.

Huamao's industrial chain, with a per capita annual income of 26, 500 Yuan.

6.2.2.3   Reducing industrial risks and helping poor households to "just make profits"

Reducing industrial risks is a guarantee for raising the poverty-stricken people's willingness to develop their businesses and for lifting them out of poverty smoothly. On the one hand, the Danfeng government has increased capital support to enhance the ability of leading companies to resist risks. The industrial insurance premiums of the six major industries including broiler farming are subsidized by the county-level industrial poverty alleviation development fund. In 2019, the local government formulated the *The Key Supporting Measures for the Development of Six Major Industries in Danfeng County*[1], which uses financial special poverty alleviation funds to support leading enterprises in the six major industries with the standards of 1 to 5 million Yuan for each enterprise. At the same time, the leading enterprises in the six major industries can apply subsidies for their loans. The county-level industrial development fund provides interest discounts at 3% of the total bank loans. The county-level industrial development fund will provide interest discounts at a rate of 3% of the total bank loans for three consecutive years with a cap of 900, 000 Yuan per enterprise each year. On the other hand, leading companies have enhanced the ability of poor households to withstand risks through chicken repurchasing and insurance coverage. Huamao places orders to purchase the broilers raised by the farmers in a unified manner, and the purchasing price of chicks at every batch is set at a protective price of 1 Yuan each, guaranteeing the minimum profit. For the free-range chicken farmers, they can sell the broilers by themselves according to market conditions. If they have difficulties in sales, Huamao can help the farmers to sell the broilers with a certain amount of profit guaranteed. In addition, the company has covered property insurance for chicken houses built by poor households. Through social fund-raising, company funding and farmers'

---

[1]   "Danfeng Introducing Development Support Measures for Six Industries", 2019-02-20, http://www. shangluo. gov. cn/info/1057/80628. htm.

fund-raising, a risk fund and a board of directors have been set up to compensate farmers for losses caused by diseases, disasters and accidents after assessment and approval. When such an event happens, the fund not only compensates the losses of the farmer, but also offers 0. 6 Yuan per chicken to the farmer as production and living expenses. Wang Guishui of Tumen Town had two chicken houses and in 2017 there was a sudden power outage when the broilers were to be slaughtered. Over half of 20, 000 chickens were smothered to death overnight. He got 110, 000 Yuan from the risk fund, which helped him overcome the difficulties.

6. 2. 3   Experiences and enlightenment

For successful poverty alleviation, we must strengthen social synergy. Danfeng County focuses on the promotion of leading enterprises' ability to reduce poverty and benefit the poor, and exerts its advantages to enhance the ability of poor people to develop industries and achieve stable poverty alleviation.

First, optimizing services to provide strong support to leading enterprises. Farmers are familiar with the businesses of agricultural enterprises which are directly linked to the farmers' interests. Such companies have the natural advantage of poverty alleviation. However, the characteristics of large investment, long cycle, and high risk in the agricultural industry determine that the development of enterprises cannot be separated from the strong support of the government. In the concentrated impoverished areas in particular, the small-scale agricultural enterprises are weak in market competitiveness and do not have much ability to alleviate poverty of local farmers. While actively introducing large enterprises with strong competitiveness outside the region, the government should also target local enterprises with development potential and strong sense of social responsibility, deepen government-enterprise cooperation, and give these enterprises more preferential policies and support so as to effectively cultivate local leading agricultural enterprises, just like growing "weak seedlings" into "big trees". The leading enterprises should play an important role in industrial development and poverty alleviation and enhance the ability of the poverty alleviation industry to resist risks.

Second, diversifying development channels and increase incomes. Leading agricultural enterprises need to innovate industrial development models, choose multiple development paths, extend industrial chains, connect enterprises, large-scale farming households and cooperatives, link the ever-changing large market with thousands of small farming households, and integrate production, processing, distribution, management and services. They should try to improve their own quality and profits, and implement multiple support models to maximize the PA effect through various forms such as "enterprise + cooperative + base + poor households".

Third, innovating mechanisms to link interests and promote a win-win result. Only when the poor have practical benefits in the development of the industry can they continue the enthusiasm to participate in production. Only when enterprises benefit from the PA campaign can they be more enthusiastic to continue the efforts. Only in this way can we realize the stable and long-term poverty reduction drive led by the enterprises in their own sustainable development. Leading enterprises are guided to lead poor households to develop their industries, which needs to find precise entry points for poverty alleviation in the industrial chain, grasps the connection points of interest in the development of industrial integration, finds the profit points of enterprises in the process of industrial poverty alleviation, and explores the establishment of a close interest connection mechanism that benefits multiple parties. We need to give full play to the leading role of leading enterprises, adhere to the principles of mutual benefit between enterprises and farmers, win-win results for economic and social benefits, and fully mobilize the enthusiasm of the government, enterprises and the farmers so that we can achieve the multi-win goals of industrial growth, enterprise development, and farmers' income increase.

Fourth, exploring ways to prevent risks and ensure long-term effectiveness. Due to weakness in capital and technology, poor households are less able to resist market risks than ordinary farmers, and effectively resisting market risks is a problem that must be solved to stabilize poverty alleviation. To guide agricultural enterprises to promote the development of industries for the poor, the companies should not only provide farmers with jobs and promote the development of industries, but also ensure the sustainability and reliability of their income. Through a variety of measures such as protective price purchase and the special risk fund, close links are established between enterprises and poor households in the sales process. Sustained and stable income growth is the key to industrial poverty alleviation. To achieve real poverty alleviation, while developing production it is necessary to explore and establish multiple guarantee mechanisms so that production development can really lift the poor out of poverty and become well-off.

6.3   Designated-area Poverty Alleviation in Donglu Village by CASS

The fixed-point poverty alleviation originated in 1986 constitutes an important composition in poverty alleviation with Chinese characteristics. Fixed-point poverty alleviation uniformly deployed by the Central government refers to the paired tailoraid preference and support in terms of funds, materials, technology, talents, projects, and information to designated impoverished counties by the central and state agencies, central committee of the democratic parties and the All-China Federation of Industry and Commerce, people's organizations, public institutions and large state-owned key enterprises, state-owned financial institutions, state key education and research institutions, military and armed forces. Chinese Academy of Social Sciences (CASS), with Danfeng County as its fixed-point poverty alleviation target[1], has concretely undertaken its given mission since 1993. Especially after 2016, in active answer to call of the CPC Central Committee, the Chinese Academy of Social Sciences and its staff have fully dedicated to the anti-poverty work, actively exerted their own advantages, innovated the poverty alleviation approaches, and harvested remarkable achievements in the fixed-point poverty alleviation in Danfeng County and designated poverty alleviation in Donglu village via measures like the

---

① " Fixed-point   poverty   alleviation ",   http://f. china. com. cn/2017-06/19/content _ 41055351. htm.

long-term poverty reduction platform establishment and endogenous development power cultivation, highlighting the important value of fixed-point poverty alleviation undertakings.

6. 3. 1   Assuming social responsibilities for fixed-point poverty alleviation

Fixed-point poverty alleviation distinguishes itself in the establishment of stable relations between alleviating agencies and impoverished areas and in promoting the normalized, long-term and institutionalized tailoraid assistance from the fixed donor to recipient. General Secretary Xi Jinping made important directives on the fixed-point poverty alleviation of government agencies, enterprises and institutions, emphasizing that fixed-point poverty alleviation endeavors by party organizations, government and military agencies, SOEs and public institutions makes up an important part of the cause of poverty alleviation and development with Chinese characteristics, and embodies political and institutional advantages of China. [1] Since 1993 when Danfeng County was designated as the poverty alleviation and development target of the Chinese Academy of Social Sciences, CASS has exerted its own superior resources and launched related programs for poverty alleviation in line with the actual situation of Danfeng County. As of 2015, a total of more than 100 million Yuan has been self-raised, introduced and channeled and over 300 poverty alleviation projects implemented for reducing poverty in Danfeng. [2] Since the fight against poverty, the Chinese Academy of Social Sciences has continued to assume its social responsibilities in active respond to the initiatives of the central government and to proceed with the in-depth poverty alleviation assistance.

---

[1]   "Xi Jinping Instructions on the Targeted Poverty Alleviation work of Government Enterprises and Institutions", 2015-12-11, http: //www. xinhuanet. com/politics/2015-12/11/c_1117436649.

[2]   Lv Sha, "CASS and its Poverty Alleviation in Danfeng", *Special Issue of the Chinese Academy of Social Sciences*, No. 288, March 20, 2015.

6. 3. 2   Optimizing unit strength for innovative ways out of poverty

6. 3. 2. 1   Innovative thinking and long-term platform for poverty alleviation

In the fixed-point poverty alleviation assistance, the Chinese Academy of Social Sciences strove to innovative thinking for long-term benefits, worked hard in mechanism and platform construction, and conducted a series of good practices with sustainable contributions. One is the formulation of the overall working mechanism. CASS formulated after exploration an overall working mechanism featuring "the leadership by the party, organization by of the leading group for poverty alleviation, first responsibility to appointed cadres and the first secretary in the village, and joint contribution from subordinate institutions ", [1] effectively pooled strength, coordinated various forces, and promoted the concrete implementation of poverty alleviation projects. The second is the innovation on patterns of industry assistance. Drawing on the "miro-credit" experience from Bangladesh, short-term, small, unsecured and uncollateralized lending were issued to the poor farmers. "Poverty Alleviation Cooperatives" integrating production and operation, village affairs management, public welfare carried out in Danfeng County under the leadership of the village CPC branch changed the traditional lump-sum loan issuance and repayment by weekly installment payments without guarantees, resolved the contradiction between the loan application and lack of guarantee and raised the industrial development capabilities of the impoverished population. More than 20 million Yuan of poverty alleviation loan issued by the " Poverty Alleviation Cooperatives" in County by far has greatly reduced the financing costs of the poor households. [2] The third is the consumption platform for poverty alleviation. In order to better link production supply and sales demand of

---

[1]   Ming Haiying, "Join Forces to Tackle the Problem-Interview with Wang Xiaoxia, Director of the Poverty Alleviation Office of the Chinese Academy of Social Sciences", *China Social Science News*, 2020-01-17.

[2]   Lv Sha, "CASS and its Poverty Alleviation in Danfeng", *Special Issue of the Chinese Academy of Social Sciences*, No. 288, March 20, 2015.

farm and sideline products, CASS joined the Bank of China in building an "CASS Public Benefit" e-commerce platform to purchase agro-products as holiday gifts for employees by labor unions from Danfeng County of Shaanxi Province and Shangyou County of Jiangxi Province (another designated County in poverty alleviation). As of the end of December 2019, CASS purchased a total of 2.47 million Yuan of agro-products online and offline and solidly improved effectiveness of poverty alleviation through consumption.

6.3.2.2　Endogenous Development Drive Cultivation Based on Think-tank

Fully playing its own think-tank advantages, CASS closely connected its experts and scholars to poverty alleviation practices in various training and investigations to assist the public quality improvement and social-economic development and to cultivate endogenous drive for self-development of the impoverished areas. One option is to hold training for the officials and general public. CASS organized distinguished experts with in-depth academic research on different disciplines to deliver various training and top-notch lectures such as "Interpretation of the Central Document No. 1" and "Chinese Culture of Clean Governance" for the cadres and the masses in multiple forms including the "Social Science Forum". Besides, a total of 130 copies of "China Social Science Today" were gifted to cadres at all levels and related schools in Danfeng County to elevate their awareness and expand their horizon. The second is to develop local resources in depth. Experts and scholars from CASS Institute of Rural Development, Urban Development and Environment Institute, the History Research Institute and the Financial and Economic Research Institute were invited to conduct thematic surveys in the county to promote the utilization of the historical and cultural resources along the Shangluo-Neixiang ancient merchant road and the development of tourism in Danfeng. Experts advised on key development projects such as beautiful countryside and characteristic towns construction and thanks to their guidance, Wanwan village of Dihua Town was named the "National Model Beautiful Village, National Key Support Village for Tourism and National Civilized Village"; Taohuagu valley of Zhulinguan Town was named "National

Water Conservancy Scenic Area and National Soil and Water Conservation Technology Demonstration Park". The third is to develop the industries in line with local conditions. The one-stop chicken farming industry developed by the "company + cooperative + poor households" model supported a total of 100 poor households and 371 poor people in Zhaogou Village of Longjuzhai Town and Longquan Village of Tumen Town to raise scattered chickens and earned each poor household an annual net income of about 3, 000 Yuan. Supported by the tea companies, the same industry model was applied to integrate funds and resources to support poor households to eliminate poverty by tea planting and making. The first secretary sent by Chinese Academy of Social Sciences to Donglu Village of Zhulinguan Town, a typical poverty-stricken village, conducted in-depth investigation of the whole village with the task force and cadres of the village, established a number of professional cooperatives for quality peppercorns and tea cultivation and rural tourism development, and effectively guaranteed the income of the poor population by long-, medium-and short-term industries projects. E-commerce was set as an effective move for targeted poverty alleviation and a three-tier e-commerce service system in counties, Towns and villages was established to stir up the entrepreneurship passion and clear the difficulties for product sales. In 2018, Danfeng County was approved as the national demonstration county for countryside e-commerce.

6. 3. 2. 3　Overall and genuine dedication to improving living necessities

Poverty alleviation shall start from grounding work and genuinely serve the daily demands of the impoverished population. The Chinese Academy of Social Sciences has effectively launched a series of moves such as infrastructure construction, educational poverty alleviation and health aid to solve the living difficulties of the poor. First is to support infrastructure construction. The Chinese Academy of Social Sciences actively participated in the infrastructure projects closely related to people's lives including the road and bridge construction, river embankments and dangerous houses restoration, and safe drinking water projects, etc in Danfeng County. Examples are the 5. 9 kilometers of cement roads and 36. 1 kilometers of sandstone roads built in altogether 9

villages and 6 towns including Donghe Village of Longju Town and Jieping Village of Taoping Town which greatly facilitated the lives of local people. In Taer Village of Yuling Town, 2. 3 kilometers of destroyed river embankment were restored and the private cultivated land of 1342 villagers and 358 households were protected from river floods. ①
The second is enhance educational poverty alleviation. "CASS Education Fund" and "Excellent Teacher and Student Award" were set up in CASS Hope Primary School of Danfeng County and Wanwan Primary School in Diwan Town; teaching materials and instruments were purchased for various schools including Caichuan K1-K9 School; and financial support were offered to poor students at different schooling age. The third is to carry out multiple ways of health aid. The Chinese Academy of Social Sciences has organized experts to Danfeng County for voluntary clinics to care for the health and deliver medicine and medical services to the poor population. Tens of thousands Yuan of drugs have been distributed for free, training and teaching observation were held to improve the diagnosis and treatment technology of local medical staff. The fourth is to present selfless commitment and sincere donation. All CASS members sincerely devoted and actively contributed to practising poverty alleviation. The "CASS Care Pack" with walkman, velvet blanket, umbrella, hand warmer, scarf and other items inside was designed and given to poor mothers in the mountains. A large number of CASS experts and scholars actively donated money and materials to the poor population. The former CASS deputy dean Ru Xin and his wife Xia Sen have continuously done their best in donation for many years. In 2013, Xia Sen donated 1 million Yuan for the education fund named after her and the couple donated nearly 1. 3 million Yuan cumulatively in years to help the poor students. ②

① Zhong Dai, "Fixed-point Poverty Alleviation of CASS in Danfeng County since the 18th CPC National Congress", *Special Issue of the Chinese Academy of Social Sciences*, No. 326, January 8, 2016.
② Lv Sha, "CASS and its Poverty Alleviation in Danfeng", *Special Issue of the Chinese Academy of Social Sciences*, No. 288, March 20, 2015.

6. 3. 3   Enlightenment of poverty alleviation by CASS

6. 3. 3. 1   Practical and innovative anti-poverty approaches based on think-tank

In the fixed-point poverty alleviation undertakings, the Chinese Academy of Social Sciences set up pilot "Poverty Alleviation Cooperatives" and "CASS Public Benefit" e-commerce platform, innovated effective forms of poverty alleviation by industries and consumption, trained the local officials and general public in poverty-stricken counties on their knowledge and capacity, and advised and guided the sustainable development through in-depth research and professional specialties, etc., all which displayed the strength and contribution of think-tank for colleges, universities and research institutes to participate in poverty alleviation. Taking its own professional advantages as unique superiority, HEIs on one hand shall be courageous enough to innovate and keep searching new models and paths to effectively combat the poverty and concretely implement policies of central government through the combination of theory and practice. Equally important are the various forms of training held to transmit advantageous resources to help improve the quality of local population and better cultivate endogenous development power in poor areas.

6. 3. 3. 2   Systematic governance of fixed-point poverty alleviation

Since the 18th National Congress of the Communist Party of China, the central government and various state departments have taken fixed-point poverty alleviation as a major political task to fulfill, fight and act. As of August 2019, 1, 727 temporarily-positioned cadres and the first secretaries in the village have been appointed, 71. 37 billion Yuan of assistance fund invested and introduced, 649 thousand officials and technicians trained, 63. 67 billion Yuan of agro-products purchased and helped sold, and 89 poverty-stricken counties, 19, 000 poor villages and

13 million impoverished people lifted out of poverty. [①] Fixed-point poverty alleviation by government agencies and institutions constitutes an important component of the poverty alleviation mission with Chinese characteristics. Tackling poverty is a systematic project involving active participation of and devoted contribution from all walks of life. All sides shall join this great cause in an effective, orderly, and efficient manner, fully play their professional features and advantages, and establish the working mechanism and architecture in the systematic management of poverty alleviation. After eliminating poverty, it is necessary to systematically explore the effective approaches for long-term fixed-point assistance by government agencies, enterprises and institution to consolidate the achievements and combat the relative poverty through institutionalized programs.

6. 3. 2. 3   Long-term institution-county cooperation for mutual benefits

Practice and achievements of fixed-point poverty alleviation of CASS in Danfeng County mirrored the significant value of strengthened bonds and profound cooperation between research institutions and the designated counties. To begin with, institution- County cooperation can promote the social responsibility and provide practical platform for research work of institutions, deepen their understanding of national conditions at the grass-roots and practical level, link their scientific research with grounded practice to maximize the effectiveness of scientific research. On the other hand, the advantages and resources of the institutions can work as "brain bank" and "think tanks" for regional economic and social development to inject new ideas and vitality into local economic and social development from a broader perspective. The feasible approaches and effective models for establishing mutually-beneficial cooperation between research institutions and designated counties shall be constantly push forward in the exploration and practice for advancing the modernization of the national governance system and

---

① " Dedicated to the Original Aspiration-Exhibition of Fixed-point Poverty Alleviation Achievement by Central and State Agencies", 2019-08-19, http: //dangjian. people. com. cn/n1/2019/ 0819 / c117092-31302187. html.

governing capacity.

6.4   Alignment of Poverty Alleviation and Living Security Policies in Danfeng County

Poverty management in China is driven by dual programs of poverty alleviation and development projects and rural minimum living security policy. The cohesive alignment of the two policies on poverty alleviation and rural minimum living security is an important issue to be continuously coordinated in the process of poverty management. Early in the "Twelfth Five-Year Plan" period (2011 – 2015), Shangluo City has contributed its successful experience in effectively converging the two programs in poverty management practice for the whole country. Since the fight of poverty alleviation, Danfeng has improved and upgraded the two programs on the basis of former experience, and achieved remarkable results in pooling the resources and efforts for poverty alleviation and insightful enlightenment to advance the modernization of national governance.

6.4.1   Background of two major policies for anti-poverty undertakings

On July 11, 2007, the *Notice on Establishing a Rural Minimum Living Security System in the Countryside issued by the State Council* (SC Doc. [2007] No. 19) marked the new era of "two-wheel" drive by subsistence allowance policy and poverty alleviation and development project in the anti-poverty campaign in China. The rural minimum living security policy is to guarantee the subsistence of the poor, while poverty alleviation and development project highlights tackling the development obstacles of the impoverished people and areas. These two programs varied in terms of policy orientation while joined each other consistently for the optimal target of ensuring and improving people's livelihood. [1] In

---

[1]   Xiang Yangsheng, "Alignment, Evaluation and Reform of Poverty Alleviation Development and Rural Minimum Living Security Systems", *Guizhou Social Sciences*, 2013 (12), pp. 82 – 86.

real practice, the two policies formed through different institutional proceedings are implemented by two respective departments following different identification standards, methods and procedures for different numbers and groups of poor population, demonstrating low degree of interlacing, matching and coverage. [1] Once the two policies cannot be effectively aligned, the efficient use of poverty alleviation resources and orderly advancement of anti-poverty work might be detained or delayed. The Third Plenary Session of the Seventeenth Central Committee of the Communist Party of China ever instructed to maintain an "effective alignment between the rural minimum living security policy and the poverty alleviation and development project". On May 7, 2010, *Notice on Forwarding the Instruction of the Poverty Alleviation Office and Other Departments on Pilot Alignment between Rural Minimum Living Security Policy and the Poverty Alleviation and Development Project* (SC Office Doc. [2010] No. 31) issued by the General Office of the State Council vigorously promoted pilot work of policies alignment between these two programs. Since the launching of anti-poverty campaign, the rural minimum living security as a cushion net set for poverty alleviation has played a significant role in solving the poverty problem of the most needed. On September 17, 2016, the General Office of the State Council forwarded the "Notice on Guidelines on the *Effective Alignment between the Rural Minimum Living Security System and the Poverty Alleviation and Development Policy* (SC Office Doc [2016] No. 70) by Ministry of Civil Affairs, emphasizing "the effective alignment between the rural minimum living security system and the poverty alleviation and development policy to ensure that the rural poverty-stricken people under the current poverty alleviation standards will be lifted out of poverty by 2020, "[2] and proposing higher requirements for the convergence of the two policies.

---

[1]　Zuo Zing, He Li, "Integration: A comparative study of the two systems of rural minimum living security and poverty alleviation development", *Public Administration Review*, 2017 (3), pp. 7 – 25 + 213.

[2]　"Notice on Effective Alignment between the Rural Minimum Living Security System and the Poverty Alleviation and Development Policy", SC Office Doc [2016] No. 70.

6. 4. 2   Practice of Danfeng on alignment of living security and anti-poverty development policies

To fulfill the requirements by the central government, Danfeng County actively carried out effective exploratory trials on the two policies alignment at its full initiative and resulted positive impact during the twelfth and thirteenth five-year plan periods.

6. 4. 2. 1   Practice and experiences attained in the twelfth Five-year Plan period

Since the pilot alignment of the rural minimum living security policy and anti-poverty development project, Shangluo city has been exploring and accumulating systematic and effective practical experiences in the twelfth five-year plan period. In implementing the alignment, the four-stage working procedures of "preparation, identification, registration and policies fulfillment" in accordance with the "targeted and household" policy requirements was verified, the eight-step operation standard including " indicators determination, team review, household application, household identification, democratic appraisal, review and approval, registration entry, and policies formulating and implementing" was established and specified. In consideration of actual work proceeding, a "low-income households ranking method" was developed in which the village representatives determined in public the low-income households in the descending order, and a negative list of 6-exclusions was formulated in determining the poverty identification, namely, exclusions of "households living in multistorey buildings or commercial housings" "households with motor vehicles and large agricultural machinery" " households with full-time job and stable income " "households with public employees" "households with higher daily consumption level" and "households with long-term employees for production and business activities". [①] In August, 2011, the national site meeting of alignment between the two policies was held in Shangluo and hundreds of participants from all over the country visited Jianzi Village

---

① "Two Measures of Shangluo on Policies Alignment Promoted as National Experience in Poverty Alleviation", 2011-08-19, Http: // www. shangluo. gov. cn/info/1054/3949. htm.

and Youfangjie Village in Danfeng County for the implementation of the pilot alignment of the living security policy and anti-poverty development project and the above practical experiences effected positive contribution to the whole country.

6.4.2.2   Optimization and upgrading of the policies alignment in the 13th Five-year Plan Period

Since 2016, poverty alleviation through social security system has been included as an important division of the five-batch anti-poverty strategies. On the basis of the earlier experience, Danfeng County furthered the alignment of the two policies by enrolling all the registered impoverished households stricken by illness, disability or disaster, with no labor force, and those cannot reduce poverty through industrial development or employment, etc., in the coverage and range for catch-all security and assistance, which increased the precision of living security provision and channeled rural minimum living security policy to exert better role in assisting the most impoverished more effectively.

Danfeng County further defined the "responsibilities at four levels", namely, the responsibility of Towns (sub-districts) for verification, the responsibility of country civil affairs bureau for approval, the responsibility of industry sectors for coordinated supervision, and the responsibility of village organizations for assistance and cooperation, strictly followed the "six standards"[1] in the six key links of policy implementation, verification procedures, democratic appraisal, approval and publicity, fund distribution, and file management, publicize the review process for the application of the living securities or "five-guarantees (guarantee the poor with food, clothing, medical care, housing and burial expenses)" and the photos and basic information of the beneficiaries with the results "ensured by the entrusted cadres to the village and signed by the investigator". At the same time, the supervision process was further strengthened via the normalized 100% household investigation on the beneficiary by the township agencies, random checking of no less than 30% of beneficiaries by the county civil affairs

---

[1]   "Danfeng county Building a Guarantee Net in Poverty Alleviation", 2017-11-30, http: // www. danfeng. gov. cn/xwzx/dfyw/18363. htm.

department, the supervision by the general public[1] to improve the precision of living security distribution.

Meanwhile, information technology was applied to reduce work costs and improve the accuracy and dynamics of identification and assistance. An information verification management platform with needed index system on household economic conditions was established and inter-connected with information resources from functional departments for business registration, payroll management, vehicle management, pension insurance, public welfare positions, tax management and others for accurately screening and determining the income, property, family structure and other information of the applicant and automatically generating the verification report. [2] The report results were timely used for policy beneficiaries identification and adjustments to promote the inclusion of all the qualified applicants and exclusion of disqualified beneficiaries. As of November 2019, 13,616 people in 5,013 households were secured by the rural minimum living allowances, an increase of 3, 716 people in1,735 households year-on-year, and the coverage rate for the impoverished increased to 5.55% of the total. [3]

6.4.3 Experiences and enlightenment on synergistic governance and local vitality activation

6.4.3.1 Systematic poverty alleviation by united efforts

Poverty alleviation is by no means the duty of a certain department, nor to be possibly resolved by a single anti-poverty policy independently, which adds to the importance of the alignment between policies and departments in the process of poverty alleviation. [4] Poverty alleviation as

---

① "'Five-ones and Five-solutions' Mechanism in Poverty Alleviation", 2017-09-14, https://www.sohu.com/a/192199259_100000034.

② "The Bottom line for Securing all the Impoverished-reports on the Poverty Alleviation Practice of Danfeng", 2018-08-03, https://www.sohu.com/a/245079338_100000034.

③ "Security Net in Danfeng County to Guarantee a Happy Life", 2019-11-18, http://www.sxslnews.com/pc/index/article/76213.

④ Zheng Hangsheng, Li Mianguan, "Individual and Society in the Process of Poverty Alleviation in China—An Interpretation of Social Mutual Construction Theory", *Teaching and Research*, 2009 (6), pp. 5 – 10.

a systematic project is secured by the effective participation and in-depth cooperation of multiple subjects and implementation of a lot of public policies. For establishing a large-scale poverty alleviation structure and aggregate the joint efforts to combat poverty, it is vital to coordinate the cooperation between different departments, different subjects and different public policies, to manage the alignment between poverty alleviation policies in avoidance of policies disagreement, and to eliminate poverty in an efficient and orderly manner.

6.4.3.2   Synergistic governance through policies alignment

The alignment between anti-poverty development projects and living security policies highlights the concept of targeted and differentiated poverty alleviation, and marks a further transformation of rural poverty governance paradigm in China. [1] The policies alignment significantly impacts not only in poverty governance, also in the overall social governance issues like that between urban and rural basic medical insurance and medical aid, environmental impact assessment and pollution discharge permit, etc. and even national governance like the cooperation among industry sectors or alignment among different public policies. In all, the effective policies alignment and the synergistic governance are of high value to improve the governance of the whole country.

6.4.3.3   Practical experiences on local vitality activation

Under the poverty alleviation governance architecture "planned by central government, headed by provincial government and implemented by cities and counties government", Chinese poverty governance to a large extent depends heavily on "top-down promotion" in which the central government issues policies to guide local poverty alleviation practices. Under the premise of honest implementation of the central government policy, the local vitality shall be vigorously generated because the wisdom and dedication of the grassroots workers are the key

---

① Xiang Deping, Liu Xin, "Constructing Diversified Anti-poverty Policy: Effective Alignment between Rural Minimum Living Security and Poverty Alleviation and Development Policies", *Social Work and Management*, 2014 (3), pp. 54 – 61 + 100.

to solve the problems in the implementation of the policy in line with actual conditions in different regions and to maximize the efficiency and effectiveness of the central policies. The institutional vitality and local experiences shall be activated and motivated in the poverty governance and even the overall national governance to explore innovation in practice, refine and promote the good experiences and practices in effective mechanisms and forms, and synergize policies for collective force to advance the modernization of national governance.

Conclusion
From Poverty Alleviation to Rural Revitalization

General Secretary Xi Jinping pointed out that absolute poverty which has existed for hundreds of years in China will be historically solved in our generation if the target of eradicating poverty is met as planned. [①] Being lifted out of poverty is not an end in itself but the starting point of a new life and a new pursuit. In response to the change of principal contradiction in China, it is necessary to clarify the working ideas and push on the poverty reduction strategy and the smooth transformation of the work system. Besides, all of these changes should integrate into the rural revitalization strategy and establish the system and mechanism which takes a holistic approach, and addresses both symptoms and root causes. [②] China will persistently elevate the development capacity of the low-income population in underdeveloped and rural areas, and strive to achieve common prosperity at an early date by addressing relative poverty and implementing strategies of rural revitalization.

1.1 Poverty Alleviation in China from the Perspective of the Practice in Qinling-Bashan Mountainous Region

The main battlefield of targeted poverty alleviation is in the mountainous area and Qinling-Bashan Mountainous Region, one of

---

① Xi Jinping, "The speech at the symposium on getting rid of poverty accurately", *QIUSHI*, 2020 (9).

② Xi Jinping, "The speech at the forum on decisive battle to overcome poverty", *People's Daily*, 2020-03-07(2).

China's 14 contiguous areas of extreme poverty stretching mainly across Shaanxi Province, is a typical example. Shangluo City in southern Shaanxi Province used to be the hardest nut to crack for the provincial government because of the extensiveness and seriousness of poverty and a large number of impoverished rural residents. From the foregoing of this report, poverty alleviation is a requirement of the times and a historical mission, and history shows that since the reform and opening-up, and especially since the 18th National Congress of the Communist Party of China, in order to win the battle against poverty and to finish building a moderately prosperous society in all respects, efforts and targeted measures were made in the Qinling-Bashan Mountainous Region with historic achievements. In September, 2018, the People's Government of Shaanxi Province authorized four counties (districts) to be removed from the poverty list, including Yanchang County, Hengshan County, Dingbian County, and Foping County. Foping County is just located in Qinling-Bashan Mountainous Region, becoming the first poor County which had been removed from the poverty list in southern Shaanxi Province. On May 7th, 2019, the provincial government issued announcement on poverty alleviation of twenty-three counties including Zhouzhi County, [①] including Liuba County in Hanzhong City, Zhenping County in Ankang City and Zhen'an County in Shangluo City. Thereinto, Zhen'an County not only became the first county in Shangluo City to get out of poverty, but also the first county in eleven of extremely impoverished areas in Shaanxi Province. According to the *Reply on Approving the Poverty Alleviation of Twenty-nine Counties (districts) including Yintai District of Tongchuan City* ([2020] No. 22) issued by the People's Government of Shaanxi Province on February 27th, 2020, Nanzheng District, Chenggu County, Yangxian County, Mianxian County, Xixiang County, Lueyang County, Zhenba County, Ningqiang County in Hanzhong City, Hanbin District, Pingli County, Xunyang County, Shiquan County, Ziyang County, Baihe County, Hanyin County, Ningshan County, Langao County in Ankang City, Shangzhou District, Luonan County, Shanyang County, Danfeng

---

① "Announcement About Twenty-three Counties Including Zhouzhi County Removed From the Poverty List", 2019-05-07, http://www. shaanxi. gov. cn/gk/zfgg/139020. htm.

County, Shangnan County, Zhashui County in Shangluo City had all been lifted out of the current poverty line, marking a historic achievement in poverty eradication among poor counties in the region for all twenty-seven counties (districts) in Hanzhong, Ankang and Shangluo in Shaanxi Province to win the battle of poverty alleviation. At the same time, poor counties in Qinling-Bashan Mountainous Region of Henan Province, Hubei Province and Chongqing Municipality, along with Wudu District, Wenxian County, Kangxian County, Chengxian County, Huixian County, and Liangdang County in Longnan City, Gansu Province all shook off poverty at the end of 2019. Furthermore, Dangchang County, Li County and Xihe County in Longnan City, Gansu Province will also be removed from the poverty list by the end of 2020.

From the foregoing of this report, it is clear that governments in Qinling-Bashan Mountainous Region remain committed to poverty alleviation as their central task and pursued the economic and social development in a coordinated way. Governments at all levels focused on ensuring that rural poor people do not have to worry about food and clothing and have access to compulsory education, basic medical services and safe housing. Meanwhile, they also fully implemented the requirements of "Eight Batches" and "Six Precision" and did their utmost to overcome the solid block of deep poverty. As a result, the basic production and living conditions in poor areas have been significantly improved, the income of the poor increased, and the development of economic and social in poor areas obviously accelerated. By strengthening party building and promoting poverty alleviation, grassroots organizations in poor areas have been consolidated, and the skills of cadres at grass-roots level have been markedly improved, thus consolidating the Party's ruling foundation in rural areas. By the end of 2019, the number of impoverished people in Shangluo City had been decreased to 15,300, and the poverty headcount ratio was controlled at 1.3%. From 2016 to 2019, the number of the impoverished people in Ankang City was reduced by 548,300, and the poverty headcount ratio dropped to 1.3% percent from 23.5%. At the end of 2019, 645,000 people in Hanzhong City had came out of poverty and the incidence of poverty had fallen to 0.9%, achieving a great success in "Winning the Battle Against Poverty".

The practice and effect of poverty alleviation in Qinling-Bashan Mountainous Region is a microcosm of China's practice to get rid of absolute poverty. Poverty alleviation is an effective way to eliminate and control poverty filled with Chinese characteristics, explored and practiced positively and bravely under the leadership of the CPC. The Chinese experience in the field of poverty alleviation is at least reflected in the following four aspects:

Firstly, upholding the Party's centralized and unified leadership is the fundamental guarantee for the success of poverty alleviation in China. The CPC is the core of leadership in contemporary China and the Party exercises overall leadership over all areas of endeavor in every part of the country. The Party always regards the eradication of poverty, the promotion of people's livelihood and the realization of common prosperity as the essential requirements of socialism. The Party also regards wholeheartedly pursuing happiness for the people as its original intention and historical mission. " Strengthening Party's leadership is the foundation for poverty alleviation. It is necessary to make full use of the role of Party committees at all levels in controlling the overall situation and coordinating all parties and put first-violin's responsibilities for poverty alleviation into effect. Besides, the implementation of the responsibilities of secretaries at all levels should be highly valued. The above practices provide a strong political guarantee for poverty alleviation. "[1] Taking the political advantages of Party's leadership, relying on Party's strong leadership and giving play to the core function of Party organization ensured the smooth development of poverty alleviation. In the practice of poverty alleviation in Qinling-Bashan Mountainous Region, which is a great and arduous battle, the Party always stood at the forefront of poverty alleviation and penetrated Party's ideology into the whole process of poverty alleviation. The systematic thinking model of Party Building Plus has become the best way for Party organizations at all levels to carry out their original missions in Qinling-Bashan Mountainous Region. Party's leadership inspired endless fighting power. Sticking to the absolute leadership of the Party over poverty

---

[1]   Research Institute of Party History and Documents of the Central Committee of the CPC, *Xi Jinping's Thesis of Poverty Alleviation*, Central Party Literature Press, 2018, p. 50.

alleviation is determined by the superiority of the Party, which has a strong political mobilization ability and advantage, being able to mobilizing all forces and resources quickly and efficiently, concentrate its efforts on fighting annihilation, gnaw the "hard bones" in poverty alleviation, and finally achieve the goal of poverty alleviation.

Secondly, adhering to the notable advantage of the socialist system with Chinese Characteristics is the key to success in poverty alleviation. "Poverty alleviation is the common responsibility of the Communist Party of China and the whole society. It is necessary to mobilize the whole society to participate in. "[1] Based on its national conditions, the Chinese government gives full play to the political advantage of the system of socialism with Chinese characteristics capable of pooling all necessary resources to solve major problems and introduces the working mechanism of "Party Leads, Government Guides, Society Participates" to integrate poverty alleviation project into the overall national developing strategy, so as to form a poverty alleviation system with the participation of multiple subjects, including departments, regions, industries and the whole society. By coordinating manpower, material, financial and intellectual resources necessary, China has made concerted efforts to develop a path of poverty alleviation with Chinese characteristics and acquired innovative achievements in the practice of socialist poverty governance based on basic national conditions

Thirdly, insisting on combining the precise strategies with targeted poverty alleviation and ambition promotion is an effective way to success in poverty alleviation. One of the important factors in the success of poverty alleviation in China is adhering to "Six Precision", the basic strategy of poverty alleviation proposed by General Secretary Xi Jinping, who called for policies and programs of assistance to be tailored for the needs of individual families in conjunction with targeted funding and village-specific expert support, and to be pursued with a results-oriented focus. By doing so, a precise work system for poverty alleviation was established and questions like "Who need support?" "Who to support?" and "How to support?" were answered. General Secretary Xi Jinping

---

[1]　Research Institute of Party History and Documents of the Central Committee of the CPC, *Xi Jinping's Thesis of Poverty Alleviation*, Central Party Literature Press, 2018, p. 99.

believes targeted approach will determine the success of the poverty alleviation drive, and it is necessary to find out the root of poverty, and make tailored and specific plans. [1] Not only attention should be given to giving material assistance, but also to stimulating the endogenous impetus of the poor. Besides, it is also important ensure that market plays the positive role in allocating resources, attracting capital and stimulating vitality in poverty governance. The impoverished people are not just the targets, but also the center of poverty alleviation. [2] Insisting on combining the ambition promotion with intellectual enhancement and technology improvement, converting limited resources into assets through market and using multiple methods simultaneously which include improving education, providing better health-care, developing e-commerce, promoting tourism in poor areas, implementing projects of poverty alleviation, offering properties, developing PV and so on, China effectively stimulated the internal impetus of poor areas and the poor to fight against poverty.

Finally, insisting on combining reformation with development and poverty alleviation is the basis for success in poverty alleviation. Reform and opening up is not only the path to a stronger China, and is also way to wipe out poverty. The reform and opening up in China has yielded huge dividends which promised a rapid economic growth and a solid financial ground year by year, and laid a solid material foundation for poverty alleviation. On the one hand, by increasing investment in poor areas, the infrastructure conditions there were greatly improved, thus creating conditions for the poor to get rid of poverty. On the other hand, by increasing transfer payments to poor areas financially, the government was able to increase the supply of public goods and services there and provided a guarantee for poverty alleviation. As the result of the economic development and the enhancement of comprehensive national strength, people's well-being has been constantly improving. China's national basic public service system has also been perfecting in ensuring people's

---

[1] Research Institute of Party History and Documents of the Central Committee of the CPC, *Xi Jinping's Thesis of Poverty Alleviation*, Central Party Literature Press, 2018, p. 72.

[2] *The selected documents since 18th National Congress of the Communist Party of China*, Vol. 2, Central Party Literature Press, 2018, p. 37.

access to childcare, education, employment, medical services, elderly care, housing, and social assistance. In a word, by strengthening the construction of inclusive programs helping improve livelihood and providing social welfare assistance in poor areas, multiple levels and diverse needs of the people have been guaranteed and the achievements of poverty alleviation have been consolidated.

1. 2   From Absolute Poverty-extinguishing to Relative Poverty-alleviating

Poverty alleviation is of vital importance in state governance in the world and all time. China insists on following the path of common prosperity to achieve overall poverty alleviation and comprehensive poverty eradication in poor regions. China's successful practice of poverty alleviation has further strengthened the confidence in the path, theory, system, and culture of socialism with Chinese characteristics and provided a new option for those countries and peoples in the world hoping to accelerate their development while maintaining their independence.

At present, China is only solving the problem of absolute rural poverty (i. e. 2, 300 Yuan per person per year at constant 2010 prices, with "two no worries and three guarantees" as the standard for poverty alleviation). In reality, it is still difficult to consolidate the gains made in poverty reduction. Among the regions and populations that have emerged from poverty, questions still exist, such as weak industrial base, homogenized industrial projects, unstable employment, high policy income ratios, the risk of returning to poverty, and the risk of causing poverty among marginalized populations respectively. For example, "relocation" of migrants is initially solved, but efforts are still needed to ensure their settlement, employment and progressive enrichment.

For the counties, villages and people who just have removed the label of poverty, China will maintain the overall stability of its existing policy—giving them a leg up to get them going. General Secretary Xi Jinping stressed while lifting people out of poverty was the first step, efforts should be made to ensure the relocated residents can settle down, which means that poverty-relief policies and poverty-relief teams should be retained for a period of time, so as to find ways and means to develop industries and strengthen the collective economy, ensuring that they can have jobs, earn money and lead better lives. [1] At the same time, the strict implementation of the "four not to take off" (not to take off the responsibility, not to take off the policy, not to take off the help, not to take off the supervision) should be required, and the coordinated promotion of the balanced development of poor and non-poor villages, poverty-relief households and non-poor households should also be introduced. We need to make sure that efforts, capital investment, policy support, help, supervision and assessment are not reduced, and continue to maintain zero poverty, consolidate the results of poverty alleviation, solidify the basis of development, strengthen the management of infrastructure and the follow-up management of relocation, continuously improve production and living conditions, ensuring that the rural poor population under the current standards all out of poverty, and that the results of the poverty alleviation campaign stand the test of history and people.

After completely eradicating absolute poverty, China will center more on addressing relative poverty. The Fourth Plenary Session of the 19th Central Committee of the CPC clearly put forward the idea of "resolutely winning and consolidating the achievements of the battle to alleviate poverty, and establishing a long-term mechanism to resolve relative poverty". This provides a direction for poverty alleviation after 2020 and marks a shift in the focus of China's poverty alleviation efforts from the elimination of absolute poverty to addressing relative poverty.

After comprehensively completing the task of poverty alleviation, China will enter the post-poverty alleviation era, when China will transform poverty alleviation from mainly solving income poverty to solving expenditure-based and capacity poverty in a comprehensive manner; from relying solely on the "three rural areas" for resources to promoting poverty alleviation and development jointly with urban and

---

[1]   "Xi Jinping stressed during his visit to Gansu Province, firm confidence in innovation, real work and unity to create a new situation of wealthy people and prosperity", 2019-08-22, http://www. xinhuanet. com/2019-08/22/c_1124909349. htm.

rural resources; from relying mainly on the Government for promotion to building a new pattern of governance for poverty reduction that combines the Government, society and itself; and from establishing a sound long-term mechanism for solving relative poverty, thereby promoting social progress.

1.3　From Winning the Battle Against Poverty to Achieving Rural Revitalization

Poverty alleviation is the precondition and foundation of rural revitalization and rural revitalization is the next target of poverty alleviation. It should be noted that China's poverty reduction programs and achievements have been widely recognized by the international community. According to the World Bank's poverty line of 1.9 US dollars per person per day, China has contributed more than 70 percent of the global poverty reduction effort. China has lifted more people out of poverty than any other country, and is the first country to reach the poverty reduction goal in the UN's Millennium Development Goals. Upon completion of the poverty eradication task this year, about 100 million poor people in China will be eradicated from poverty and China will achieve the goals set in the United Nations 2030 Agenda for Sustainable Development 10 years ahead of schedule, which is of great significance to both China and the world, as no country in the world has ever lifted so many people out of poverty in such a short period of time, so it's natural that the international community has highly praised China's poverty reduction efforts. According to United Nations Secretary-General Guterres, a precise poverty alleviation strategy is the only way to help the poor and achieve the ambitious goals set out in the 2030 Agenda for Sustainable Development, and China's experience can provide useful lessons for other developing countries. In the "Belt and Road" international cooperation, many developing countries wish to share China's experience in poverty reduction. [1]

---

[1]　Xi Jinping, "Speech at the Symposium on the Battle to Defeat the Poverty Alleviation Offensive", *People's Daily*, 2020-03-07 (2).

The cause of socialism with Chinese characteristics led by the CPC is a grand blueprint. "Following the blueprint through to the end", with perseverance and continuous efforts. China will also continue to promote effective linkages between comprehensive poverty reduction and rural revitalization, as being lifted out of poverty is not an end in itself but the starting point of a new life and a new pursuit. The elimination of absolute poverty is a state of the development of the Qinling-Bashan Mountainous Region. The full realization of a moderately prosperous society is just a wave in the long river of development in the area. According to the report of the 19th Communist Party of China National Congress, issues relating to agriculture, rural areas, and rural people are fundamental to China as they directly concern our country's stability and our people's wellbeing. Addressing these issues should have a central place on the work agenda of the Party for rural revitalization. What are the prospects of rural revitalization in the Qinling-Bashan Mountainous Region? In terms of social form, it will offer a sustainable and pleasant living environment, with culture and civilization moving in tandem, and with consumer advantages or attractiveness to the outside world; in terms of economic form, it will enjoy a steadily and sustainably growing economy, with development and environmental friendliness, and the ecological economy becoming a regional highland. This economic form will enable this region to remain stable and prosperous, effectively solve the problems arising from economic and social development, effectively develop its the culture, and promote the optimal civilization of the social form of the area, so that this region can be the forefront and compete for the upper reaches in the construction of the two "centennial goals". In addition, in response to the evolution of the principal contradiction in poverty reduction, China will further clarify the working ideas, push on the poverty reduction strategy and the smooth transformation of the work system, integrate all of these changes into the rural revitalization strategy, and establish the system and mechanism which takes a holistic approach, addressing both symptoms and root causes. In this way, China can better elevate the development capacity of the low-income population in underdeveloped and rural areas, and strive to achieve common prosperity by addressing relative poverty.

Looking to the future, China will focus on cracking the binary structure of urban and rural areas, innovating mechanisms of poverty alleviation between the two in a coordinated way. In April 2020, General Secretary Xi Jinping pointed out during an inspection tour in Shaanxi Province that "Being lifted out of poverty is not an end in itself but the starting point of a new life and a new pursuit. " The next step is to focus on rural vitalization, promoting the comprehensive revitalization of rural industries, talents, culture, ecology, organizations and so on. [1] China's rural revitalization efforts are bound to be in full swing. China will continue to deepen its exploration of poverty alleviation reforms, reform the collective property rights system in rural areas, improve the rural land management system, revitalize and put to good use rural assets, and stimulate rural development vitality. China will also update the policy on the deployment of talents to the countryside and call for more young people and social resources to start businesses and employment in the countryside to drive innovative agricultural development. At the same time, based on the new requirements of rural governance, China will innovate governance models for poverty reduction. By following a rural governance system that is led by sound party organization and that combines self-governance, rule of law, and rule of virtue, China will encourage the general public to play an active part, enhance rural governance capacity, highlight the Party's efforts to build up and alleviate poverty and promote the effort, implement the "Leading Goose Project" and train entrepreneurs in agri-business.

Once rural revitalization is normalized, more attention will be paid to introducing markets, enterprises and farmers, as well as social forces, into the long-term work of rural revitalization. The construction of villagers' autonomous organizations, collective economic organizations, peasants' cooperative organizations and various social service organizations will be enhanced, and the systems of grass-roots organizations at the village level will also be improved under the leadership of the CPC. Various ways and modalities will be employed to develop and grow the collective economies, increase the income from

---

① "Xi Jinping stressed in Shaanxi during his visit to do a solid job of ' six stable' work to implement the ' six protection' task and strive to write a new chapter of Shaanxi in the new era to catch up and surpass", *Shaanxi Daily*, 2020-04-24(2).

collective economic undertakings and improve the public service capacity at the village level. A beautiful rural area with thriving businesses, pleasant living environments, social etiquette and civility, effective governance, and prosperity will gradually come in sight, and China's wisdom on rural revitalization will be shared.

References

Xi Jinping, *A New Vision for Development*, Hangzhou: Zhejiang People's Publishing House, 2018.

Xi Jinping, *Getting rid of poverty*, Fuzhou: Fujian People's Publishing House, 1992.

Xi Jinping, "Speech at the symposium on decisive battle and decisive victory from poverty", *People's Daily*, 2020-03-07 (2).

Xi Jinping, "Speech at the symposium on getting rid of poverty accurately", *QiuShi*, 2020 (09).

Xi Jinping, *Speech at the Symposium on Poverty Alleviation in Deep Poverty Regions*, Beijing: People's Publishing House, 2017.

Xi Jinping, *Xi Jinping on Governance: Volume One*, Beijing: Foreign Language Press, 2014.

Xi Jinping, *Xi Jinping on Governance: Volume Two*, Beijing: Foreign Language Press, 2014.

Bian Huimin, et al., "A study on the synergistic development of poverty alleviation and rural revitalization in contiguous poverty-stricken areas", *Rural Economy*, 2019(04), pp. 40 – 46.

Cao Junhui, et al., "Satisfaction of farmers to accurate poverty alleviation policy and its influencing factors", *Journal of Northwest A&F University(Social Science Edition)*, 2017(04), pp. 16 – 23.

Chen Xiyun, "An investigation from Pingwu County in Sichuan Province about the dilemma and countermeasures of targeted poverty alleviation in mountain industry", *Rural Economy*, 2016(05), pp. 87 – 90.

Dang Guoying, "Several major guiding issues of rural revitalization", *Social Science Front*, 2019(2), pp. 172 – 180.

Dang Guoying, "The types of poverty and the choice about poverty reduction strategy", *Reform*, 2016(8), pp. 68 – 70.

Deng Weijie, "Difficulties, countermeasures and path choice of targeted poverty alleviation", *Rural Economy*, 2014(06), pp. 78 – 81.

Dou Shulong, and Ye Jingzhong, "The organic connection and mechanism construction of rural revitalization and poverty alleviation", *Reform*, 2019(01), pp. 19 – 29.

Gao Fei, and Xiang Deping, "Policy implication of precision poverty relief from social administration angle", *Journal of Nanjing Agricultural University(Social Sciences Edition)*, 2017(04), pp. 21 – 27 + 156.

Guo Sujian, Wang Pengxiang, "Rural governance elites and rural revitalization in China", *Nankai Journal (Philosophy, Literature and Social Science Edition)*, 2019(04), pp. 62 – 75.

He Degui, *A study on the implementation of relocation policy for disaster avoidance in mountainous areas: taking the area in southern Shaanxi Province as an example*, Beijing: People's Publishing House, 2016.

He Degui, Dang Guoying, "A study on the implementation deviation of relocation policy in Western Mountainous Areas: based on the investigation in Southern Shaanxi Province", *Journal of Chinese Academy of Governance*, 2015(06), pp. 119 – 123.

He Degui, et al., "The structural restriction and transcendence of targeted poverty alleviation in contiguous and extreme poor areas: based on empirical analysis of immigrant relocation in southern Shaanxi Province", *Local Governance Research*, 2016(01), pp. 31 – 45.

He Degui, *Farewell to poverty: a record of relocation and targeted poverty alleviation in southern Shaanxi Province*, Xi'an: Xi'an Map Publishing House, 2019.

He Degui, *Getting rid of poverty: the description of relocation in Shaanxi Province*, Beijing: Intellectual Property Publishing house, 2018.

He Degui, *The way to govern poverty: relocation and targeted poverty alleviation*, Beijing: Intellectual Property Publishing house, 2017.

He Degui, Xu Rong, Gao Jianmei, *A reader for grassroots cadres and masses to win the battle against poverty*, Beijing: People's Publishing House, 2019.

He Degui, Xu Rong, "The dimension of grassroots organization construction in the process of poverty governance: based on General Secretary Xi Jinping's important exposition on poverty alleviation",

Journal of Liaoning Academy of Governance, 2019(3) , pp. 5 – 10.

He Degui, Zhang Shuo, "Practical inspection and national integration of rural governance from the perspective of comprehensive poverty alleviation", *Journal of Henan Normal University (Philosophy and Social Sciences Edition)*, 2019(4) , pp. 24 – 29.

He Guangliu, "The correlation between precise poverty alleviation and aiding the will and wisdom", *Reform*, 2017(12) , pp. 36 – 38.

Huang Chengwei, "' Four Persistence' and ' Three Emphases' to achieve high quality poverty alleviation", *People's Tribune*, 2018(21) , p. 18.

Huang Chengwei, "Research on China's path of development-oriented poverty reduction: review and prospect", *Journal of China Agricultural University Social Sciences*, 2016(05) , pp. 5 – 17.

Huang Chengwei, "Summary of innovation on poverty eradication theory and practice since the 18th national plenary session of the communist party of China ", *Journal of China Agricultural University Social Sciences*, 2017(05) , pp. 5 – 16.

Huang Chengwei, "Theory and practice of stimulating the endogenous force of poverty alleviation ", *Journal of Guangxi University for Nationalities(Philosophy and Social Science Edition)*, 2019 (01) , pp. 44 – 50.

Huang Chengwei, "Xi Jinping's poverty-relief thoughts of socialism with Chinese characteristics in the new era ", *Journal of Nanjing Agricultural University (Social Sciences Edition)*, 2018(03) , pp. 12 – 18 + 152.

Huang Xisheng, He Jiang, "On the linkage between the construction of ecological civilization and the system of poverty alleviation of Western Area in China: an investigation taking ecological compensation as the ' Interface' ", *Academic Forum*, 2017(01) , pp. 105 – 110.

Institute of Party History and Documentation of the CPC Central Committee, *Abstract of Xi Jinping's Poverty Alleviation Discourse*, Beijing: Central Document Press, 2018.

Institute of Party History and Documentation of the CPC Central Committee, *Abstract of Xi Jinping's work on the "Three Rural Areas"*, Beijing: Central Document Press, 2019.

Institute of Party History and Documentation of the CPC Central Committee, *Selected Important Documents Since the Eighteenth*

National Congress (Part 2) , Beijing: Central Document Press, 2018.

Institute of Party History and Documentation of the CPC Central Committee, *Selected Important Documents Since the 18th National Congress (Part 1)* , Beijing: Central Document Press, 2014.

Li Bo, Zuo Ting, "Encountering relocation: The discussion about poverty alleviation migration relocation policy implementation logic from the perspective of Precise poverty alleviation—Take Wang village in southern Shaanxi for example", *Journal of China Agricultural University Social Sciences*, 2016(02), pp. 25 – 31.

Li Xiaoyun, Wu Yifan, Wu Jin, "The targeted poverty alleviation program: a practice of the new governance framework of China", *Journal of Huazhong Agricultural University (Social Sciences Edition)*, 2019(05), pp. 12 – 20 + 164.

Li Xiaoyun, Yuan Junjun, Yu Lerong, "The prospects on the China's Post-2020 rural poverty reduction strategy and policy: transformation from ' Poverty Alleviation' to ' Poverty Prevention' ", *Issues in Agricultural Economy*, 2020(02), pp. 15 – 22.

Li Xueping, " Anti-vulnerability development: the new paradigm of poverty governance in poverty-stricken areas", *Journal of Central China Normal University(Humanities and Social Sciences)*, 2016(03), pp. 24 – 29.

Liu Jiansheng, Chen Xin, Cao Jiahui, "Research on the mechanism of industry's precise poverty alleviation", *Chinese Population, Resources and Environment*, 2017 (06), pp. 127 – 135.

Liu Mingyue, Feng Xiaolong, Wang Sangui, " A Study on Poverty Vulnerability of Peasant Households Relocated to Help Poverty Alleviation", *Rural Economy*, 2019 (03), pp. 64 – 72.

Liu Wei, Xu Jie, Li Jie, "A Study on the Livelihood Adaptability of Peasant Households Relocated to Poverty Alleviation—A Case Study of Immigrant Relocation in Southern Shaanxi", *China Agricultural Resources and Regional Planning*, 2018 (12), pp. 218 – 223.

Liu Yongfu, " Guided by General Secretary Xi Jinping's important discussion on poverty alleviation as a guide to resolutely win the fight against poverty", *Administration Reform*, 2019 (05), pp. 4 – 11.

Lu Fang, Cheng Feng, Mei Lin, " The ' precision' dilemma and reflection of poverty management in counties", *Journal of Hohai*

University (*Philosophy and Social Sciences*), 2017 (02), pp. 47 – 52 + 91.

Lu Hanwen, "East-West Cooperation on Poverty Alleviation and the China Road", *Frontiers*, 2019(21), pp. 62 – 68.

Lu Hanwen, "Stimulating the endogenous impetus of the poor", *Social Science in China*, 2017-12-15(5).

Shi Yucheng, "Ecological Poverty Alleviation: A Combination of Precision Poverty Alleviation and Ecological Protection", *Gansu Social Sciences*, 2018 (06), pp. 169 – 176.

Wang Sangui, Feng Zixi, "Organic connection between poverty alleviation and rural revitalization: logical relationship, connotation and key content", *Journal of Nanjing Agricultural University (Social Science Edition)*, 2019 (05), pp. 8 – 14 + 154.

Wang Sangui, Hu Jun, "From Survival to Development: Seventy Years of Anti-Poverty Practice in New China", *Agricultural Economic Problems*, 2020 (02), pp. 4 – 14.

Wang Sangui, Liu Mingyue, "Function mechanism of health poverty alleviation, implementation dilemma and policy choice", *Journal of Xinjiang Normal University (Philosophy and Social Sciences Edition)*, 2019 (03), pp. 82 – 91 + 2.

Wang Yang, "Tightly Focusing on Precise Poverty Alleviation and Precise Poverty Eradication Deeply Advancing the Poverty Alleviation Offensive", *Administrative Reform*, 2016(04), pp. 4 – 13 + 2.

Wang Yulei, "Digital going to the countryside: technical governance in rural targeted poverty alleviation", *Sociological Research*, 2016 (06), pp. 119 – 142 + 244.

Wang Yu, Wang Sangui, "Analysis of clustering of rural poor and poverty reduction strategies", *Journal of China Agricultural University (Social Science Edition)*, 2015 (02), pp. 98 – 109.

Wang Zhizhang, Liu Tianyuan, "Endogenous causes and solutions of intergenerational transmission of rural poverty in contiguous destitute areas", *Rural Economy*, 2016 (05), pp. 74 – 79.

Wan Jun, Zhang Qi, "' Internal and External Integration ' : Development, Transformation and Improvement of the Precision Poverty Reduction Mechanism", *Journal of Nanjing Agricultural University (Social Science Edition)*, 2017 (04), pp. 9 – 20 + 156.

Wan Jun, Zhang Qi, "Thoughts on targeted poverty alleviation and poverty alleviation in contiguous poor areas in China from the perspective of regional development", *Journal of China Agricultural University (Social Science Edition)*, 2016 (05), pp. 36 – 45.

Wu Guobao, "Achievements and Experiences of China's Rural Poverty Alleviation and Development in the 40 Years of Reform and Opening Up", *Journal of Nanjing Agricultural University (Social Science Edition)*, 2018 (06), pp. 17 – 30 + 157 – 158.

Wu Guobao, "Innovate poverty alleviation governance and curb poverty alleviation and fraud", *People's Forum*, 2017 (10), pp. 55 – 57.

Wu Guobao, "Poverty Alleviation Cooperation Poverty in East and West China and Its Solution", *Reform*, 2017 (08), pp. 57 – 61.

Wu Jingnan, "Study on the realization path of rural tourism targeted poverty alleviation", *Rural Economy*, 2017 (03), pp. 99 – 103.

Wu Lijuan, Li Ding, "Research on the Impact of Financial Capital on Farmers ' Income Increase under the Background of Precision Poverty Alleviation—Based on the Perspective of Internal Income Stratification and Regional Differences", *Agricultural Technology and Economy*, 2019 (02), pp. 61 – 72.

Wu Xinye, Niu Chenguang, "Tension and Relief of the Poverty Alleviation and Relocation Community", *Journal of South China Agricultural University (Social Science Edition)*, 2018 (02), pp. 118 – 127.

Xu Hong, Wang Caicai, "Rethinking on targeted poverty alleviation under the strategy of rural revitalization", *Rural Economy*, 2018 (03), pp. 11 – 17.

Xu Yong, "Endogenous motivation to stimulate poverty alleviation", *People's Daily*, 2016-01 – 11 (7).

Yang Yanlin, Yuan An, "Precision industry selection mechanism in targeted poverty alleviation", *Journal of South China Agricultural University (Social Science Edition)*, 2019 (02), pp. 1 – 14.

Yuan Mingbao, "Poverty Alleviation and Governance: Suspension in the Implementation of Targeted Poverty Alleviation Policies and the Dilemma of Grassroots Governance", *Journal of Nanjing Agricultural University (Social Science Edition)*, 2018 (03), pp. 57 – 64 + 153 – 154.

Zhang Bei, "The Endogenous Motivation and Practical Path of Promoting Precision Poverty Alleviation by Supporting Zhizhi and Supporting Intelligence", *Reform*, 2017 (12), pp. 41 –44.

Zhang Liming, Shuai Fang, *Dongping's Overcoming: Overcoming Difficulties in the Decisive Stage with Property Rights Reform*, Beijing: Social Science Literature Press, 2019.

Zhang Yuqiang, Xiang Li, "A Comparative Study on the Models of Accurate Poverty Alleviation in Concentrated Continuously Poor Areas in China—Based on the Practice of Dabie Mountainous Area, Wuling Mountainous Area and Qinba Mountainous Area", *Hubei Social Sciences*, 2017 (02), pp. 46 –56.

Zuo Ding, Liu Wenjing, Li Bo, "Gradient advancement and optimization upgrade: Research on the effective connection between poverty alleviation and rural revitalization", *Journal of Huazhong Agricultural University (Social Science Edition)*, 2019 (05), pp. 21 –28 +165.

Introduction to the authors

He Degui　male, Born in Youxi, Fujian province; PhD in Management; doctoral supervisor, associate professor and dean of the Department of Public Management in Northwest A&F University; mainly research on public policy and local governance. HE is currently Council Member of the Special Committee of Immigration Sociology of the Chinese Sociological Society, Council Member of Shaanxi Provincial Political Association, Secretary-General of Shaanxi Health Poverty Alleviation Expert Advisory Committee, Council Member of Contemporary Shaanxi Research Association, Council Member of Shaanxi Provincial Economic Association, Member of Decision Advisory Committee of Yangling Demonstration Zone, etc.; HE presided over and finished over 20 projects supported by National Social Science Fund, etc or commissioned by various local governments, won 4 provincial and ministerial scientific research awards and many of his contribution have been approved by national, provincial and ministerial leaders, adopted and applied by relevant departments.

Yao Guimei　senior research fellow of Division of economic Studies and Chief for the center of southern Africa studies of the Chinese Academy of Social Sciences (CASS); visiting scholar at the center for African studies in University of Illinois at Urbana-Champaign, USA; master's students supervisor of University of Chinese Academy of Social Sciences; lead researcher on innovation projects of CASS including Research on China 's Investment Strategies in Africa and Research on Production Capacity Cooperation between China and Africa. Specifically, she has been devoted to the studies for more than 30 years on African economic development, regional economic integration in Africa and the economic cooperation and trade relations between China and African countries. She has visited more than a dozen African countries, chaired and participated in over ten research projects from governmental organizations, and submitted dozens of think-tank reports. Among them, China-Africa Direct Investment and Cooperation won "the CASS Award for the Excellence national think tank report of 2018". From 2012 to 2018, she won the CASS Award for the Excellence in Countermeasure Studies twice for the second prize, and three times for the third prize.

China-Africa Institute

On September 3, 2018, while giving remarks at the opening ceremony of the Beijing Summit of the Forum on China-Africa Cooperation (FOCAC), the Chinese President, His Excellency Xi Jinping proposed that "China will proactively implement the Eight Major Initiatives" and that China decided to establish a China-Africa institute to enhance exchanges with Africa on civilization". To establish the China-Africa Institute (CAI) topped the agenda of "People-to-People Exchanges" of the "Eight Major Initiatives" on China-Africa relations. The CAI was inaugurated in Beijing on April 9, 2019, when His Excellency, President Xi Jinping sent a congratulatory letter to commemorate its establishment.

The CAI is a national and international intellectual hub for African studies in China and China studies in Africa, and is committed to strengthening the exchanges between China and Africa on governance and development experiences through a wider exploration of academic resources in both China and Africa and a more comprehensive China-Africa mutual understanding. The CAI provides intellectual support for China's cooperation with African countries within the framework of the "Belt and Road Initiative" (BRI), so as to build a comprehensive strategic China-Africa partnership for the future, and a stronger China-Africa community with a shared future.

The CAI has four main functions: a platform for academic exchanges between China and Africa; a research base to support studies regarding China-Africa cooperation on the BRI; a hub to gather and train high-end talents and professionals for China-Africa friendship; and a window for people-to-people exchanges between China and Africa.

The CAI is set up on the basis of the Institute of West Asian and African Studies (IWAAS) of the Chinese Academy of Social Sciences (CASS), a national-level and the top Chinese research organ and think tank which has been dedicated to studies regarding the Middle East and Africa since its establishment in 1961. The CAI temporarily shares same physical institutions and operation mechanism with the IWAAS, including leadership, research divisions, academic personnel, international exchanges and cooperation, research management, and administration.

China Social Sciences Press (CSSP)

Established in June, 1978, China Social Sciences Press (CSSP) is sponsored by Chinese Academy of Social Science. CSSP is a national level publishing house focusing on academic publications mainly in the field of humanities and social sciences. In 1993, CSSP won the honorary title of "national outstanding press" granted by Publicity Department of CPC Central Committee and National Press and Publication Administration.

Large numbers of exellent monographs and book series have been published by CSSP since the 40th anniversary of its establishment. Among the publications, hundreds of these won various national book prizes and rewards. In the "Chinese Citation Book Index" published by Institute for Chinese Social Sciences Research and ssessment of Nanjing University CSSP ranked fourth among the nearly 600 publishing houses in China. In "the Influence Assessment on World-renowned Books from China" published by Evaluation Center for the "Going Global" of Chinese Culture, CSSP takes the first place.

In recent years, on the basis of traditional book brands such as "the Cambridge History of China" and "Selected Works of Scholars of Chinese Academy of Social Sciences", CSSP has also created new book brands, such as "CSSP Think Tank Series", "China Insights Series", "Chinese System Research Series" and so on. CSSP has developed into an important publishing base for Marxist theory and philosophy and social sciences, a significant publication platform for the achievements of national high-end think tank. CSSP is playing the vital role in promoting the "Going Global" of Chinese academic achievements.

The China-Africa Friendship Group of the CPPCC National Committee

The China-Africa Friendship Group of the National Committee of the Chinese People's Political Consultative Conference (CPPCC) was established on June 19, 2018.

Featuring the uniqueness and strengths of the CPPCC and composed with a wealth of expertise on international affairs and other fields of the CPPCC National Committee, the Group is a mechanism for advice and consensus building and for promoting friendly ties with Africa and building a closer China-Africa community with a shared future.

With a view to implementing the outcomes of the 2018 Beijing Summit of the Forum on China-Africa Cooperation (FOCAC), the Group is dedicated to engaging in dialogue and consultation with correspondent African institutions, regional organizations, think tanks, media and important figures on issues of common interest, including amongst others, poverty reduction, sustainable development, people-to-people exchanges in culture, education, sports, health care and respective experience in state governance.

The Group organizes exchange of visits, conducts studies and surveys and holds conferences and seminars to pool wisdom and strength to enhance mutual understanding and mutually beneficial cooperation between China and Africa.